The Oyster

THE

OYSTER

*The Life and Lore
of the Celebrated Bivalve*

ROBERT A. HEDEEN

Drawings by Lynne N. Lockhart

TIDEWATER PUBLISHERS

Centreville, Maryland

Library of Congress Cataloging in Publication Data

Hedeen, Robert A. 1928-
    The oyster: the life and lore of the celebrated
bivalve.

        Bibliography: p.
        Includes index.
        1. Oysters.   2. Oyster fisheries—Chesapeake Bay
Region (Md. and Va.)   3. Mollusks—Chesapeake Bay Region
(Md. and Va.)   4. Chesapeake Bay Region (Md. and Va.)
I. Title.
QL430.6.H43   1986   594'.11   86-5861
ISBN 0-87033-358-5

Manufactured in the United States of America

First edition

To my three sons
Robert Jr., Michael, *and* Scott
who have taught me more
than I sometimes care to admit

CONTENTS

PREFACE

THE oyster is not a beautiful animal, except perhaps to another oyster, and, as a matter of fact, it does not even resemble a typical member of the animal kingdom. Yet this nondescript mass of protoplasm living between two calcareous shells has greatly influenced human civilization. Wars have been fought over the right to catch these animals, and many a man has met his death when he went to sea to retrieve them from the depths.

Societies have arisen that were totally dependent on the oyster for their existence, and a special breed of humans, the oysterman, evolved to catch them. Many politicians, both important and not so important, have met their nemesis because they did not recognize how important oysters were to the people they represented.

In parts of the United States where the oyster is king, almost any item of news pertaining to this animal is eagerly snapped up by the media—frequently ending up on page one of the local newspaper. In doing the research required to write this book, I consulted extensively the newspaper collection in the Maryland Room of the library of Salisbury (Maryland) State College. This collection consists of clippings on various subjects of local interest, which some assistant librarian has for years tediously and methodically clipped out of each issue of local newspapers. I was stunned to find a file of clippings pertaining to the oyster that occupied half of a regular file cabinet drawer. The newspaper extracts, dating from the 1950s to the present, were taken from the *Salisbury Times*, the *Cambridge Banner*, and the *Easton Star-Democrat*,

The Oyster

three of the more popular newspapers on Maryland's Eastern Shore. Wondering how many clippings there actually were, I proceeded to spend an hour and a half counting the 2,272 separate items. Apparently, editors on the Eastern Shore think oysters are newsworthy.

Oysters have been of great importance to Maryland from the beginning of her existence, and there are more people who make their living from them in Maryland than in any other state. Though the industry in the state has been on a more or less steady decline for the last hundred years, the impact of oysters on the overall economy of Maryland today is great. As we look back into the history of the industry in this state, certain dates stand out as being significant and should be mentioned:

1820 The first oyster-related law was enacted by the legislature. Dredging was prohibited; so was the transport of Maryland oysters in ships that had not been owned by Marylanders for at least the preceding year.

1830 The One-Acre Planting Law was enacted, allowing citizens to use one acre of bottom for planting and growing oysters.

1854 Dredges were legalized in certain waters of Somerset County for county residents who had obtained a fifteen-dollar license. This was the first oyster-license law in Maryland and one of the first in the nation.

1865 The One-Acre Planting Law was expanded to five acres.

1868 Creation of the infamous "Oyster Navy" or "Oyster Police."

1878–79 First scientific study of the oyster beds in Maryland. Francis Winslow was in charge of the study, which made definitive, long-range recommendations.

1882 An Oyster Commission consisting of three men, including Dr. W. K. Brooks, was created to "examine the oyster beds of Maryland and advise as to their protection and improvement." Later this group was known as the Brooks Commission.

1890 The Cull Law, considered by oyster biologists to be the most important piece of legislation yet to come out of the legislature as far as oysters were concerned, was passed after a long and bitter fight. Two and a half inches was set as the minimum legal size, and undersized oysters, as well as items of cultch, had to be returned to the bed from which they were taken.

Preface

1906 The Haman Oyster Bill was enacted in spite of considerable opposition. This act permitted individuals to lease up to thirty acres of barren bottom in county waters and up to one hundred acres in the Chesapeake Bay beyond county limits for oyster propagation. This law is still in effect today.

1906–12 Survey of the natural oyster bars in Maryland by the U. S. Coast and Geodetic Survey. The so-called Yates Survey, as amended, forms the basis for the delimitation of the natural rocks to this day.

1914 Passage of the Shepherd Bill which, in effect, nullified the Haman Bill of 1906. Three or more residents could dispute a barren-bottom designation by stating under oath that they had caught oysters there previously. The bottom in question would most likely then be placed on the maps as natural rock, and, therefore, not available for leasing.

1927 Mainly through the efforts of Dr. R. V. Truitt, the minimum size of harvestable oysters was increased from 2½ inches in height to 3 inches.

1951 Oyster shuckers and processors were required to sell 50 percent of their shucked shell to the state to be used in rehabilitating the cultch on public beds and to furnish a base for the setting of seed oysters in designated areas.

And here the significant dates end. Very little has been accomplished in the last thirty-five years. One of the primary purposes in writing this book was to bring together under one cover some of the facts known about the enigmatic oyster at the present time and to interest as many people as possible in the importance of this animal to the economy and ecology of the Chesapeake Bay. If even a small amount of additional interest is generated, I will consider my efforts to have been worthwhile.

In preparing the manuscript, countless sources of information were utilized, and I have taken the liberty of including the major reference works as an appendix for consultation by anyone who may wish to delve further into the matter. The unpublished word, however, is sometimes more valuable than the printed page, and I would like to thank the following Marylanders who orally shared their knowledge of the oyster with me: Ed Bedsworth, Nanticoke;

The Oyster

Quincey Blevins, Nanticoke; Max and Flo Chambers, Tyaskin; Louis Griffin, Tyaskin; Don, Jr., and Jane Insley, Tyaskin; Kenneth Lappe, Tyaskin; Cornelius and Wilbur Messick, Bivalve; Mike Manning, Salisbury; Robert L. Mitchell, Jr., Salisbury; William Price, Salisbury; Jodie Whitelock, Salisbury; Dr. Reginald V. Truitt, Great Neck.

Finally, I would like to express my appreciation to Dr. Osmond P. Breland, late Professor of Zoology at the University of Texas, for critically reading portions of the manuscript and for his inspiration and encouragement throughout the years.

Robert A. Hedeen

Tyaskin, Maryland
February 1986

The Oyster

CHAPTER ONE

Introduction

The man had sure a palate cover'd o'er
With brass or steel, that on that rocky shore
First broke the oyster's pearly coat,
And risked the living morsel down his throat.

John Gay

WHOEVER that man was, he should be saluted and awarded a medal for courage. I suspect this brave individual lived in the dim prehistoric past, and, once he had sampled the oyster's delectable flavor, he was addicted to the shellfish for the rest of his life. Great heaps of oyster shells occur in various parts of the world and attest to the oyster's popularity in the diets of the members of most ancient civilizations.

Perhaps no bygone civilization enjoyed oysters more than that of Rome. Cicero, Horace, Juvenal, and many other Roman writers and historians recorded the glories of the oyster, and Pliny the Elder left a record of cultivation attempts as early as the first century B. C. When the Roman legions marched into Britain they were delighted with the oysters they found in that primitive land. One soldier expressed his reaction to the conquered land thus: "Poor Britons—there is some good in them after all—they produce an oyster." That the oyster produced in the colder waters surrounding England was considered far superior to the one from the warmer Mediterranean is shown by the occurrence of the shells of English oysters in the ruins of Rome. The savory English variety must have been relished by the conquerors so much that they loaded them in sacks filled with close-packed snow and sent them home.

The Oyster

Almost every historian describing the culinary practices of Rome has something to say about the oyster's place in the diet. Roman orgies have usually been associated with sexual and other excesses, and I doubt if many people have ever heard of an oyster orgy. But in a record kept of the numerous feasts held in the palace of Sergius Orata, it is noted: "Oysters occupied the place of honor . . . at every feast thousands of them were consumed. Satiated, but not satisfied, these gourmets were in the habit of retiring to an adjoining room, where they relieved the stomach of its load by artificial means, and then returned to indulge again their appetite with a fresh supply of oysters."

That anyone could consume so many oysters may be amazing to the nonconnoisseur, but there is another record of a Roman who swallowed as many as a thousand during an all-day binge. Once in England, in more modern times, a man made a wager that he could eat twelve dozen oysters while the town clock was striking twelve. He won the bet by placing a dozen oysters in each of twelve wine glasses, and, having swallowed the contents of one glass, he washed the mollusks down with a glass of champagne and quickly proceeded to the next glass.

Once in a raw bar in the city of New Orleans I watched a modern-day oyster glutton devour five dozen on the half-shell in little less than an hour while sipping two bottles of beer. Though this individual was applauded for his accomplishment by the patrons of the seafood establishment, he would have been considered a rank amateur by the voracious Romans or other true oyster hogs.

The all-time oyster gastronome, however, is a modern-day Marylander by the name of Tommy "Muskrat" Greene of the waterfront community of Deale. In July of 1985 Muskrat's stomach earned him a place in the Guinness Book of Records when he polished off 288 oysters—weighing a total of six pounds—in a minute and thirty-three seconds. Friends who were familiar with the capacity of Greene's belly were not surprised at his feat because, after all, in 1981 he had established another record by gulping down 350 snails in garlic butter at a Washington, D. C., restaurant.

Oyster gourmands have been publicized ever since
history has been recorded.

The Oyster

When the Romans left England, a long period ensued in which little or nothing was recorded about oysters in that country or on the continent for that matter. In 1319 Edward II established St. Denys's Fair, which, according to legend, was the opening of the oyster season in Colchester. In 1599 a man by the name of Butler wrote a treatise entitled *Dyet's Dry Dinner* in which he stated: "It is unseasonable and unwholesome in all months that have not an R in their name to eat oysters." Butler, then, is responsible for the present day taboo against eating oysters in *r*-less months. This superstition has no basis in fact, as we will discuss later. After Butler's proclamation, English literature becomes filled with references to the oyster. Everyone, it seems, had something to say about it, from Shakespeare to Byron to Dickens. Surely the inhabitants of the British Isles enjoyed oysters before the Romans came and continued to eat them in great numbers after the legions left, but why they didn't record their impressions and reactions to this food staple for an extended time is a mystery.

When the first Europeans arrived in North America they were as much surprised at the oyster fauna of the New World as the Romans had been when they first set foot on English soil. Having been accustomed to the small (about one-quarter the size of the American variety) and (by comparison) tasteless European oyster, it was like finding manna from heaven for many of them.

Francis Louis Michel, a Swiss, visited Virginia in 1701 and recorded the following concerning oysters in that colony: "The abundance of oysters is incredible. There are whole banks of them so that the ships must avoid them. A sloop, which was to land us at Kingscreek, struck an oyster bed, where we had to wait about two hours for the tide. They surpass those in England by far in size, indeed they are four times as large. I often cut them in two, before I could put them in my mouth."

Many of the new arrivals, however, were not overly impressed with the abundance of oysters clogging the waterways around their new homes. At that time in England, oysters were so plentiful and inexpensive that members of the upper echelons of society considered them food for the lower classes and would not eat them. In *The Pickwick Papers* (1836), Charles Dickens described the attitude of the Englishmen of his day concerning the oyster:

Introduction

"It's a wery remarkable circunstance, sir," said Sam, "that poverty and oysters always seems to go together."

"I don't understand, Sam," said Mr. Pickwick.

"What I mean, sir," said Sam, "is, that the poorer a place is, the greater call there seems to be for oysters. Look here, sir; here's a oyster stall to every half-dozen houses. The streets lined vith 'em. Blessed if I don't think that ven a man's wery poor, he rushes out of his lodgings and eats oysters in reg'lar desperation."

Later, overfishing and pollution destroyed a large part of the English oyster beds, and the animals that had previously been so common became hard to obtain. Only then, when they became scarce and expensive, did the British gourmets recognize their value. A similar situation occurred in the colonies of Maryland and Virginia in respect to the diamondback terrapin and canvasback duck. These delicacies were so common during colonial days that laws prohibited slaveowners from feeding their slaves these foods more than a certain number of times a week.

Though the colonists were familiar with oysters in the old country, they were unprepared for the different habits of the species they found in America. The oysters of Europe grow on tidal flats that are subject to the fluctuating tides. One had only to wait until low tide to go to the oyster bed and easily take all that could be carried away. For the most part, the American oyster lives in deeper water and usually remains submerged in at least a few feet even at low tide. The Indians, who had been harvesting oysters for as long as they had occupied the land, taught the colonists how to make and use tongs to retrieve the shellfish from the bottom. The instruments used by the Indians are not much different from the tongs (widow-makers as they are called) used by oystermen today.

As noted, many of the early colonists looked down their noses at oysters as food and refused to consume them unless they had nothing else. Jamestown was besieged by famine on more than one occasion, and in one instance a group of the settlers swallowed their pride and moved to the mouth of the James River, where they fended off starvation by subsisting for several months on oysters and a small amount of Indian corn. If one has any doubts about the nutritional value of the oyster, the survival of these individuals should prove otherwise.

7

The Oyster

Certain Indian tribes along the Chesapeake Bay eked out an existence at certain times of the year by living mainly on oysters, which they devoured in the raw state or roasted in the shell. Large middens of oyster shells discarded by Indians are common throughout the region.

On the Nanticoke River near the village of Tyaskin on Maryland's Eastern Shore where I have a house, the evidence of the extensive use of oysters by the Indians and early settlers is apparent to even the casual beach stroller. As the river has eaten away at the fast ground over the centuries, various distinct strata are exposed and offer an insight into the way of life of the people who occupied the area when the particular stratum was at ground level. One such chronicle of the past is a cliff some twelve feet high that reveals three distinct layers of oyster shells. An amateur archaeologist friend who is familiar with the area examined this profile in time and estimated that approximately one hundred years were required for the deposition of each three feet of the cliff. Using this estimation as a yardstick and relying on the geological Law of Superposition, which says the oldest strata are toward the bottom and the younger layers are above, I calculated that the lowest oyster midden was created around 1600—probably by Nanticoke Indians who were indigenous to this region. The next layer of shells was dated about 1800, and the uppermost one (very close to present-day ground level) had to have been deposited in the early 1900s.

It is interesting to note that the intrepid Captain John Smith explored this exact region of the Nanticoke in June of 1608. Few things escaped the pen of Smith, and in his diary he mentions the abundance of "crabs, shrimps, creveces, oysters, cocles, and muscles." He also records an encounter with "savages" in the region "where the great river narrows." This is where the villages of Tyaskin and Bivalve are found today. Smith named the Indians the Nantiquakes, and a scrimmage with them, which left several Indians wounded, convinced him to explore no farther up the river. Perhaps if the encounter had been friendlier, Smith and his men would have been invited to dinner, and we could fantasize that a few of the shells in the "1600" midden had been cast there by the Englishmen.

Introduction

Though many of the colonists appreciated the availability of the oysters and ate them raw, roasted, stewed, or pickled, it was not until the nineteenth century that oysters were recognized as a valuable natural asset. One can imagine, however, that shortly after the first log cabins were erected conflicts over the ownership of the oysters in the vicinities of the settlements erupted. Eventually, the infamous oyster wars of the Chesapeake occurred, and, in a limited way, continue today.

Basically the problem goes back to 1785 when Virginia held ownership to the entrance to the Chesapeake Bay and exacted a heavy toll from Marylanders seeking access to the sea. Maryland owned the entire Potomac River and retaliated by forbidding residents of Virginia from fishing there. It just happens that the Potomac River is one of the finest oyster-breeding grounds in the world. Its rocky bottom makes it an ideal place for oysters to grow. It was only natural for the Virginians to lust after the large and plentiful oysters that grew in waters lapping at their shoreline, so an agreement between the two states was reached, the so-called Compact of 1785. Under this treaty Virginia residents would be allowed to fish in the Potomac but would be subject to Maryland rules and regulations. This uneasy accord continued in force (with certain modifications from time to time) until 5 December 1962 when President John Kennedy signed the Potomac Fisheries Bill, reaffirming the governing of the river by a bistate commission. Only then did the oyster wars more or less end.

Many have forgotten that the conflict between Marylanders and Virginians raged for almost two hundred years—almost up to the minute the bill was signed. Evidence of this is to be found in an article appearing in the *Washington Post* of 4 November 1947. The author, Mr. F. B. Rhein, wrote:

> Already the sound of rifle fire has echoed across the Potomac River this year. Only fifty miles from Washington, men are shooting at one another. The night is quiet until suddenly shots snap through the air. The dark sky is ripped by a spotlight which drops down to jab at the water. . . . Possibly a man is dead, perhaps a boat is taken, but the oyster war will go on the next night and the next. The air patrol will go out day after day. The governors of Virginia and Maryland

9

will write notes and issue proclamations. But until the laws are changed, the river people will go on breaking them.

It is hard to conceive of the violence men resorted to—all to acquire ownership of one of the most tranquil of all animals.

CHAPTER TWO

Form and Function

I suppose that when the sapid and slippery morsel—which is gone like a flash of gustatory summer lightning—glides along the palate, few people imagine that they are swallowing a piece of machinery (and going machinery too) greatly more complicated than a watch.

T. H. Huxley

ONE of the first things students of basic zoology are taught is the surfaces or directions into which the body of an animal can be divided. Anterior is toward the head, posterior is opposite of anterior, dorsal refers to the back or upper side, ventral to the underside or belly, and lateral is to the side.

In most animals studied in the laboratory or field, such as insects, worms, and frogs, it is a comparatively easy task to orient the animal in respect to these directions. But when a bivalve mollusk, such as an oyster or clam, is presented for study, many students find themselves at a loss and experience difficulty determining which end is up.

Bivalves are different from the majority of higher animals in that there is no distinct head region, and one really has no reference point from which to start. Nevertheless, the bivalve possesses the same body positions as you and I—they are just not as apparent.

As I describe the anatomy of the oyster, both externally and internally, I have several specimens in various states of dissection before me to aid in the descriptive process. Perhaps the reader may wish to obtain a specimen and follow along.

The Oyster

As we examine the oyster we will note, of course, that the animal is covered by the two characteristic valves that are more pointed at one end than at the other. The pointed end is called the beak, or umbo, and is associated with the anterior end of the creature. The beak represents the oldest part of the oyster and can show considerable variation. For example, very narrow, straight, or slightly curved beaks are usually formed by oysters that grow on soft, muddy bottoms, but other shapes of the beak cannot be definitely associated with any particular environment. Now that the general anterior region has been determined, we know the opposite, wider, and rounded end is posterior in position. Looking at the inner part of a valve, the posterior position is indicated by the oval-shaped, pigmented area termed the muscle scar. This represents the site of attachment of the large adductor muscle that holds the two valves together and is always located posteriorly in position.

If we hold the oyster in such a way that the beaks are visible and point up toward the observer, it is apparent that the two valves are shaped differently. The flatter of the two is the right valve or lid, and the cup-shaped one is the left. The beaks point to the dorsal side, and the ventral part of the animal is opposite. If the lid or right valve alone is examined with the beak pointing away from you, the anterior end is at the right side of the valve, and the posterior is at the left.

As far as the average person is concerned, the most important dimension of an oyster is its "length." Oyster experts insist, however, that what the layman calls the length of the oyster is really its height. The height, then, of an oyster is determined by measuring the distance between the extreme part of the beak and the ventral margin of the valves. Length is defined as the maximum distance between the anterior and posterior margin measured parallel with the axis of the hinge, and width is the greatest distance between the outsides of the closed valves.

The Shell

The valves of an oyster are articulated by an effective hinge mechanism located just behind the beaks. The part of the hinge

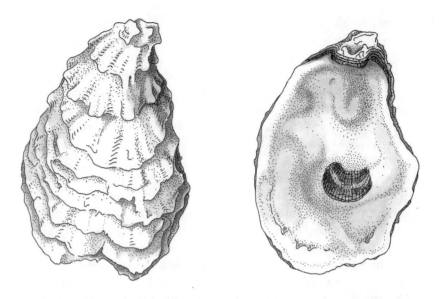

Blue Point oyster *(C. virginica)* from Long Island, New York. This oyster is about five years old. *Left,* outside surface of left valve. *Right,* inner surface of right valve showing adductor muscle scar.

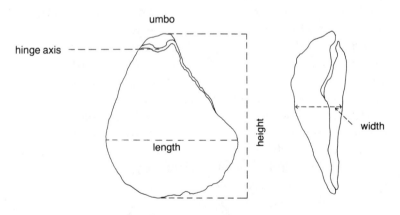

The dimensions of an oyster.

located in the right valve is a projecting structure called the buttress, which fits snugly into a seemingly custom-made depression in the left shell. A band of horny and elastic material, the ligament, joins the valves at the hinge and is capable of expansion and contraction when the shells open and close. How far the valves can open and close for feeding and respiration is determined by the angle between the two beaks and is, naturally, of considerable importance to the oyster.

The shape and thickness of the shell of *Crassostrea virginica* is quite variable, but in general it corresponds to the surroundings in which the oyster grew. For example, oysters having a rounded and thickened shell usually developed singly on hard bottoms and can be found anywhere in the distribution range where these conditions are met. Sometimes specific "brands" of oysters, like Blue Points or Chincoteagues, are said to have a definite shape or thickness, and these features are used for marketing purposes. The Blue Point is advertised as being rounded with a thick shell, but many of these special and frequently more expensive oysters sold to discriminating gourmets are actually taken from the Chesapeake Bay. As noted previously, the brand or trade names of *C. virginica* refer to the specific areas in which they were caught and have nothing to do with the anatomy of the animal.

The only significant difference in the shells of *C. virginica* taken from various geographical locations is the color of the inner shell, and this difference is by no means absolute. The inner part of the shell of an oyster taken from waters of the North Atlantic is devoid (or almost so) of pigment, with the exception of the dark muscle scar. In those caught in the South Atlantic and the Gulf of Mexico, the inner part of the valve is tinged with brown or reddish-brown hues.

The shells of bivalves are manufactured by the mantle, a versatile organ that is characteristic of the phylum Mollusca. (The outer covering of a squid or octopus, for example, is the mantle, which protects the internal parts because the shell has been lost to the forces of evolution.) In the oyster, and other bivalves as well, it is represented by a double fold of the body wall that lines the inner surfaces of the valves and encloses and protects the other organs of the body. This is the first organ to greet us when we open the valves of the oyster.

Special glands within the mantle are responsible for extracting a wide variety of elements from the water and converting them into the complex constituents of the shell.

The margin of the mantle has three folds, the inner one of which is muscular. The muscular part of one side of the mantle presses against the inner part of the other when the valves close. The area of the shell where the muscles of the inner folds are attached is represented by a thin line (the pallial line, or scar, in technical terminology) located a short distance back from the margin of the shell.

The middle fold of the mantle bears sense organs, and the outer fold, along with the general surface of the mantle, is responsible for laying down the shell.

The shell is one of the most salient features of mollusks (exceptions previously noted), and its formation has been the subject of many scientific investigations. Such phenomena as crystal formation and deposition, calcification, growth patterns, and synthesis of components have intrigued researchers for years, especially those interested in the life of the oyster.

In 1964 Paul S. Galtsoff published *The American Oyster*, Crassostrea virginica, a 480-page treatise encompassing everything known about the oyster at that time. The shell itself is considered in 42 pages of the publication, and not the smallest detail, no matter how technical, is neglected. For example, complex mathematical expressions are given to determine such arcane features of the shell as the shape of the logarithmic spiral and the plane of closure of the valves. Galtsoff's monumental work should be consulted by anyone giving serious consideration to becoming involved with the oyster on either a commercial or scientific basis.

Needless to say, I will not attempt to go into even a fraction of the detail to be found in that publication when I describe the structure and physiology of the oyster.

The outer layer of the shell is called the periostracum (there is no common name) and is composed primarily of an organic material called conchiolin. The primary purpose of the outer layer is to protect the other parts of the shell from the corrosive action of the salt water. Conchiolin, incidentally, is the principal ingredient in the ligament that holds the shell hinge together. In *C. virginica* the periostracum is poorly developed, and practically nonexistent in older oysters. The middle layer of the shell is termed the prismatic layer and is composed of several tiers of crystalline calcium carbonate, each layer alternating with a layer of conchiolin. The calcium carbonate is first laid down as small crystals, which grow to form columns. The columns are formed at right angles to the innermost layer, which is laminated like the pages of a book.

The inner layer is frequently called the nacreous layer and is deposited as plates of calcium carbonate, which reflect the light. This is the so-called mother-of-pearl, or nacre; it has some commercial value and was called wampum by many of the early Indians. The shells were strung in strands, belts, or sashes and used as money, ceremonial pledges, and ornaments.

If a foreign substance becomes lodged between the nacreous layer and the inner part of the mantle, concentric, successive layers of nacre are secreted around the foreign object to protect the soft parts of the oyster from irritation. The resulting sphere is a pearl.

Though pearls can be produced by all shell-bearing mollusks, only those with a nacreous layer can produce pearls of commercial value. The finest natural pearls are manufactured by the pearl oysters that inhabit the waters of the warmer Pacific areas. The pearls produced by *C. virginica* are of poor quality and have little or no value on the jewel market.

Bead pearls are produced by inserting a small piece of shell bead into a bona fide pearl oyster, and a nacreous layer approximately one millimeter thick is laid down around the bead. Most cultured pearls are started by transplanting a year-old bead or seed pearl into another oyster and waiting for about three years to obtain a pearl of marketable size.

In the formation of the three layers of the shell, the mantle extracts a variety of elements from the environment, combines them into chemical compounds, and deposits them in the proper order. Calcium carbonate makes up about 98 percent of the shell and may occur as either calcite or aragonite, which are chemically identical but have different systems of crystallization. About 1½ percent of the shell is composed of various compounds of the following elements: sodium, magnesium, sulfur, silicon, and strontium. The remaining ½ percent is made up of chemical concoctions of a number of "trace" elements: chlorine, aluminum, iron, copper, phosphorus, manganese, fluorine, potassium, titanium, boron, zinc, bromine, and iodine.

Over 250 years ago the French biologist de Réaumur discovered that shells grow by accretion of material deposited at the edges, and since that time numerous investigations of the process have confirmed his original observations. If we look at the outer surface of an oyster shell, growth rings will be noted. These rings represent the shape of the shell at the various stages in the oyster's life. The rings nearest the umbo are the oldest and those at the margin of the shell are the youngest. In an unreliable way, the number of rings present can be used to estimate the age of the oyster. *C. virginica* from the region of the Chesapeake Bay normally experience two growing periods during the year. One of these periods is during April and May and the other usually occurs sometime in October. Temperature, which affects the overall rate of metabolism, is the governing factor in respect to shell growth. At about 40 degrees Fahrenheit all shell growth ceases, but as the temperature of the water climbs into the 50 to 60 degree range in April and early May growth becomes accelerated. Experiments performed at the Woods Hole Biological Laboratory in Massachusetts showed that shell growth in the winter will begin immediately after oysters are transferred from the cold ocean to much warmer seawater in the laboratory.

Very little growth is experienced during the summer months because the oyster's physiology has a more important chore to perform—reproduction. All physiological processes in an animal require the expenditure of adenosine triphosphate (ATP)—energy units that have been produced from the food taken in, digested, and eventually assimilated. The process of reproduction in the oyster is such a massive operation that there is precious little energy left over after the testes and ovaries have produced millions and millions of sperm and eggs. At the termination of the

17

spawning season in the fall, the oyster is spent and devastated—a mere shadow of its former self. After a period of recuperation at the end of the reproductive period, energy derived from the food can be used again for shell growth and tissue rebuilding.

Internal Anatomy

The internal parts of an oyster can be compared to the pages of a book. Having made this comparison, it must be stated that the book is a hard one to open. The valves are held together by a single large adductor-type muscle that must be cut before the living oyster can be opened. A special oyster knife is usually inserted between the valves on the ventral margin, and by deftly moving the blade back and forth inside the shell the muscle can be severed. When an oyster dies, the adductor muscle relaxes, and the valves fall open.

When an oyster is shucked the valves are opened and the body or meat of the animal is removed. Each year at the Annual Oyster Festival held in St. Mary's County, Maryland, the National Oyster Shucking Contest is held. In this main feature of each year's festival the finalists in both the men's and women's contests win separate cash awards plus a plaque. For the last few years the winner of the shuck-off between the sexes received an all-expense-paid trip to Galway, Ireland, to represent the United States in the international contest held there in the fall. A special trophy, usually presented by the governor of Maryland, is displayed in the winner's home state for the year of his or her reign as champion.

In 1983 Sarah Hammond of Urbanna, Virginia, defeated the men's champion, Francis Cullison of Tall Timbers, Maryland, to become the National Champion. Sarah won the coveted title by shucking twenty-four oysters in two minutes and thirty-eight seconds, but with penalty time added for nicking the oysters and the presence of shell in the meat, her official time was recorded as three minutes and thirty-seven seconds, good enough to beat Mr. Cullison by a few seconds.

Now that we have parted the oyster's valves—probably with considerable difficulty—it is possible to open the "book," take a look at the internal organs, and learn something about how they function. If the beginning zoology student experienced trouble in establishing the basic body regions on the exterior of the animal, he is usually dumbfounded when he first gazes on the body of the animal contained within the valves. There seems to be no distinct differentiation of the body parts, and, to add to the confusion, there is no head. The oyster has no similarity to any other animal the student has studied previously. Once I heard a freshman remark, "The whole mess just looks like a big blob of undifferentiated tissue." The student's initial reaction to the oyster's anatomy is typical, but after draping back the folds of the mantle, turning to the next set of pages so to speak, definite structures can be delimited. As mentioned previously, the mantle is a double fold of the body wall of the animals and encompasses the other organs, making up what is termed the visceral mass, which lies in the mantle cavity. The oyster has few sense organs, but those it has are located on the middle fold of the mantle's edge. Numerous small tentacles, just visible to the unaided eye, are responsive to touch or tactile stimuli, and small pigmented spots also along the margin are said to be sensitive to light. As the adult oyster is not going anywhere, it has no need for eyes. It does have its preferences as to the amount of light it desires to bask in at various times, and an oyster whose valves are ajar will close them if a shadow is passed over it.

If one side of the mantle is folded back while the oyster is on the half-shell the most obvious structures to appear are the striated gills, which are double on each side. (Oysters examined during the height of the spawning season will look different. The large gonad, testis or ovary, will obscure most of the other organs.)

The gills of oysters and other bivalves perform several vital functions and are extremely complex in structure. Respiration, or gas exchange, is accomplished mainly by the gills, but the overall surface of the broad mantle participates in this function in a limited way. As in almost all animals, oxygen is required for the burning of sugar by the cells of the body to obtain energy—to stoke the fires of the processes of life. As the gills are profusely supplied with blood vessels, oxygen diffuses from the water into the bloodstream to be transported to every cell of the body. When sugar is burned in the cell and the indispensable energy is re-

The Oyster

leased, carbon dioxide is produced. Carbon dioxide is toxic to
living protoplasm and must be eliminated before it can build up to
dangerous concentrations. As the blood delivers oxygen to the
individual cell it takes up carbon dioxide and returns it to the gills,
where it is given off to the environment to be recycled into many
basic molecules.

The life of an oyster is dependent on a current of water flowing
through its body to provide oxygen and food and to carry away the
by-products of metabolism. For many years biologists tried to
figure out how this essential flow was established and maintained.
Finally, the puzzle was solved when it was discovered that the
surface of the gills was covered with untold numbers of microscopic, hairlike structures called cilia. The cilia, with a constant
and coordinated beat, draw the water in at one point and expel it
at another.

Oysters are known as filter, or ciliary, feeders. The current of
water passing through the body contains countless numbers of
living organisms that make up the plankton of a body of water. The
plankton is composed primarily of one-celled plants and animals
and microorganisms such as bacteria. These minute organisms are
trapped by the oyster in a sticky mucus secreted by certain gland
cells in the gills and transformed into fine ropes of particles, which
are passed to the mouth for ingestion. As the water passes through
the network of tentacles found along the mantle's edge, large,
unusable particles such as grains of sand are filtered out and
prevented from making contact with the delicate surface of the
gills.

One can readily understand why silt (a suspension of minute
particles of minerals and clay) can be disastrous to an oyster
population. The particles found in the silt are too small to be
filtered by the oyster, and, having gained entrance to the mantle
cavity, they will be engulfed by the mucus-laden gills and block
the food-transport system. Though the oyster has no head, and
really nothing that can be called a brain, it somehow perceives
that its existence is in peril when an excessive amount of silt is
present. The valves are tightly closed, and the oyster shuts down
operations. Sooner or later (depending on the temperature,
which largely controls the rate of metabolism), however, the

20

oyster must open up and reestablish the life-giving current. The buildup of carbon dioxide in the tissues, and not the lack of oxygen or food as one might suspect, is the primary factor involved in the decision to reopen the valves. The same sort of thing happens when we voluntarily hold our breath. Young children sometimes threaten to commit suicide by holding their breath if the parent does not accede to their wishes. The parent should have no concern for this aspect of the problem as it is impossible to kill oneself in this manner. As carbon dioxide concentrates in the blood of the child (or the oyster) it is converted to carbonic acid, and the delicate acid-base (pH) balance is upset. The body then involuntarily reacts to alleviate the problem—the child starts breathing or the oyster opens its valves.

Damage to the oyster results if the period of siltation is prolonged, and deleterious material is taken in when the valves reopen.

The gills aid the reproductive process of *Crassostrea* by providing the means by which the sex cells are distributed at the time of spawning. Sperm produced by the males and eggs by the females are liberated into the mantle cavity, where they are flushed out of the oyster by the continuous current. In incubatory oysters, such as the common European species, *Ostrea edulis*, the eggs are caught and retained by the gills of the female, where they are fertilized by sperm introduced with the incoming current. After fertilization the young oysters are incubated for a time in special brood sacs located in the tissue of the gills.

The mucus-encased strands of food prepared by the gills are moved forward toward the rather obvious hatchet-shaped and double-folded palps that guard the entrance to the mouth. If there is too much indigestible food or extraneous material in the food package, it is rejected and is propelled back to await elimination. A sort of cesspool or backwater is created at the rear of the animal, which serves to collect undesirable products and other types of waste materials. When the oyster closes its shell the water of the cesspool is forcibly ejected, carrying with it the undesirable material.

Nestled between the lobelike palps is the mouth, which is connected to the stomach by a short esophagus. When the ropes of food arrive in the stomach there is an additional sorting of the particles. The stomach lining is coated with tracts of cilia, which keep the food in a constant state of agitation.

Attached to the stomach are two organs essential to the digestive processes of the oyster—the crystalline style and the digestive gland. The style is essentially a gelatinous rod secreted by the glandular style sac when the oyster is actively feeding. This unique structure is as close in shape to a wheel as you will find in all of the animal kingdom and is found only in filter feeders of the phylum Mollusca. The style rotates, acting as a capstan, and winds the strands of food about itself. As it turns, the tip is brought into contact with a hard structure called the gastric shield, which is embedded in the stomach wall. As the tip of the style is abraded away by the shield, large quantities of the digestive enzyme amylase are liberated. Amylase is the enzyme or digestive ferment found in all animals, from sponges to man, which is responsible for the chemical reactions occurring during the digestion of starch to usable simple sugars. Other enzymes that help in the breakdown of fats and proteins are known to be associated with the tip of the style.

The style is a transient structure not present in nonfeeding oysters. During the winter months when metabolism is reduced to a standstill, it is usually not present, but for some unknown reason a few of the dormant oysters retain it. Likewise, during the warm months a significant number of nonfeeding oysters retain the style while others in the same category lose it. The presence or absence of the style is, therefore, not an infallible method to be used by the oyster biologist to determine if an oyster is feeding or not.

The other organ associated with the stomach is the digestive gland, or digestive diverticula, which may appear to the observer as an irregular mass of tissue, yellow to dirty green to dark brown in color. In many cases the color is not visible through a creamy-white layer of animal starch (glycogen). Though this organ has been called a liver or a liver-pancreas by some, it has none of the functions usually associated with these organs in higher animals.

Most animals digest their food first and then absorb and assimilate it. In the human stomach, for example, some types of food

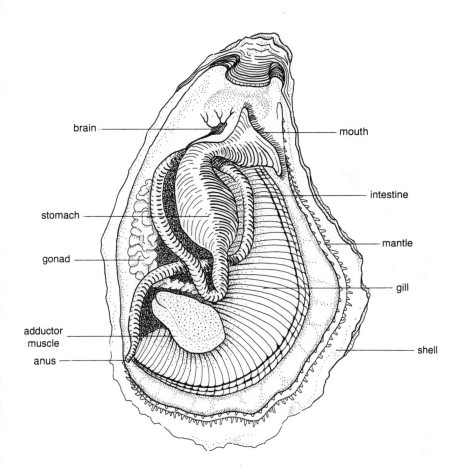

brain

mouth

intestine

stomach

mantle

gonad

gill

adductor
muscle

anus

shell

Internal anatomy of *Crassostrea virginica*.

The Oyster

are broken down by enzymes contained in the gastric juice to the basic molecules, which are absorbed into the bloodstream for assimilation throughout the body. The oyster accomplishes the same thing, but in reverse—first absorption, then digestion.

Amoebocytes are cells found in many types of animals and have the ability to wander to and fro around the body and ingest other cells and bits of organic matter. White blood cells are amoebocytes and are in fact, quite similar to the ones occurring in the digestive gland of the oyster. These voracious cells leave their place of origin in the digestive gland and make their way to the stomach, where they proceed to engorge themselves with food items—organic matter and the partially digested remains of the plankton-laden ropes.

After ingesting as much food as possible, the amoebocytes retire to the lining of the digestive gland to fully digest the food intracellularly with the aid of enzymes they manufacture. Carbohydrates are finished off to glucose, proteins are reduced to amino acids, and fats are broken down to fatty acids and glycerol; these fundamental building blocks of life are then shared with the other cells of the oyster.

The remainder of the digestive system consists of the midgut, rectum, and anal opening. Though the digestion and absorption of food are basically intracellular processes taking place in the stomach and digestive gland, it seems likely that they occur to a limited extent in the midgut. Numerous amoebocytes are present, and small quantities of enzymes have been reported as occurring in this region. The midgut, or intestine, is a short, loosely coiled organ that is difficult to see in the dissected specimen, as are the stomach, style sac, and rectum. As there is no layer of muscle built into the midgut, the fecal material is moved along toward the rectum and anus by the beating of countless cila. The anal opening is located near the right side of the adductor muscle, and the feces are discharged into the mantle cavity in the form of a slightly flattened ribbon which, to me at least, resembles a tapeworm. The fecal ribbons settle in the cesspool mentioned earlier and are eventually discharged along with filtered items and other waste materials.

24

Form and Function

Just above the adductor muscle is the heart, whose function is to keep the blood circulating around the body. In the oyster it will be noted that the rectum is located along the side of the heart, whereas in the clam it passes through the center of the organ.

The heart of an oyster consists of three chambers, two auricles and a ventricle, and may beat as many as fifty times a minute or as few as six times per minute. The physiological state of the oyster at a given time determines the rate of heartbeat. Blood is forced out of the ventricle to the gills, where it is oxygenated after releasing its supply of carbon dioxide. Some of the blood is directed to the mantle, where it takes on an additional supply of oxygen and eventually is returned to the auricles of the heart after the oxygen has been delivered to the body cells. A portion of the blood, however, circulates through cavities or sinuses and passes in a vein to the small U-shaped kidneys for purification. Certain waste products of metabolism, such as toxic nitrogenous compounds, are extracted from the blood as it passes through the kidneys.

Oysters are literally blue-blooded. In animals with red blood, iron is a vital element in the molecule of hemoglobin that carries the oxygen and some of the carbon dioxide content of the blood. For some reason, iron has been replaced in the hemoglobin of the oyster by copper, which gives the blood a bluish tinge. (The same thing occurs in crabs.)

No one has ever claimed the oyster was one of the more intelligent members of the animal kingdom, and when we examine its tiny, unspecialized nervous system, the reason becomes obvious. About the closest thing to a brain the oyster can claim is either one of two aggregates of nerve cells called ganglia located rather close together. Small nerves radiate out from each ganglion and are in communication with all parts of the oyster, but there is no central command post or true brain. Parts of the nervous system are next to impossible to locate unless one is a trained oyster anatomist.

Depending on the state of reproductive activity, the size of the gonad, or sex organ, will vary tremendously. In oysters that have just completed the spawning process, the testis or ovary will be quite small and difficult to identify. When reproduction is in full swing, however, these organs will have become so enlarged with sperm and eggs that they obscure most of the other parts of the body.

The young male oyster has two testes, and the juvenile female is the proud possesser of two ovaries, but as the oysters mature, the double gonads unite and fuse to form a single body—combining forces, perhaps, to face the upcoming task of producing the many millions of sex cells by which the species will, one hopes, be perpetuated.

In the mature gonad, the outer covering is stretched so thin by the internal contents that it is translucent, and one can readily see the treelike branches of the system of canals that will conduct the sperm and eggs to the outside. About the only indication that the oyster's single gonad was originally composed of two organs is the presence of the branches of the canals on each side.

About now, I think most of us will say that Huxley was certainly right. That slippery, living, morsel that glides so easily down the palate is more complicated than a watch.

Zoological Status

As noted earlier, in the system of biological classification, oysters belong to the phylum Mollusca. The name *mollusca* means "soft body" in Latin, but the members of this group have certain other definite characteristics in common.

Over one hundred thousand different species of mollusks have been described over the years; they include such familiar forms as snails, squids, octopuses, chitons, and those with two calcareous shells, the bivalves. Only one other phylum is larger than the Mollusca from a standpoint of number of species and number of individuals. This group is, of course, the Arthropoda ("jointed-leg"), which encompasses the insects, crustaceans, ticks, mites, spiders, and a host of other forms. Well over one million different species of insects alone are known to science, and, from an evolutionary standpoint, there can be no doubt that this has been the most successful group of animals ever to appear on the face of the earth.

Form and Function

But the mollusks, with only a fraction of the number of species of arthropods, are not doing too badly in the struggle for existence that all animals face. This becomes apparent when we consider that the members of the phylum Chordata, the animals that possess at least a trace of a backbone at some time during their life, can boast only a few thousand different types.

The Swedish naturalist Carolus Linnaeus is known as the Father of Taxonomy (classification of living things); in his monumental work of 1758 he devised a system to bring order to the biological world, and his ideas remain little changed today. He described most of the animal and plant phyla, as well as many of the species included in the broad groupings. He is also responsible for establishing the binomial system of naming individual species. Under the binomial scheme the scientific name of an organism consists of two parts, the genus and the species to which it has been assigned. This method of giving an animal or plant a single name to be used universally has been employed by scientists ever since Linnaeus first proposed it. For example, man belongs to the genus *Homo* ("man") and the species *sapiens* ("knowing"), so the correct scientific name of man is *Homo sapiens*. Similarly, the scientific name of the oyster with which we are most familiar and which is the main character in this book is *Crassostrea virginica* ("thick shell, of Virginia").

At first, Linnaeus created the genus *Ostrea* to include all oysters and a variety of other mollusks that obviously were not oysters. In 1801, the French zoologist Jean Baptiste de Lamarck, who is better known for his early theory of evolution of species by means of acquired characters than for his study of oysters, removed the nonoysters from the genus and set down a description of what an oyster really was. According to Lamarck, to be qualified as an oyster and be named *Ostrea* the mollusk had to possess the following characteristics: adhering, unequal valves (shells); valves irregular in shape, with divergent beaks that with age become unequal; hinge without teeth; hinge ligament half internal. Though considerable controversy over the classification of oysters has raged over the years, especially when fossil forms are considered, Lamarck's basic description of what constitutes an oyster is as good as any advocated since his time.

27

The Oyster

In this book our primary concern is the species *C. virginica* and a brief background of this and other species found in the coastal waters of the continental United States is in order.

Crassostrea virginica.   This is the principal edible oyster of the Atlantic and Gulf coasts and is the star of this production. As *C. virginica* enjoys such a wide distribution, from the Gulf of St. Lawrence to the Gulf of Mexico and the West Indies, biologists were unable to decide on the correct name until 1955. Chincoteague oysters come from Chincoteague, Virginia, and Blue Point oysters originate in New York, but they are the same species, *C. virginica,* as are those that bear the label of Florida, Louisiana, or Texas oysters. Of course, fans of the Blue Point will insist that their variety of *C. virginica* is superior to the Chincoteague type and vice versa, but, in reality, they are talking about the same animal.

   C. virginica is called a nonincubatory oyster in that the sex cells are deposited to the outside and fertilization and development takes place in the water. (An incubatory species retains the eggs within the body of the female, where fertilization and early development occur.)

   The right valve is smaller than the left and the beaks of the valves are elongated and strongly curved. Adults vary from 2 to 14 inches in height depending on the age of the animal and the environment it occupies. The shape, sculpture, and pigmentation of the inner side of the shell vary greatly.

Crassostrea gigas.   This is the Japanese or Pacific oyster; it was introduced many years ago into coastal waters of the western United States, British Columbia, and the panhandle of Alaska. *C. gigas* is a long, straplike oyster that may be several inches larger than *C. virginica,* though the valves are much thinner and quite variable. This nonincubatory species has been successfully cultivated in Pacific waters for many decades and is the oyster one is most apt to purchase in the seafood section of a supermarket anywhere in the country.

Crassostrea rivularis.   This species is another import from the Far East that has established itself in Puget Sound. It is similar to

C. gigas but is much smaller. It is a nonincubatory oyster of limited commercial value.

Ostrea edulis.   Where the members of the genus *Crassostrea* have a cuplike configuration of the lower shell that houses the bulk of the animal's body, species of the genus *Ostrea* have both shells relatively flattened. *O. edulis* is the oyster common to Europe, and the one that so delighted the Romans when they came to England. An incubatory species of medium size, it was introduced into the coastal waters of Maine many years ago at Boothbay Harbor. Though it survived and reproduced in the cold New England sea, it has never become numerous enough to warrant commercial harvesting.

Ostrea lurida.   *O. lurida* is called the California, or Olympia, oyster and is native to the coastal waters of the Pacific. This small, incubatory oyster lost most of its commercial value to the Japanese import, which is much larger and, its propagators claim, tastier.

Ostrea equestris.   Sometimes called the horse, or crested, oyster, this is a small, noncommercial bivalve found from the Atlantic states to the Gulf of Mexico and to the West Indies. Laymen often mistake it for the young of *C. virginica*. Its average size is only about 2 inches, but occasional specimens measuring up to 3½ inches are found. *O. equestris* is incubatory and frequently occurs in large numbers on commercial beds in association with *C. virginica*.

Ostrea frons.   Sometimes called the coon oyster, this one is a common sight in the southeastern states, where it is found attached to branches and roots of the mangrove tree. Because of its small size, it has little if any market value. As far as its taste goes, there is a sharp division of opinion. On several visits to Florida in the past, I have "picked" them in their natural habitat, and, after seasoning them with brackish water, found the taste to be very good.

But, as far as I am personally concerned, no oyster in the world can match the taste and succulence of *C. virginica* taken from the Chesapeake Bay. Living on the southwestern coast of France for

The Oyster

several years, I frequently devoured large numbers of the so-called Portuguese oyster (the one most often served at Roman banquets) and found them to be delicious. It was not until I returned to the United States and became reacquainted with our native species that I realized I had forgotten what a real oyster tasted like.

For years it was the custom in my boyhood home in Texas to have oyster stew for supper on Saturday evenings during the "*r*" months of the year. My father would stop by a local fish market on his way home from work and purchase a pint of Gulf Coast oysters, and with milk, butter, pepper, and celery salt he would concoct a delicious stew. Routinely, however, he would withhold two or three oysters from the stew pot, and, after placing them on Saltine crackers, devour them with much gusto. I think I was about eight years old when he first offered me the opportunity to share a raw oyster with him. Reluctantly I accepted the invitation, and, after closing my eyes, let the slippery morsel stimulate my taste buds. At that precise moment I became addicted to the glorious oyster, and my affection for them has only increased as the years have passed.

Many years later my father lay in a hospital bed stricken with a virulent form of leukemia, and I asked him if there was anything at all he wanted. After thinking about my offer for a moment, he replied, "Some raw oysters would be nice." It did not take long to locate a seafood restaurant that provided carryouts, and I quickly returned to his bedside with a dozen on the half-shell. I will never forget the pleasure on his face as he ate them.

A few days later he was dead, and I feel sure he carried the memory of those oysters with him to the very end. Such is the relationship of oysters and men.

CHAPTER THREE

To Be or Not to Be:
Life Cycle and Development

An oyster may be cross'd in love—and why?
Because he mopeth in his shell,
And heaves a lonely subterraqueous sigh,
Much as monk may do within his cell.

Lord Byron

AN oyster is capable of functioning as a male at one time during its life and as a female at another period. An animal like this is called a hermaphrodite by zoologists. Greek mythology holds that the first hermaphrodite was created when Hermaphroditus, the son of Hermes, united with the love goddess Aphrodite and entered the body of the nymph Salacis. With the male and female capacities united under one roof, the process of procreation was greatly simplified.

Hermaphroditism is the normal way of life for many invertebrate (without backbones) animals and some vertebrate (with backbones) species. This mode of reproduction is common among the mollusks, though many of them have separate sexes. Most of these types are termed *true hermaphrodites* because both male and female sex organs are present in the same individual, and sperm and eggs are produced at approximately the same time.

Barbut, in his *Genera Vermium*, published in 1788, was the first to call attention to hermaphroditism in oysters, but in fact they, as well as a few other members of the animal kingdom, are not true hermaphrodites but are referred to as *protandrous* ("first, male") *hermaphrodites*. In these animals the diversified sex organ may be male, female, or neutral at a given time. Usually one individual has the capacity to go either way and cannot simultaneously produce sperm and eggs, but a few *Crassostrea* in the laboratory have been reported to function as both male and female at the same time. This phenomenon, however, is considered to be a rare and abnormal occurrence.

C. virginica becomes sexually mature (capable of forming functional sperm or eggs) at about one year of age. This is not an ironclad figure, however, for the emergence of the oyster's puberty; some have been reported capable of reproducing as early as six months after hatching or as late as two or three years. These latter observations were made on laboratory specimens maintained under controlled conditions and may or may not be indicative of what goes on in a natural environment.

When the oyster does become sexually qualified, it almost always plays the male role first. Exceptions to this rule frequently have been noted, however, and reports of *protogynandrous* ("first, female") oysters are common in the scientific literature.

One of the cardinal principles of science is that nothing is absolute, and this very important tenet is difficult for non-scientists to understand. When the scientist uses such terms as "usually," "normally," "almost always," or "in a majority of the cases," he is sometimes accused of "copping out." Because all living organisms are genetically different (with the exception of identical twins), the science of biology is inexact at best, and any biologist who makes a perfect or absolute statement when commenting on some aspect of the living world is either ignorant of the nature of the science itself, or is a fool. I hope the reader, keeping these thoughts in mind, will be tolerant of statements that appear to vacillate, hesitate, or compromise as we consider the intimate aspects of the life of the enigmatic oyster.

After the oyster has played the role of the male in its first spawning season, his testis undergoes radical anatomical and physiological changes, and, as if by magic, transforms into a functional ovary which will produce unbelievable numbers of eggs for the remainder of the creature's life.

One would think this unusual arrangement of the sex life of the oyster would be well known to the people who have spent their lives bringing them up from the bottom, but such is not the case.

Oystermen of the Chesapeake (and elsewhere, I imagine) are notoriously ignorant of the basic biology of the animal they so avidly seek. Out of ten oystermen on Maryland's Eastern Shore I queried concerning the sex life of the oyster, eight thought the oyster led a "normal" existence, that is, separate sexes that do not change. One respondent replied that he had heard homosexuality was involved, and another knew they were hermaphroditic ("morphodites" as he called them), but he was not aware of the protandrous nature of their hermaphroditism.

As a rule of thumb, the sex of an oyster may be determined by its height. Generally speaking, a specimen of 3 inches or more in height is probably functioning as a female, while those smaller than 3 inches are biological males. This method of sex determination is based on the fact that oysters gain about an inch in height during each year of their existence. Presumably, an oyster 3 or more inches in height is at least three years old and has completed its tenure as a male. In the common European oyster, *Ostrea edulis,* sex change is an ongoing event, with the male stage alternating with the female phase each year of the mollusk's life.

From a standpoint of biological efficiency, protandrous hermaphroditism is highly advantageous to the species which have evolved this mode of life. In true hermaphroditism, where sperm and eggs are produced by the same individual at approximately the same time, there is always the possibility of biological incest as fertilization may be accomplished with sex cells from the same individual. Offspring resulting from such a union would be genetically identical to the parent. This routine is called self-fertilization, or selfing.

From a standpoint of population genetics and evolution, self-fertilization is detrimental to the species. Cross-fertilization, on the other hand, combines the DNA (genetic material) of two different individuals to form the offspring. In all probability, different genes have arisen by mutation in the individuals of a population, and, we hope, at least a few of these genetic sports will key the development of advantageous characteristics in the organism. With cross-fertilization, these changed or mutated genes are shared with the other members of the population and more adaptable oysters (or anything else) will result. Selfing prohibits the free exchange of these mutated genetic determiners and suppresses variation and adaptability.

If all members of a population were identical, the forces of natural selection and evolution would have nothing on which to operate, and the vast diversity of living forms we observe in nature would not exist. With the sharing of genes by cross-fertilization, nature insures that no two individuals, be they oysters or men, will be exactly alike. This fundamental concept was first recognized by Charles Darwin more than 125 years ago, and it played a very important role in his formulation of the theory of evolution of species by means of natural selection. (The oyster was one of the many animals Darwin studied intensely in formulating the theory.)

Cross-fertilization has been so vital to the evolutionary process of animals that even true hermaphrodites have developed ways to keep selfing to a minimum. About the only species in which self-fertilization routinely occurs are solitary parasites such as large tapeworms. Some of these freeloaders may reach a length of up to thirty feet or more, and the digestive tract of the unfortunate human, pig, or cow that plays host to such monsters simply cannot support more than one of these elongated worms. Consequently, with only one individual present, selfing is obligatory. Even in the instance of these primitive but highly specialized parasites, however, the mixing of the genes of different individuals may occur. Some tapeworm experts do not consider the worm to represent a single individual. Rather, the plausible theory has been advanced that a tapeworm represents a colony of many worms, each of which is represented by a single segment of the "tape." This makes sense. When we examine the anatomy of the tapeworm it is readily apparent that each of the thousands of segments of the body contains a complete set of male and female reproductive organs. Eggs produced by one segment of the body may be fertilized by sperm from another, resulting in cross-fertilization.

Tapeworms and oysters, as well as all other species of animals, produce more offspring than can possibly survive. Only a select few will survive to sexual maturity and serve as the breeding stock for the next generation. This principle of overproduction applies to all species and was recognized by Darwin and others as being the primary driving force of the evolutionary process. The reasoning: As more offspring are produced than can possibly survive because of the finite nature of the necessities of life, intense competition results. Those individuals with a genetic makeup that provides an advantage over its competitors will have a better chance of surviving to become the parents of the next generation. Those which lack the genetic advantage will have less of a chance to contribute their genes to the continuity of the species.

The chance variations, created by cross-fertilization, will be preserved from one generation to the next if they are of an advantageous nature to the individual. Conversely, if a variation generated by the mixing of the DNA of two animals results in a character of an inferior or disadvantageous nature, the individual will have little hope of surviving to reproductive maturity.

A female oyster may produce up to five hundred million eggs during a single year of her life. If all these ova were fertilized and grew to maturity and reproduced, and the same thing happened through five succeeding generations, mathematical experts calculate the number of oysters resulting would equal a volume 250 times that of the earth. Fortunately for the inhabitants of this planet, it can be safely said that no more than a dozen from these matings would survive.

I mentioned these figures to a retired waterman of my acquaintance, and, after pondering the numbers for a minute or two, he replied, "We are having a hard enough time as it is to find the shuckers to take care of the arsters we got now. Where in the world would we find enough to shuck a batch like that?"

In the region of the Chesapeake Bay, *Crassostrea* begin spawning about the first of June when the water reaches a temperature of about 20 degrees Celsius (68 degrees Fahrenheit). At a temperature of 72 degrees Fahrenheit the process shifts into high gear and gradually tapers off as the water gets warmer. At about 85 degrees F. reproductive activities cease.

By late spring the sex organs are mature and contain great numbers of sex cells which are characterized by the fact that they have only half the amount of DNA of the other cells of the body. A special type of cell division (spermatogenesis in the male; oogenesis in the female) has occurred to reduce the characteristic amount of DNA exactly in half. As each sperm or egg carries only

35

half of the genes of the individual who produced it, fertilization restores the correct amount of hereditary material in the new individual.

When the oyster is ready to spawn, the sex organs are bulging with sperm and eggs and more or less obliterate the other organs of the body. Still, it is impossible to determine the sex of the animal with the naked eye. If, however, the gonad is pricked with a sharp needle a milky exudate will issue forth. Microscopic examination of this fluid at a magnification of about one hundred times will quickly answer the question. If the animal is a male, large numbers of sperm will be readily apparent. The male cells resemble dancing tadpoles as they thrash about with the aid of their elongated tails. Eggs of the female have no tails and resemble a kernel of corn, the interior of which is translucent because it contains a considerable amount of yolk.

When spawning is actually taking place, the female behaves differently than the male. She will be observed to open and close her valves in a clappinglike motion every few minutes. With each opening and closing a puff of eggs is discharged, in much the same way an old-time steam locomotive belches forth clouds of smoke. The egg-laying process requires about fifteen to twenty minutes. No one knows for sure just how many eggs are released during each spawning session, but the number is very large. Oyster researchers report numbers of between fifteen and one hundred million eggs being released at a single act of oviposition, and I imagine the age and physical condition of the animal involved, as well as environmental factors, play a large role in determining how prolific a female is at any given spawning period.

A male oyster does not clap his valves when he ejaculates into the water. Once the emission process is started, the sperm cells, surrounded by the seminal fluid, ooze out in a steady stream through the partially opened valves. When one considers the number of sperm cells shed by a single male during a spawning session, the female oyster is put to shame. Dr. Reginald V. Truitt of the Chesapeake Biological Laboratory at Solomons Island, Maryland, and one of the pioneer oyster researchers of the Bay area, was able to estimate the number of sperm an oyster, "whose testis was not especially distended," produced on one occasion.

Dr. Truitt measured sperm production of this particular mollusk at approximately 2,960,000,000!

With both male and female oysters it seems that certain chemical messengers called pheromones stimulate the spawning process. A pheromone is similar to a hormone in action, but in the case of the former the "magic bullet" is shed to the outside and produces its effects on other animals, whereas in the latter the compound operates within the body of the individual producing it. When a set of forces, many of which are not known, induce the male or female to commence spawning, it has been observed that the other males or females on the bar (or in the laboratory) will quickly follow suit. It is believed pheromones are discharged by the first oysters to ejaculate or ovulate, and these stimuli goad the others to perform their biological duty.

The production of large numbers of gametes (sex cells) is characteristic of animals that practice external fertilization and development. Most of the sperm and eggs emitted will never come in contact with each other. The staggering numbers produced, however, ensure that at least a few of them will meet and create a limited number of new oysters, if not at this spawning session, perhaps at the next, because the oysters will repeat the act of propagation several times during the summer months.

The female of *Ostrea edulis* produces far fewer eggs than her American cousin, *Crassostrea*. This is correlated with the fact that the European is an incubatory oyster and does not discharge her eggs into the hostile environment of the sea. They are caught and retained by the gills, where they are fertilized by sperm brought in by the current. With internal fertilization and subsequent development of the early stages in protective brood sacs, *Ostrea* offspring have a better chance of survival. Wrapped in the protective valves of the mother until they become adolescent, the young oysters are able to fend for themselves much better when they finally face the trials and tribulations of life on their own. In all probability, however, the same number of European and American oysters make it to sexual maturity.

The definitive act of fertilization consists of the penetration of the egg membrane by the sperm and the subsequent uniting of the egg and sperm nuclei. Though only one sperm cell actually

37

fertilizes an egg, the success of this crucial process requires the participation of a large number of the male cells.

If oyster eggs and sperm are mixed together in a container in the laboratory (*in vitro* fertilization) and a microscope slide is prepared for viewing, the process of new oysters being created may be readily observed. Minutes or even seconds after sperm are added to a suspension of eggs, the individual egg is seemingly under attack by hundreds of the tailed sperm. In this condition the egg looks like a pincushion with many pins sticking into its surface at all angles. It will be noted that the egg membrane is surrounded by a protective coating of a jellylike substance that must dissolve before access to the interior by a sperm is possible. Apparently, the heads of the sperm cells, which are in reality the nuclei of the cells and contain the DNA, secrete an enzyme whose sole function is to digest the coating of the egg. One or two sperm heads cannot supply sufficient enzyme to do the job, so the output of many cells is required. The enzyme, hyaluronidase, performs its task well, and, in fact is the same enzyme found in the heads of the sperm cells of man and many other animals, both vertebrate and invertebrate. Its function is apparently the same as in the oyster.

Eventually the coating of the egg is destroyed, and a single sperm cell penetrates the egg's membrane, discarding its tail on the way in. A series of mechanical and physiological changes occur in the membrane that preclude the entrance of any additional male cells. Supposedly, the strongest sperm is the one that enters and thus assures the vigor of the next generation. The weaker cells, having contributed their part to the perpetuation of the species by supplying the excess hyaluronidase required, are left out in the cold to perish. After entrance, the head of the lucky sperm quickly moves to the nucleus of the egg and fuses with it. A single cell results, and at the exact moment of fusion, when the DNA of the father is combined with that of the mother, a new oyster is created.

Once fertilization is accomplished, the egg loses its resemblance to a kernel of corn and becomes globose or spherical in shape. This change in contour is striking, and an observer may readily distinguish between a fertilized and an unfertilized egg.

To Be or Not to Be

The fertilized egg, or zygote as it is now called, drops to the bottom of the river or bay to begin the complicated process of development.

About an hour after fertilization, cleavage, or cell division, begins. First 1 cell becomes 2, then 4, 8, 16, 32, 64, 128, 256, and so on, almost ad infinitum. After a period of about four hours, the young oyster arrives at a stage that resembles a Ping-Pong ball; embryologists call this a blastula. Hundreds of cells make up the blastula, but the size of the small, hollow ball is only slightly larger than the single-celled zygote. In the development of an animal, it is essential that while the cells increase in number they decrease in size during the early stages. If cell division in the early phases of an oyster's life resulted in daughter cells that were as large as the mother cell, the blastula would be as big as a tennis ball. Actually, it is very small and cannot be seen without the aid of a microscope. And, if subsequent development involved no size reduction in the millions of cells that must be produced before the oyster is complete, we would have oysters that weigh hundreds of pounds and stand 35 to 45 feet in height. (If you think it is difficult to shuck a 4- to 5-inch oyster, how would you like to tackle one of this size?) Actually, about the largest oyster one is apt to run into around the Chesapeake Bay will be about a foot high and weigh no more than 2½ pounds—and, you are not going to encounter too many in this size range.

During the blastula stage cell division takes place at a rapid pace, and the hollow sphere consists of an inner and outer layer of cells. All these cells are essentially alike and have not differentiated into the special types required to build organs such as the kidneys, blood vessels, or gills. Recall, however, that all these cells are the direct descendents of the fertilized egg and contain the DNA recipe for a complete oyster. But each of these cells does not go on to become a complete oyster. In the next stage of growth some genes in each cell will be "turned on" and some will be "turned off." In a way that represents one of the great unsolved mysteries in biology, certain cells will be programmed to form the building blocks of the gonads, others designated to become amoebocytes, while still others will be assigned to the construction of the mantle. What controls this process of differentiation

39

has puzzled biologists for a hundred years, and, though research in recent times has cast some light on the problem, the exact nature of the process is, in reality, little understood.

For many years scientists believed each cell of the developing embryo was allotted only a portion of the total DNA complement, and it was those genes that determined whether the cell ended up forming a part of the kidney, intestine, or heart. In 1969, experiments performed in England demonstrated conclusively that all cells of the body of an animal contain a full allocation of the genetic material. Dr. J. B. Gurdon of Oxford University successfully grew a frog from the nucleus of an intestinal cell that had been transplanted into an egg from another frog in which the nucleus had been destroyed by radiation. The art of animal cloning had been discovered, as Gurdon's frog proved once and for all that each cell has hidden within its nucleus the capacity to grow into an entire new individual.

Since 1969, many other animals have been cloned, and from time to time one hears that this type of asexual reproduction has been accomplished in humans in some secret laboratory. This is probably untrue, but, with recent advances in the art of creating test-tube babies, transplanting embryos, and creating artificial uteruses, the cloning of human beings is not far in the future. The morality and ethics of such a procedure, as well as the tactics being used at present to circumvent the normal reproductive process, are subjects of heated debates at this time, and no explicit resolution of the problem is in sight.

In the minds of many, cloning conjures up visions of a despot creating an army of perfect foot soldiers from cells taken from a prototype and incubated in the laboratory, or the formation of a basketball team consisting of eight-foot giants cloned from cells scraped from the inside of the mouth of a superstar. To others, cloning suggests a way to propagate untold numbers of super-oysters from the cells extracted from an oyster selected to be the parent on the basis of its size, vigor, and resistance to disease organisms. What seems like science fiction today frequently turns into reality tomorrow. It could very well be that in the not too distant future oysters will be reared by the process of cloning. Researchers are now involved in the preliminary experiments needed to accomplish this procedure economically, and the end result of their work could result in the salvation of the oyster industry in many parts of the world. Though many scientists, theologians, philosophers, moralists, and laymen vociferously condemn tinkering with humans in this way, it is doubtful if too much objection would be raised to the sexual manipulation of oysters. Until such procedures have been perfected, however, life on the oyster bar continues on, as it has for over four hundred million years.

A little more than four hours have passed in the life of the new bivalve, and the differentiation process of tissues and organs begins. At one end of the embryo a row of tiny cilia appears, and the rudiment of the shell makes its debut at the other extreme. The tiny cilia start to beat, and the larva, as it is now called, swims to near the surface of the water. At this stage, zoologists term the larva a *trochophore* ("wheel-bearer"). Careful observation will reveal that a groove has started to form on one side of the body; this will eventually become the digestive tract. The process of gastrulation has begun and will develop into what is called the gastrula stage of development.

During the gastrula period of the life cycle, a third layer of cells will form between the two tiers characteristic of the blastula. From this third bank of undifferentiated cells the kidneys, gonads, muscles, and heart will form. The gastrula stage is peculiar to all animals that develop from three basic cell layers and has been cited by students of evolution as one bit of evidence showing the common ancestry of different species. Likewise, the trochophore larva of the mollusks is very similar to the larval form of the segmented worms, which are considered to be below the mollusks in the scale of evolution. This phenomenon is generally taken as prima facie evidence that mollusks evolved directly from this group of worms, which includes such familiar creatures as the earthworm, sandworm, clamworm, bloodworm, and leech. It should be noted, however, that other evidence exists supporting the theory that these two great groups of animals are closely related. Biologists long ago recognized they were on thin ice when embryological evidence was the sole criterion for declaring one group gave rise to some other.

41

The Oyster

Development of the young oyster greatly accelerates during the next eighteen to twenty hours. The digestive tract becomes complete, with a mouth at one end and the anus at the other, and the larva feeds voraciously. The mouth formed from an invagination of the blastula that rapidly grew inward to become the precursor of the entire system. In most invertebrate animals this initial point of invagination eventually ends up as the mouth, but in the group that includes the starfish, sea urchin, and sea cucumber this tiny aperture (correctly called the blastopore) forms the anal opening. In vertebrates, including man, the fate of the blastopore is also the posterior opening to the digestive system, and this has long been interpreted as denoting a close affinity of starfish and their kin to the animals with backbones.

By the end of the first day of life the larval oyster is called a veliger. With a complete digestive system, foot, mantle, sensory spots that function as primitive eyes, two complete valves, and a padlike organ, called the velum, bearing cilia for swimming, the young oyster closely resembles a miniature clam. During the next four days it continues to grow rapidly and assumes a characteristic D shape. The veligers scatter from near the water's surface to occupy various depths of the environment. After dispersal, the larvae actively swim about, stuffing themselves with microscopic algae and other organisms. Millions of them perish during this period, and it is surprising that any of them survive to reach the stage where they resemble oysters more than clams. Predators of all types must take a tremendous toll, and even a slight change in environmental conditions, such as a shift in wind direction or temperature, can spell disaster for the fragile and defenseless creatures. As they are extremely numerous at the various levels, the intense competition for the necessities of life, emphasized by Darwin as being of prime importance in the struggle for existence, takes place. Truly, only the strongest and best adapted (maybe an inferior gets lucky every now and then) will be able to survive the selective forces of nature, but the few who manage to eke out an existence will pass on their recipe for success to the members of the generation they will eventually sire.

The veliger stage occupies a period of about fifteen days, and at the end of this time it is recognizable as an oyster and not a clam, albeit a small one. It is about 1/64 inch in size and appears to the

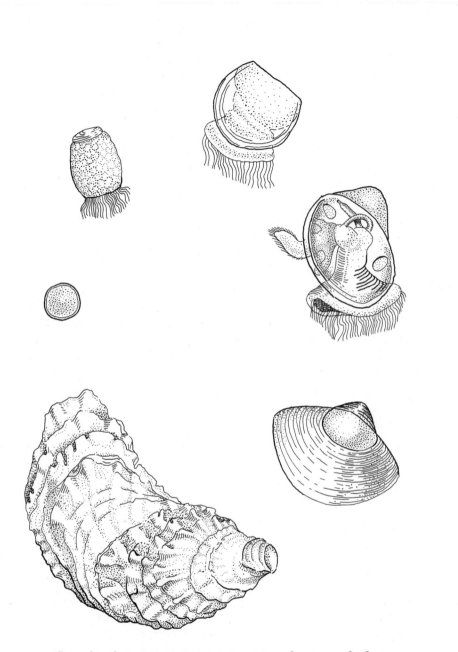

Life cycle of *Crassostrea virginica*. From bottom, *clockwise:*
Adult; egg; trochophore larva; hinged or "D"-shaped larva;
veliger or "eyed-larva"; spat.

unaided eye about as big as a fly speck. The oyster has now reached a major crossroad in its young life and is ready to abandon its carefree, motile way of life and undertake a sessile life style where it will attach to an inert object and spend the rest of its days watching the world flow by.

The act of migrating to the bottom and attaching to a permanent homesite is called spatting, settling, spat falling, or simply settling down. Some individuals refer to the oyster at this time as a spat, but technically it does not become a spat until it immutably adheres itself to its chosen homestead. *Cultch* is the name given to the object on which the veliger decides to affix itself, and spatting on the cultch is an extremely critical time in the life of the oyster. Again, sudden changes in the environment can deter or prevent this necessary part of the life cycle. Apparently, the veliger about to spat has a relatively short period in which this may be accomplished. If spatting is delayed for more than a few hours, physiological changes occur that preclude its attachment. An entire crop of oysters can be (and frequently is) lost because of a sudden drop in temperature that persists for a day or so.

If all systems are go, the veligers settle to the bottom and, with luck, land on a suitable piece of cultch. Almost any settling surface can be utilized if it is permanent, free of detritus, hard, and fairly smooth. Studies have revealed that young oysters prefer to spat on other oysters, or at least on the shells that once encompassed other oysters. They will, however, spat on glass, brickbats, slag, rocks, and pebbles in that order of preference. Untold numbers of the veligers are destroyed when they are unable to locate a bit of cultch and are enveloped by the mud and muck of the bottom. Perhaps now one can better understand why it is necessary that untold millions of gametes be produced in order to get a few oysters to carry on the family name.

When the fortunate veliger reaches an acceptable bit of cultch, it immediately begins to make itself comfortable. Feeling the surface ever so gently with its protruding foot, the veliger scuds across the cultch, testing the surface to ascertain the desirability of the site. If an area is chosen, the oyster attaches itself temporarily at the tip of the foot. Around this point of adhesion it draws its tiny body up and around the length of the foot. For some unknown reason, the tip of the foot is then released and makes contact with a spot nearby. The body is again drawn up to the protruding foot, and this performance is repeated several times before the creature finds the exact spot that suits him. As this location on the cultch will be the oyster's home for ever more, it is not surprising the creature is such a careful and discriminate househunter.

Finally, it comes to rest with the left valve (recall this is the cup-shaped one that holds the bulk of the animal's body) against the surface of the cultch and the body tilted somewhat toward the opening of the valves. As the croupier in the gambling casino says when the roulette wheel is spun and no more wagers are permitted, "Les jeux sont faits"—the bets are made, the decision has been made. The oyster is forever bound to that spot.

Darwinian competition again comes into play during the act of spatting, as, in addition to being able to secure enough food and oxygen, the larva must be able to find a spot on the cultch he can call his own. Sometimes great numbers of larvae land on the same piece of substratum, and there is not enough surface area to go around. Only the strongest will survive, and the weaker siblings will be crowded off. One oyster propagator describes a successful spatting by likening a bit of cultch laden with young oysters to a piece of coarse sandpaper with each grain of sand representing a spat. A few of the unfortunate individuals who are denied spatting privileges may accidentally end up on another bit of cultch after being evicted by their stronger neighbors and be able to reestablish themselves. The number who are able to salvage their existence in this manner is probably small.

The byssus gland of the veliger is located at the base of the muscular foot, and it is the primary function of this organ to provide the strong cement that will be used to weld the oyster permanently to the cultch. The adhesive produced is extremely strong and effective, and, despite numerous attempts to synthesize it in the laboratory, its exact composition and mode of action are largely unknown. Man could produce the world's best superglue if the chemistry of this substance could be discovered.

The Oyster

The byssus gland is present in other mollusks and performs a similar function in them. The long, threadlike projections that firmly attach the familiar blue and ribbed mussels to wharf pilings are secreted by this gland.

Soon after setting the spat resorbs its foot, and some authorities believe the cement used in the setting process comes from chemicals making up the foot which are converted to the adhesive. Most oyster students, however, are convinced the byssus gland is the organ primarily involved in the manufacture of the sticky substance. Once the oyster is firmly attached, it almost requires a stick of dynamite to break it loose. The waterman is able to separate bouquets of oysters with the aid of a unique instrument called a culling hammer. This utensil is bladelike on one side and will effectively separate undersize oysters from "keepers" if considerable force is applied by the user's elbow.

Observations were made more than fifty years ago that proved oyster larvae set in much greater numbers on shells that already had spat adhering to them. Shells from which the spat had been removed were less attractive. This gregarious tendency is most marked when a light spat fall occurs. When numerous larvae were settling they quickly covered occupied and bare shells with equal enthusiasm, but when only a few were involved in the spatting process, the shells with few or no spat attached were virtually ignored. Apparently veligers in the cultch-seeking process proceed more rapidly with the spatting maneuver if there are already spat nearby. This behavior probably occurs as an olfactory response to some waterborne pheromone released by the spat already attached. The many ways animals communicate are sometimes strange indeed.

After adhesion has been accomplished the veliger larva can now be correctly called a spat. They are 1/64 inch long and can be detected on the cultch only by those with acute vision. After setting, the spat grows rapidly and many anatomical and physiological changes occur. The foot and velum disappear quickly as a result of powerful digestive enzymes, and the eye spots fade away (veligers about to spat are sometimes called "eyed-larvae"—the light-sensitive spot is obvious). The spat will never locomote again, so it has little use for either organs of motion or sensory receptors to tell it where it's going. The output of shell doubles in the first twenty-four hours of attachment, and the young oyster gains some degree of protection from would-be enemies.

At the end of three months, the spat will have grown to the size of a dime if the food supply has been adequate and the temperatures favorable. It is at this stage that many watermen are first able to recognize the presence of spat on cultch, so it is understandable why most of those who toil to bring the oyster to market believe the oyster does not spat until it is the size of a ten-cent piece. The trochophore and veliger stages in the oyster's life cycle are generally unknown to these professionals. Frequently the oysterman will check bars to determine their productivity by counting the number of spat attached to the cultch he tongs or dredges up. As only the large spat are counted, an erroneous conclusion as to how successful or unsuccessful the spat set has been can easily be made. If a strong hand lens, or better yet a dissecting-type microscope, is used to examine the cultch, a much more accurate assessment of the potential numbers of oysters present can be made.

If food is plentiful and the environment has been favorable, the spat will reach sexual maturity in about a year, but, as mentioned previously, this time period can vary. Maximum reproductive potential is reached between the fourth and seventh years of life, and after that time (if the oyster has not been snatched from its home by a pair of tongs or fallen victim to a predator or disease agent) its fecundity tapers off. No one knows how long an oyster may live in a natural setting but a good guess for *C. virginica* is about ten to twelve years. Under favorable conditions, the oyster will grow an average of 1 inch in height up to the third year of its life. After the third year, the rate of growth becomes progressively slower as old age catches up with the oyster. When one considers that Chesapeake Bay oysters in excess of 10 to 12 inches in height are rarely taken, the figure of ten to twelve years for the life span seems to coincide nicely. There is a report of an *Ostrea edulis* living to the ripe old age of twenty years in a laboratory tank in England, but it is highly doubtful if this geriatric bivalve could have attained its advanced age if it had been subjected to the trials and tribulations of a natural environment.

There is no sure way to calculate the age of an oyster taken from the depths. The growth rings on the shell are easily counted, but, unlike the growth rings of a tree, are not a reliable measure of age. The best way to calculate the approximate age of an oyster is to measure its height, giving, as indicated, one year for each inch.

Centuries ago, Pliny the Elder stated, "Generally speaking oysters increase in size with the size of the moon," and this thesis was reiterated by other classical observers such as Lucilius, Manilius, and Horace. Annianus remarked, "The moon is now in truth waning, and on that account the oyster, like other things, is lean and void of juice."

Investigations into the biology of the oyster long ago left little doubt that temperature was an important factor in the spawning process. When the oyster is ready to spawn it is fat and succulent because of its ripe and distended gonad; it becomes lean, watery, and scrawny after releasing its gametes. As the phase of the moon influences the tides, it stands to reason that as the tides get lower the temperature of the water will increase and spawning will be instigated. Though some scientific evidence for the correlation of moon phase and spawning with the European oyster has been presented, no relationship between the spawning activities of *Crassostrea virginica* and the lunar phases has ever been documented.

Once the sperm and eggs have been released, the oyster is a mere shadow of its prespawning self and really has nothing to be proud of. An oyster taken immediately after spawning would be rated as a "Class 1" specimen, the bottom of the line. Oyster specialists and enthusiasts have agreed generally on the following rating system that anyone can use to evaluate oysters placed before them in a raw bar:

Class	Distinguishing Features
1.	Condition glassy, very watery, no substance
2.	Firm, thin, no apparent glycogen (animal starch) in the digestive gland, somewhat watery

3.   Glycogen evident in the digestive gland (yellow-brown color), gonad apparent, firm

4.   Fat, glycogen-laden digestive gland hidden by massive gonad, firm

5.   Very fat and plump, gonad massive, glycogen content high

The next time you are tempted to order oysters from the menu of a restaurant, try to determine in advance what category of oysters is being served that day. To a real oyster epicure a 3+ will win acceptance, even praise. Not many of us have had the pleasure of engorging ourselves with 4s and 5s.

CHAPTER FOUR

The Ostraculturist of the Nanticoke

FALSTAFF: *I will not lend thee a penny.*
PISTOL: *Why then the worlds mine oyster*
                  Which I with sword will open.
                                              Shakespeare

RAISING oysters for profit can only be described as risky business. Anyone entertaining the idea of entering into such an endeavor should be aware there is little chance for success, and, in all probability, frustration, bankruptcy, and perhaps insanity await him. Very few individuals have been able to make a go of it, but still a few bold pioneers sometimes believe they have the secret ingredient that will enable them to succeed where most others have failed.

In 1945, Dr. Truitt of the Chesapeake Biological Laboratory calculated that the 15 million bushels of oysters harvested from the Chesapeake Bay in 1885 would have yielded about 120 million pounds of oyster meat. This was the equivalent of about two hundred thousand dressed steers, the entire yield from New Jersey, Delaware, Maryland, and West Virginia in 1945. Perhaps it is figures like these that conjure up visions of wealth and prosperity and lure the unsuspecting entrepreneur toward what seems to be an untapped source of easy money.

But the pitfalls are many, and the abandoned buildings and equipment of defunct operations dotting the shores of both ocean coasts as well as the Gulf of Mexico offer mute evidence of the fate of oyster-farming attempts. Bankers and governmental loan agencies know the story and have the facts and figures behind such labors, and they take a dim view of any request for money to

51

be used in the commercial rearing of oysters. The person thinking he has the right formula to win where others almost always fail is obliged to finance his project out of his own pocket or out of the pockets of individuals who are convinced his scheme has money-making potential.

Having resided off and on for several years on the Nanticoke River on Maryland's Eastern Shore, I was pretty well cognizant of what was going on in the tiny hamlets of Tyaskin, Bivalve, Nanticoke, and Waterview which dot the shoreline near the mouth of this estuary, about twenty miles west of Salisbury. Being in touch with the local network of gossip, I was rather surprised a few years ago to pick up the news that some sort of foreign character had established an "arster" farm in a marsh near the spot on the map named Waterview. The individual transmitting this tidbit of information added he was sure the man must be "tetched" to have put any time and money into such a cracked-brain undertaking. Realizing the significance of such an operation in regard to the declining oyster industry in the immediate area, and because I am a student and teacher of invertebrate zoology, I found the report of considerable interest. Though I made no effort at the time to check personally into what was going on, I frequently inquired how the operation was progressing when I tuned in on the local news channel. Invariably the report was the same: "Oh, he's still down there amongst the snakes and skeeters playing around tryin' to get the arsters to get it on."

Eventually, I found out that the man of mystery was named Max Chambers, and he was indeed spawning oysters and rearing the larvae, and had been successful in getting the spat to set on a cultch of clean oyster shells. The word was out that he had even sold some of the spat to some of the private growers for planting on sections of river bottom leased from the state. I thought it was about time I met this man to find out firsthand what was going on.

My first meeting with the aquaculturist took place during January of 1984 in his farmhouse-type dwelling near the historic port village of Whitehaven on the Wicomico River. Being graciously received and ushered into a warm kitchen dominated by a large round table, I immediately established a rapport with Max

Chambers. The hot coffee served was most enjoyable considering the temperature outside was around freezing, and the river was frozen into a solid piece of ice. It seemed a strange time to talk about oysters, but, really, not so strange as I recalled that many oystermen were waiting anxiously in port for the ice to break up so they could resume their tonging operations. Watermen count heavily on the year's oyster catch to maintain their existence. Many add to their incomes by crabbing or fishing, but the funds derived from these endeavors are not enough to pay the bills. If you don't make it on oysters, you don't make it, and each day the ice prevented the boats from going out to the bars was depriving these men of the chance to earn money that had already been spent.

I learned that Chambers was a retired military man who came to the Eastern Shore a number of years ago. Raised a farmer's son in Indiana, he found the Delmarva Peninsula to his liking and compatible with his background. Soon after arriving on the Shore, he found work at a large seafood-processing plant on the banks of the Nanticoke, but after a time his enthusiasm for the eight to five job waned. He began to develop ideas about marine biology, conservation of the area's natural resources, and especially about *Crassostrea virginica*. Someone told him that in 1884, fourteen million bushels of oysters were harvested from the Chesapeake Bay system but only a little more than one million bushels were caught in 1974. I do not know if he was familiar with Truitt's figures comparing oyster meat to beef or not, but he soon realized the oyster industry was in deep trouble with no place to go but down.

Knowing very little about oysters except what he had learned from his position in the packinghouse, and even less about marine biology, he decided in the early seventies to leave his job and attempt to raise oysters for profit. Whether he knew it or not, he had arrived at a fundamental conclusion that had been reached many years previously by the pioneering oyster biologists, Francis Winslow, W. K. Brooks, and R. V. Truitt—the oyster industry of the Chesapeake cannot endure without the aid of artificial propagation and subsequent planting of the seed on areas prepared with cultch material. Natural fecundity cannot sustain the oyster populations at a level where oysters may be harvested profitably.

Aware of the odds against establishing an economically feasible mollusk farm, Chambers embarked on a year-long sabbatical to learn everything he possibly could about the oyster and its methods of cultivation. During this period he read everything he could find concerning the oyster and visited the various state and federal agencies engaged in oyster research. He picked the brains of anyone he thought might have an iota of information on any phase of the oyster's life cycle, and he especially sought out people who had previously tried to grow oysters for profit but had failed. In this manner he was able to pinpoint the areas in which he could expect to experience difficulty. At the end of the year he probably knew as much about the biology of *C. virginica* as any Ph.D. marine biologist working in a well-equipped laboratory with access to a nice chunk of state or federal money to provide equipment and pay research assistants' salaries.

When at last he was ready to set sail on his questionable voyage, one can imagine his confidence level was high. It would be nice to be able to say FLOMAX Enterprises (Flo is Max's wife and partner) was an instant success, but such is not the case. The next seven years or so were characterized by repeated failures. Frequently the advice given by "experts" was inaccurate or simply did not prove to be workable in the FLOMAX hatcheries. The supposedly simple act of inducing the breeding stock to release their sperm and eggs under artificial conditions turned out to be a major obstacle. How does one determine if the eggs have been fertilized after the sperm have been introduced to them? Will the algae-laden water of the Nanticoke provide enough food at various times of the year for the different developmental stages, or must one establish an expensive and time-consuming algae-growing operation?

Chambers decided the best way to find answers to these and many other questions crucial to the operation was to test each procedure to determine if it worked. Needless to say, this trial-and-error method consumed a great deal of time and cut deeply into the company's limited financial reserves. Over the years, however, each specific problem was attacked and eventually solved in a manner many would recognize as the application of the principles of the scientific method. To Chambers, it was the common-sense method of obtaining answers to his questions and developing a workable protocol of operation.

Success finally came in 1981 when the first spat adhering to the shells of the cultch were finally obtained in sufficient quantity to be offered for sale to commercial growers. Many had scoffed at the operation and said it could not be done under conditions at the FLOMAX hatcheries but somehow Flo and Max had developed procedures that worked and had definite possibilities of making money for them.

As I sat at the kitchen table that cold January afternoon and listened with fascination to the story, I became filled with admiration for this unassuming man with the tenacity to push onward, in spite of repeated failures, to eventually find success. Self-reliance and hard work, as well as dedication to a cause and the elimination of the word *impossible* from his vocabulary played the significant roles in his story. Chambers, however, is the first to admit, that in addition to these admirable attributes, luck had a heavy hand in it. Excellence in any undertaking compels admiration, and this is especially true when the excellence is attained under difficult working conditions.

When I paid my first call on Max Chambers I imagined I already knew everything of importance about oysters. After all, years before in graduate school I had learned that they were hermaphroditic mollusks that passed through the trochophore and veliger larval stages before settling down to live a life of perpetual attachment to the substratum. I had made careful dissections of the internal parts according to the instructions given in the laboratory manual (cutting my finger badly the first time I tried to pry open the valves of the pickled specimen given me) and could identify any organ of the beast to which the professor might point. I knew they were filter-feeders and trapped tiny organisms on their sticky gills as the plankton-laden water of their environment flowed through their valves, and just about all the other important features of their biology. But when I left the Chambers's farmhouse after our first session I felt like the greenest of

The Oyster

freshman students who had just finished his first class in introductory zoology. I was amazed at the amount of knowledge he had managed to accrue, not only on all phases of the life of the oyster, but in other areas such as conservation and ecology. I could hardly wait for early summer to arrive to visit the hatchery to observe the rearing methods firsthand.

FLOMAX hatcheries is located on a bit of fast ground in the middle of a marsh near Waterview, Maryland. Years ago the community boasted the presence of a grandiose resort hotel on the sandy banks of the Nanticoke. Appropriately, the hostelry was named the Waterview Hotel. Visitors from Baltimore, Philadelphia, Washington, D. C., and a host of other places frequented the vacation resort during the summer months to swim, crab, sunbathe, stroll on the tiny boardwalk, and enjoy the seafood served family-style in the spacious dining room. The increased popularity of nearby Ocean City, Maryland, and the resort beaches along the coast of Delaware, as well as other circumstances, eventually took its toll. The facility was closed to its previous clientele in the 1960s and leased to the Soviet Union. For a time the facility was used as place of relaxation and recuperation by Russians fatigued by their duties in Washington and New York, and the constant coming and going of long, black limousines containing stern-looking foreigners was of considerable concern to the local inhabitants. Everyone seemed to have a theory about what the Russians were up to. Many were sure an invasion was imminent. Eventually, the Soviets tired of the sea nettles, mosquitoes, greenhead flies, and other obnoxious creatures and retreated to a more "desirable" location. The Waterview Hotel then closed its doors for the last time. Entropy was set in motion and accelerated by the harsh environment, and today only a few weather-beaten structures remain as reminders of what once had been. A portion of the abandoned property was leased by FLOMAX enterprises.

As one nears the hatchery operation (a stranger must have explicit instructions in order to find it) via the single-lane dirt road, one notices a crude sign that proclaims, "FLOMAX Hatcheries, Watch Out for Snakes!" Though there are numerous species of snakes present in the area, only the relatively rare eastern copperhead is venomous. The nonvenomous but greatly feared northern water snake and blue racer or black snake are very common. Max is well aware of the inherent (almost pathological) fear most of the residents of the community have for any kind of snake—especially the dreaded water snake, which is believed to be the deadly cottonmouth moccasin. I suspect his subtle warning on the sign serves as a more effective deterrent to would-be snoopers or vandals than would be a warning to "Beware of the dog" or that "Trespassers will be prosecuted."

The hatchery is located on the edge of a small tidal pool connected by a small gut or rivulet to the river. With each changing of the tide the water in the impoundment is renewed with fresh river water containing an abundant supply of the microscopic green algae and other organisms essential to the growth of oysters in all stages of development. Someone expecting to find a well-kept, spotless, and fully equipped facility at FLOMAX will be sadly disappointed. The hatchery itself consists of a series of connecting rooms constructed of used sheets of tin and fiberglass, juxtaposed around an old shed, which constitutes the nucleus of the operation. The dilapidated shed was the first hatchery building, and as operations expanded and additional space was needed, a new room was ingloriously fabricated from material at hand.

As I drove by the snake-warning sign and entered the grounds of the hatchery for the first time, Chambers emerged from the building and hailed me. Noting he was barefooted and dressed in only a pair of swimming trunks, I wondered how he was able to withstand the attacks of the insects frequenting the marsh that day, all of which seemed dedicated to making life miserable for any intruder. Though I was making every effort not to scratch the numerous bites I had received on the way in, the proprietor of the hatchery seemed immune (or oblivious) to the thirsty bloodsuckers. A few people have a rare body chemistry that protects them from the bites of insects, and Chambers is apparently one of the lucky ones.

It was necessary to duck my head to gain entrance to the hatchery building, and, upon emerging on the inside, I was confronted by another sign. This one stated in bold letters, "This is not a government operation. If it was I'd have twice as nice facilities and only half the production." One may interpret this somewhat sarcastic statement with its contemptuous overtone as a reflection of the operator's opinion of similar state and federal hatcheries, or you may take it as a statement of fact.

During the spring of 1984 a conference for those interested in the commercial growing of oysters was held in the nearby city of Salisbury. It was sponsored by the University of Maryland Sea Grant Program and the state Department of Natural Resources, and it attracted a large number of interested individuals. One of the participants in the program was the president of a long-established company in the state of Washington specializing in the rearing and marketing of the large Japanese oyster, *Crassostrea gigas*. This gentlemen, whose family has been in the oyster-growing business for decades, expressed a desire to visit the FLOMAX operation after he heard Chambers moderate a panel discussion. He is reported to have uttered, as he entered the hatchery building, "Good God Almighty, don't tell me the man raises oysters in a junkpile like this!"

Junkpile or not, Max Chambers, assisted only by his wife, Flo, hatched ten million oysters at the Waterview site during the year 1984. Approximately two-thirds of the survivors were vended as either "eyed-larvae" (advanced veligers) or spat attached to shell cultch to private growers; the remaining one-third was retained by FLOMAX for seeding a small site it leases from the state. In two or three years these hatchery-spawned oysters will have grown to the legal limit of 3 inches and may be retrieved from the river bottom—that is, unless they have fallen prey to the tongs or dredges of poachers or been destroyed by predators or disease organisms.

The FLOMAX recipe for spawning and rearing oysters on the Nanticoke is not classified as top secret but is available to almost anyone who has an interest in aquaculture. Max loses no sleep over thoughts of industrial thievery. After all, who would be crazy enough to want to try to raise oysters?

All oyster-growing operations follow certain basic steps from the emission of the sperm and eggs at the time of spawning to the setting of the spat two or three weeks later. It's the thousand and one details, which can drive the oyster farmer into bankruptcy or

59

The Oyster

to a mental institution, that must be reckoned with. The methods and techniques employed by Chambers at Waterview work in that particular ecological situation, but may or may not be the correct procedures to follow at another location. In other words, each operation is unique, and the operator must modify fundamental concepts to fit the individual site and environment. What works in Maine or Washington State may not be effective in Maryland or Texas.

During the winter of 1981 the residents of the area were surprised when a large tractor-trailer rig bearing Maine license plates rolled up to the end of the road at Waterview. The trailer was detached from the tractor and established in a permanent posture with concrete blocks supporting it. After much speculation about the purpose of this activity it was learned that a new oyster-rearing operation was about to go into business. One individual summed up pretty well the consensus of local opinion when he snorted to me, "Now we got two crazies round here try'n' to grow arsters."

The new operation adopted an appropriate name, SPATCO, and a young biologist arrived on the scene to take charge of the business at hand. During the spring of the year, the zone around the trailer buzzed with activity, and the biologist, who had taken up residence in a nearby house, was most cooperative in answering questions posed by the curious who stopped by. A small gut runs more or less perpendicular to the road's end and connects to the river through a marsh fronting on the Nanticoke. One would think it an ideal location for an oyster-rearing operation. Algae-laden river water from the gut was pumped into large cylindrical tanks made of plastic, located within the trailer-laboratory. Constant lighting was provided for the tanks to stimulate photosynthesis, and it was supposed the stupendous amount of algae to be produced would provide a constant source of nourishment for the growing oysters. Large rearing tanks of fiberglass were constructed outside the trailer, and plumbing connections to the flowing gut were established. The entire facility was enclosed by a wire fence, and everything seemed ready to go. I was favorably impressed and was beginning to believe SPATCO might have a reasonable chance for success. The biologist exuded optimism,

60

and there seemed to be little doubt that untold millions of spat would be forthcoming from the tanks, to be made available to an eager market in many parts of the country.

The biologist was a graduate of a university with a fine program in marine biology, and he had had considerable practical experience in the oyster-raising business in Maine. He had not, however, graduated from the school of hard knocks, and things went badly from the outset. Untold numbers of dollars were poured into the operation during 1982 and 1983, but it is a sad fact that not one oyster was ever spawned and, of course, no spat were ever produced.

In 1984, SPATCO was abandoned, and at last inspection of the doomed site I noted the tires on the trailer were flat, the wire enclosure had been breached by vandals, and someone had used the fiberglass rearing tanks for rifle practice. The biologist and his assistant disappeared, leaving the operation to the mercy of the elements. SPATCO failed because the rearing methods employed were those used in Maine. Though they were successful there, they were not applicable to the Eastern Shore of Maryland.

The successful procedures employed at FLOMAX are generally available to anyone who is interested, but they are not recorded in any scientific journal of marine biology, or any other publication. They exist only in the mind and weather-beaten notebooks of Max Chambers.

Actual spawning operations are undertaken at Waterview in June or July when the breeding stock is conditioned, that is, there is plenty of stored glycogen, and the gonads are distended with either sperm or eggs. Though visitors are welcome at the hatchery at almost any other time, Max wants to be alone when he attempts to coax the sex cells from his selected breeders. Usually, spawning is undertaken in the still of the night because he has determined that any loud noise or vibration can adversely interfere with the process.

Bloodsworth Island, located in Tangier Sound about ten miles downstream from the hatchery, is a tiny bit of real estate used by the U. S. Navy as a target-practice site for its aircraft. When bombs are dropped on the scrap ships anchored in the island's waterways, the resulting explosions may sometimes be heard in

Salisbury, twenty-five miles away. Fortunately, the aerial target practice usually takes place during daylight hours, leaving the hours of darkness undisturbed for the spawning of oysters, and perhaps other species.

Fifteen to twenty robust specimens make up the breeding stock and have been selected by Chambers for their size and apparent vigor. "Like begets like," as Charles Darwin wrote in *The Origin of Species,* and Chambers hopes to improve his offspring by using superior parents. The breeders are maintained in a broad, shallow container filled with aerated river water. With the aid of a heat exchanger, which is actually a modified domestic hot water heater Max found at the Tyaskin dump, the water in the breeding tank is slowly raised to about 80 degrees Fahrenheit and maintained at that level for an hour or so. The ostraculturist then selects one of the breeders to be sacrificed for the reproductive cause. The one chosen is opened, and the contents of the branching gonad are placed on a glass slide and examined with the microscope. (There is no way to distinguish between a male and a female oyster by their external anatomy—the gonad must be examined microscopically.) If a male has been selected, vast numbers of sperm cells are readily visible at 100× magnification. If by chance a female was selected, she is discarded (or unceremoniously dropped down Max's gullet) and another breeder is chosen. Eventually a male is found and his testis is quickly ripped apart with a sharp needle. The contents of the male sex organ are intermingled with the water in the breeding tank, and Max sits back and carefully observes the other oysters.

Certain chemical pheromones seem to be essential in the instigation of the spawning process. As noted in a previous chapter, pheromones are similar in chemical structure and action to hormones and are responsible for numerous physiological functions in animals (and plants as well). Generally, a pheromone performs its function outside the animal's body, whereas a hormone works internally. There seems to be little doubt that at least one male pheromone in oysters serves to stimulate the females to release their eggs and other males to ejaculate their sperm. Pheromones are effective in minute concentrations.

The Ostraculturist of the Nanticoke

In the hatchery spawning tank the pheromone level is much higher than would be found on a natually occurring oyster bar, and the females and males are quickly excited and release the contents of their gonads in a few minutes. One cannot help but wonder how this works in nature, where the pheromones are diluted to an infinitesimal concentration. Of course, a little bit of the chemical goes a long way, and there are many more oysters emitting pheromones on an oyster bar in the river than there are in the hatchery. One can visualize a chain reaction occurring when the first male begins the spawning activity. In a short while a tremendous amount of the magic elixir would be released as the effects of the first bit of excitant filtered down to nearby oysters and induced them to spawn and release even more pheromones. The question arises, What stimulates the first male to begin the reproductive process? This is similar to the familiar question of which came first, the chicken or the egg, and neither scientists nor laymen have a definitive answer.

When spawning starts in the tank the males are readily distinguishable from the females. The spawning female opens and closes her valves in a clapping motion, discharging a puff of eggs each time. This behavior lasts from fifteen to twenty minutes until a total of about twenty million eggs have been emitted. The male discharges untold millions of sperm in a steady stream through a crack in the valves.

As soon as a female starts releasing her eggs, she is quickly removed from the common breeding tank to an isolation container, where oviposition continues. The males are not transferred to a separate tank. When the females have exhausted their ovaries, the egg-laden water is placed in a plastic garbage-can-style container. To this medium Chambers adds a couple of fifty-milliliter cups of sperm infusion dipped from the original spawning tank. The sperm and egg mixtures are commingled with the aid of a crude wooden paddle, and, after a few minutes, a slide for the microscope is prepared to determine what percentage of the eggs have been fertilized. The unfertilized egg, as noted previously, resembles a grain of corn, but after the sperm cell has entered and the nuclei of the gametes have fused, the shape of the zygote changes to a globose or spherical configuration. If approximately 90 percent of the eggs are determined to have been fertilized, this "in vitro" method of oyster propagation is considered to be a success. If a smaller figure is determined when the slide is screened, another cup or two of the male seed is added and stirred into the mixture. Usually these extra sperm cells will bring the fertilization rate up to the desired level.

Within an hour the fertilized egg begins to cleave; this indicates the onset of cell division. The instigation of the cleavage process is used as a final check to make sure these test-tube oysters are on their long and tortuous way to maturity. Max Chambers, as well as other observers of the oyster's early embryology, has noted that the penetration of the egg by a sperm cell and the subsequent union of the two nuclei does not always mean a new oyster is assured. In some spawning sessions a significant percentage of the fertilized eggs will fail to cleave, while in other reproductive convocations almost all the zygotes will divide and embark on the pattern of development characteristic of the species.

The failure of the zygote to develop properly is found in many animal species that have been studied in detail. In matings between two different but closely related species, fertilization may occur but embryological development does not proceed in a normal fashion. Somewhere down the line the new individual will die prematurely, usually before development has progressed very far. (Sometimes this phenomenon is also observed in matings between members of the same species.) Zoologists call this occurrence hybrid inviability and recognize it as a valuable tool used by nature to prevent the successful crossing of two different species of animals and thereby destroying order in the natural world.

Regardless of what folklore may have to say about successful hybridization between two distinct species (an ostrich results from the mating of a sparrow and a camel or a pekingese dog is a result of the mixing of the genes of a monkey and a bulldog) there has never been a case known to science where two distinct species mated and produced a viable offspring capable of reproduction. The dog and the coyote are two distinct, genetically isolated, species, but many believe they are capable of mating and producing mongrel offspring. Such is not the case; even though mating, fertilization, development of the embryo, and birth may occur, no sound pups are produced. Frequently the embryos are aborted at an early stage of development, but sometimes gestation continues to term and hybrids are indeed born. In this latter case, the newborn are always defective in some way and soon die—long before they could reach sexual maturity and be capable of reproducing themselves. This is hybrid inviability carried to one extreme; the failure of the fertilized egg to divide even one time is the same sort of isolating mechanism at the other end of the spectrum.

As indicated, hybrid inviability is frequently observed in *Crassostrea virginica* at the onset of the developmental cycle, and sometimes this phenomenon is noted at later stages of the oyster's embryology. Max Chambers has witnessed these occurrences in his hatchery, and so have numerous other oyster propagators. Most often when normal development was lacking, it had been assumed something was wrong with the rearing techniques or the medium in which the oysters were living. Laboratory or hatchery conditions can only approximate the situation found in the natural environment, and in many cases the failure of the young stages can be traced to some chemical imbalance, temperature deviation, salinity aberration, or some other quality or quantity of the medium which may not be exactly right. In other instances the reason for developmental failure cannot be identified. In these instances it could very well be a form of hybrid inviability or genetic incompatibility of the gametes that is responsible for arrested or abnormal development.

Genetic incompatibility between races of the same species has been reported in many type of animals (there have been suggestions of this in humans when no cause for infertility can be found), and it probably occurs in oysters reproducing on the bottom of a river or bay. In nature, however, the gametes from many parents are mixed and enough compatible fertilizations are accomplished to insure the survival and perpetuation of the species. In the hatchery, where only a few breeders are utilized as sex-cell donors, the problem of hybrid inviability or genetic incompatibility may be magnified if the oysters used possess significant variability in their genetic makeup. Seed oysters obtained from distant populations and planted on existing bars may have reached the point in the ongoing process of evolution where most of their gametes are not compatible with those of the oysters that have occupied their own little private niche of the environment for hundreds (or maybe even thousands) of years.

In any event, at FLOMAX, sperm and eggs are mixed together, agitated, sworn at, and otherwise manipulated until the development of the larval oyster begins. Once on the road to adulthood the young oyster grows rapidly, but it must be watched carefully and receive a goodly amount of tender, loving care. The water in the thousand-liter rearing tank is maintained at a constant temperature of 80 degrees Fahrenheit and is constantly aerated. Each day the water is exchanged with a fresh supply from the river (the millions of tiny larvae are collected and held during the exchange by a fine-meshed filter), providing a new ration for the ravenous brood. Most other oyster-rearing facilities must engage in the time-consuming and complicated procedure of raising the unicellular green algae required for nourishment, but Chambers has determined that his oyster larvae do very well on the number and type of organisms found in Nanticoke River water. It seemed to me the biologist in charge of the ill-fated SPATCO venture spent most of his time worrying about raising algae rather than oysters.

Researchers have tried for years to find an artificial food for larval oysters that would satisfy their dietary requirements and simplify the rearing process, but so far no one has been successful. Though a few recipes appear to be acceptable to the oysters, the use of artificial food has not proven to be economically feasible in mass-rearing endeavors.

On my first visit to the Chambers hatchery the thousand-liter rearing tank (equivalent to about five fifty-five-gallon drums) contained about ten million two-day-old larvae. With a plastic pipette, Max nonchalantly extracted a drop of the medium and placed in on a slide for microscopic examination. I was amazed to see twenty to twenty-five trochophores gleefully swimming around in the field of vision. That was a lot of larvae to be contained in an approximately one-milliliter sample. But ten million in a thousand-liter tank was quite a concentration, so, upon reflection, it was not too surprising that the small random sample contained the number of oysters it did.

Returning two days later to check on the progress made by this batch, I found the number had been reduced to about fifteen per milliliter of rearing-tank water. These four-day-old fledglings were, however, considerably larger than they had been two days previously. The natural law of overproduction and selection of the fittest to survive was at work, and those who could not successfully compete for the available food and living space were slowly but most assuredly succumbing to the laws of evolution.

It takes about fourteen days of accommodation at the hatchery for the larvae to develop to the stage when they are ready to settle down and set up a sessile mode of housekeeping for the rest of their lives. The number in the rearing tank will have been reduced considerably from what was present at the outset, but still the ones reaching larval maturity will number about ten per milliliter of water. In hatcheries where the larvae are fed algae grown in a greenhouse, the ratio of oysters to water is in the neighborhood of one oyster to one milliliter of water. By using the "dirty" river water, the production rate is increased tenfold.

At certain times of year the water of the Nanticoke is heavily laden with algae and other minute organisms. It is aptly called "dirty water"; when a sample in a clean glass tube is held up to the light for visual examination, the fluid is translucent at best. This food-laden, cloudy liquid is pumped into the rearing tank each day, and twenty-four hours later it has, as if by magic, become clear. The larvae have filtered the water through their bodies many times during this period, and most of the suspended items of food have been extracted and digested. Upon close examination, the bottom of the rearing tank will be found to contain an inch or so of accumulated oyster feces.

Could the use of biological filters such as oysters (and to a lesser extent, clams) be of use in cleaning up the Chesapeake Bay? Max Chambers and a few others believe they could. One of the most pressing problems of the Chesapeake system at the present time is the overproduction of various species of unicellular algae

The Oyster

due to the chemical enhancement of the waters by the runoff of chemical fertilizers and other organic nutrients from adjacent farmlands and sewage-treatment facilities. The nitrates and phosphates making their way into the Bay and its tributaries stimulate excessive growth of these plants, and the quality of the water is reduced. The turbidity resulting from abnormally high numbers of these microorganisms prohibits the rays of sunlight from penetrating the surface more than a few feet. Consequently, the rooted plants such as eelgrass, wild celery, coontail, and stargrass are denied the energy of the sun essential for the fundamental process of photosynthesis. When the rooted plants die off, the animals, great and small, that depend on them for food and other requisites of life are adversely affected, and the ecology of the entire system is disrupted.

The states of Maryland, Virginia, and Pennsylvania are now engaged in a gigantic "cleanup" of the Bay (whatever that means). In 1984 the Maryland legislature appropriated millions of dollars to cure the ailing estuary, and the federal Environmental Protection Agency, as well as the U. S. Army Corps of Engineers, are pledged to assist. One of the announced major goals is to limit the contamination of the waters by organic materials. This will be difficult to accomplish, because the political and economic factors involved, such as severe building and farming restrictions, are not going to sit well with many of the people affected.

Max Chambers certainly advocates controlling excessive algal growth, but he suggests an unorthodox way to achieve this goal. Instead of restricting farming operations close to the Bay and its many tributaries and the creation or modernization of sewage-treatment plants (at a cost of unheard-of millions of dollars), he says, "Let the oyster do it."

In his rearing tank one can observe the dramatic results achieved in a twenty-four-hour period and can readily understand what Chambers means. He proposes the rearing of great numbers of oysters, planting them in biologically receptive areas, and letting them filter out and utilize as food the offending algae. The runoff of the organic materials would enhance the production of algae, which in turn would stoke the digestive furnaces of countless obese oysters, which could be harvested for a waiting and

68

anxious market. More oyster meat than beef would again be cultivated.

Dr. Roger Newell, a research scientist with the University of Maryland Sea Grant Program, has estimated that all the water of the Bay passed through the oyster population of a century ago every five days. With the present number of oysters in the Bay, he calculates five months would be required to do the same thing. On the surface the idea of the massive growing and planting of oysters would seem to be the answer to the problem, but the complexities of the natural environment are many and only infrequently does one find a relatively simple answer to an ecological enigma.

Dr. Thomas Jones, a specialist on the biochemistry of algae and a coworker of Dr. Newell, believes that more and more of the algae engendered by the nutrient enrichment from farming and sewage-disposal practices are not to the oyster's taste. His research indicates that shifts occurring in the ratios of the nutrients required by algae (nitrogen and phosphorus are very important) can result in the production of algal species that are indigestible by larval or adult oysters—starving the former and rendering the latter malnourished and incapable of normal reproduction. Additional long-range research into these fundamental questions must be accomplished before the government undertakes a program of bivalve rearing and planting in an attempt to alleviate the almost moribund condition of the Bay. This applies, too, to any other program the managers of the cleanup campaign decide to use. All too often in the past we have witnessed biological programs of one sort or another being placed into operation before sufficient knowledge of the efficacy or their aftereffects were known. In many instances these crash programs have not only failed to accomplish anything beneficial but have resulted in deleterious effects on the environment—not to mention wasting great sums of the taxpayers' money.

Meanwhile, back at the hatchery, the rearing process continues. Fourteen days have passed since spawning, and those surviving now have a well-developed eyespot and a functional foot. The veligers are now called eyed-larvae by those in the propagation business and are ready to be set (or spatted, as you prefer) on cultch consisting of previously owned oyster shells.

The Oyster

Large numbers of shells secured from the local processing plant or elsewhere are prepared to receive the tender embrace of the eyed-larva preparing to attach.

Before exposing the eyed-larvae to the cultch, however, the calcareous valves have been cleaned in a special washing device. This shell washer was invented by Chambers and reminds one of a Rube Goldberg contraption. Shells, covered with mud, dirt, and other grime, are shoveled into one end of a large, rotating, meshed cylinder made of metal. A perforated pipe running through the center of this machine delivers jets of water under pressure to the contents. The shells are washed for a period of time and the foreign material, which would interfere with the delicate process of spatting, is removed. Flo Chambers is usually waiting at the opposite end of the "plumber's nightmare," ready to catch about two hundred cleaned shells in a large-meshed plastic bag.

The bags, each containing about half a bushel of shell, are placed in the spat tank for setting. About 150 bags of shell are used, and large numbers of eyed-larvae are introduced to the tank. The spatting tank is aerated constantly for forty-eight hours, and at the end of that period the spat that have not set are filtered out. The tank is refilled, and the larvae that did not attach to one of the shells the first time are given another chance. This is their final opportunity to salvage their existence, and some of them are successful in finding a place to spat this time around. More spat set on the shell, however, than there will eventually be room for as they grow and increase in height and width. It's hoped that about ten will affix themselves to each piece of cultch in such a way they cannot be crowded off. Some, however, are evicted from the surface of the shell, and these are lost, as once an attached oyster becomes detached, it can never affix itself again. The materials used in manufacturing the cementum have been expended and cannot be resynthesized.

When it has been determined that the setting process is complete, the bags of spat-encrusted shells are transferred to wooden pallets that have been placed in the shallow water of the river's shoreline. If temperatures are optimum (as in July, August, and September), the young oysters will grow rapidly, metabolizing food around the clock and assimilating the minerals needed for

The ostraculturist of the Nanticoke and the "plumber's
nightmare" (cultch washing apparatus).

the growth of the valves; they will be ready for sale to oyster planters in about sixty days. If the young oysters were spawned in the fall, it will probably be necessary to hold them over until the next spring before they are ready for marketing. The underdeveloped spat seem to do well in a state of suspended animation during the winter months and readily survive under the ice. (Infrequently, the Nanticoke does not ice over during the winter, but whether it does or not seems to have no effect on the spat.)

Reaching a size of about ¼ inch, the spat are ready to be sold. A count of the number of spat attached to a randomly selected number of shells in a bag is used to calculate the approximate number of oysters in each lot. In 1984 each of the bags produced by FLOMAX contained about two thousand spat and was sold for eight dollars. Poor Max: In 1985 he moved his hatchery from the Waterview site (the property was sold for development) to a site on the Manokin River. Things went badly in the new area and he was not able to produce sufficient spat to offer for sale. He says he has solved the problem and will produce great numbers in 1986.

The efficiency of the Chambers system is apparent when one compares the figure of two thousand spat per bag (recall that the two hundred shells in the bag amount to about half a bushel) with the number of spat observed to be present on cultch taken from a natural oyster bar. In 1983, the state Department of Natural Resources conducted a survey of this sort of shell cultch dredged from a bar in the Manokin River near Crisfield, Maryland. Though this oyster bed had previously been classified as "very productive," the state biologists found only forty spat per bushel of cultch.

In the spots around the community where people routinely gather to exchange tidbits of information and debate the great issues of the time, the current topic of conversation is usually Max Chambers and the FLOMAX experiment. Not that Chambers's oyster-propagating wasn't a favorite subject for impromptu discussions previously, but now his name is spoken with respect and admiration. I don't know if Max and Flo are going to be able to raise enough oysters to clean up the Bay (or to stay afloat financially, for that matter), but I do know they are going to keep trying.

CHAPTER FIVE

Private Propagation

*"The Lord put them arsters here for every man. I'm
agin them private planters."*

*"Used to be a man could walk across Tangier Sound
on the arster boats. Won't never be no more."*
                                    Anonymous Oystermen

AS far as recorded history is concerned, the Roman Sergius
Orata appears to have been the first to attempt the controlled propagation of oysters. Pliny the Elder describes the efforts of Sergius to raise his own oysters in artificial beds about
ninety-five years before the birth of Christ, and, as much as he
enjoyed devouring them at his lavish feasts, it seems he was more
interested in filling his pocketbook than satisfying his tastebuds.

In his famous zoological treatise on mollusks and crustaceans,
Ulissi Aldrovandi (1522–1605) wrote regarding this early
entrepreneur:

> They were held in such high favor among the epicures of Rome that
> they were brought in wooden tubs to the very farthest districts, from
> the sea, and they were transferred from Brundisium to the Lucrine
> Lake, for they grew wonderfully fat there. We learn from Pliny that
> Sergius Orata was the first to devise oyster preserves in the Baian
> Lake (i.e. Lacus Lucrinus) . . . He did this, not out of indulgence to
> his palate, but with an eye on financial gains, for he saw that he
> would be able to make a substantial profit. He had a genius for this
> sort of thing, for he was the first to invent shower baths, making
> great profits by selling them thus decked out.

The Oyster

Sergius Orata's endeavors to grow oysters artificially involved little more than placing seed, or undeveloped, oysters in a receptive environment and waiting for them to grow to a more desirable size. Taking the next logical step in the evolution of oyster culture, one can readily imagine some primitive grower deciding his crop would grow better if he prepared the bottom with a cultch of shells before planting. The seed would be provided with a firm foundation and their forthcoming offspring would have a place to attach.

Seventeenth-century Japanese culturists refined this method by using rocks, tree branches, and other objects of a size that could be moved easily from place to place with the developing oysters attached. In 1673, Gorohachi Koroshiya, a Japanese clam grower, made the serendipitous discovery that oyster larvae would spat on upright bamboo stakes anchored in the sea bottom. Not only were the oysters so attached protected from bottom predators, but the resulting three-dimensional "bed" offered many times more surface area for attachment than a flat bottom. The next step was the development of the many types of suspended collectors, hung from floats, which are still used widely today.

In France, oysters are grown on the bottom because this method of culture is the best way to produce the regularly shaped shells preferred by consumers of oysters on the half-shell. Virtually all the oysters consumed in that country are eaten raw, on the half-shell. The French prefer the flat oyster, *Ostrea edulis*, but as few French waters are suitable for the propagation of this species, the Portuguese oyster, *Crassostrea angulata*, is a frequent substitute. Though the Portuguese variety is hardier than its flat cousin, it is valued less because of its incorrigibly irregular shell.

The oyster-farming industry of France resulted from a crisis in the natural populations during the middle of the nineteenth century. A mysterious disease almost totally wiped out the natural beds from which French oyster catchers had always been able to secure enough to meet the demands of the market. Ever sensitive to the fundamental needs of its citizens, the French government commissioned a Professor Coste of the College of France to investigate and determine how the oysters could be saved. At about the same time, another emergency arose relating to another

74

favorite product—wine. For unknown reasons, much of the wine produced was turning to vinegar as it aged, and a national crisis loomed. Catastrophe was just around the corner; for a time it appeared as if the French would find themselves with a greatly reduced wine supply and the oysters they relished so much would be prohibitively expensive because of short supply.

The scientist Louis Pasteur solved the riddle of the fermenting wine in a little over two years, and Coste quickly developed a scheme for growing oysters artificially that is little changed today.

Boosted by Emperor Napoleon III, Coste established two imperial oyster-propagation farms in the shallow Bay of Arcachon, on the southwest Atlantic coast, and set out to learn how to grow oysters. He sat the spat on half-round roofing tiles covered with a mixture of lime and sand, which gave the young oysters good footing. After spatting, the mortar with the spat attached was flaked off and placed in so-called "ambulances" which were, in reality, wooden frames resting on short legs with fine mesh wire above and below. The ambulances protected the tiny oysters from predators and the smothering action of the mud at the bottom of Arcachon Bay until they were more mature and able to cope better with the hazards of the natural world.

After reaching a size of about ½ inch, they were removed from the ambulances and transferred to relatively large "oyster parks," or rearing beds, where they were allowed to grow for two years and attain a size of about 2 inches. The final step in the production line was, as in cattle farming, the fattening process, which was carried out for about a year in special "fattening farms."

The methods for rearing oysters along the Atlantic coast of France have been little modified over the intervening years. They worked, and France presently produces so many oysters that, after the domestic requirements are met, four to five hundred million are exported each year to satisfy the connoisseurs of Europe.

In France, oysters having a greenish tint are considered great delicacies and command a much higher price than those lacking the coloring. The celebrated green oysters of Marennes receive their unique coloring after being placed for a short time in special holding beds *(claires)* that contained great amounts of green

The Oyster

plankton. Some believe the green pigment chlorophyll is stored in the body and is completely responsible for the green color. Others attribute the color to the characteristics of the clayey soil of the area. Both factors are involved in the tinting process, and the deposition of copper in the tissues certainly plays a part in the greening of the oysters. The copper content of green oysters must be carefully monitored, however, to prevent poisoning of the gourmet by excessive amounts of this heavy metal.

During my sojourn in France in the 1950s I resided, for the most part, in the vicinity of the city of Rochefort on the southwestern coast. Rochefort is, perhaps, the oyster-distribution center of France (at least the locals say it is), and on one occasion I recall a brouhaha developed when oysters containing an abnormally high content of copper were detected and seized by government inspectors in the markets of that city. Many of the oysters had been sold, however, before it was determined that many of them contained as much as two centigrams of copper each, an amount dangerous to human health. The newspapers and radio warned the populace of this potential health hazard and offered a fairly simple procedure for anyone to use to check oysters that might be suspect. The test procedure was as follows: Thrust an ordinary needle into the green part of the oyster and then immerse the creature in pure vinegar. Observe the needle after thirty seconds, and if it is covered with a red, dusty coating discard it: The oyster will contain more copper than it is healthy to consume.

I recall that during this copper scare I had purchased two kilograms of oysters in a market at nearby La Rochelle (the price was about two hundred francs, or fifty-six cents at that time) and observed that they had a greenish tint when I pried open the shells. Not wishing to become ill from copper poisoning in a foreign land, I followed the advice of the French Ministry of Health and performed the needle-vinegar test. The results of the assay were negative even after I kept the oyster submerged in the vinegar for ten minutes. Having assured myself it was safe to eat the oysters, I swallowed the test specimen and immediately rejected it. Vinegar does not enhance the taste of a Portuguese oyster, at least not in my opinion. Assuming, perhaps incorrectly,

76

that the others in the batch were safe to eat, I devoured them all in a short period of time and suffered no ill affects.

It is well beyond the scope of this book to describe the procedures employed in oyster farming in various parts of the world, but the following table of the species most commonly cultured in different countries should be of interest.

Species	Countries where cultured
Crassostrea virginica (American oyster)	Atlantic and Gulf coasts of the United States, Maritime Provinces of Canada; experimentally in Japan and California
C. gigas (Pacific, or Japanese, oyster)	Japan, Korea, Taiwan, Pacific coast of U. S. and Canada; experimentally in Australia, France, Netherlands, Portugal, Thailand, and United Kingdom
C. angulata (Portuguese oyster)	France, Portugal, Spain, Tunisia; experimentally in Japan and California
C. commercialis (Sydney rock oyster)	Australia from southern Queensland to eastern Victoria and New Zealand
C. eradelie	Philippines
C. rhizophorae	Experimentally in Cuba and Venezuela
Ostrea edulis (European, or flat, oyster)	North Atlantic coast of France, Spain, Netherlands, United Kingdom, Japan and United States (Maine and the Pacific coast)

The Situation in Maryland

After the early colonists in America overcame their reluctance to use oysters as food, it did not take very long until the once plentiful mollusks dwindled in number. By the beginning of the nineteenth century, the oyster beds of New England had become badly depleted by overfishing, and the dredgers were forced to look to southern waters to supply the Yankee damand. At first the skippers dredged the waters of New Jersey and Virginia, but, in 1811, Virginia enacted a law prohibiting dredging within the territorial waters of the commonwealth. The northern oystermen were forced to retreat north to the Maryland portion of the Chesapeake Bay. The antidredging law passed by the Virginia legislature, incidentally, has the distinction of being the earliest oyster-related law ever enacted in the United States.

The invasion of Maryland waters by the alien dredge-schooners soon caused considerable concern about such increased oyster fishing and led the Maryland legislature, in 1820, to enact its first law aimed at conserving what was now being recognized as an important natural resource—the state's oyster beds. The Maryland law of 1820 prohibited both the dredging of state waters for oysters and the transport of oysters out of state in vessels not totally owned for the preceding year by residents of Maryland. The crafty New Englanders were not to be deterred, however, and simply moved a branch of their oyster-packing operation to Baltimore and established residence. After the required year, the ships were free to transport "Maryland's Finest" to the waiting markets in the Northeast.

Transportation to the West was being greatly improved with the opening of turnpikes and the Baltimore and Ohio Railroad, and additional markets were quickly opened for the "pearls of the Chesapeake." The demand for Chesapeake oysters rose in proportion to the amount supplied, as evidenced by the growth of Baltimore-based processing establishments (raw and steam packers, canners). One such plant existed in Baltimore City in 1834; by 1868 the number had risen to eighty. By 1875, the approximate harvest from the Chesapeake was fourteen million bushels with a peak of fifteen million bushels in 1885. The catch has gone downhill since then.

Having finally awakened to the fact the oysters beneath Maryland waters represented a great economic asset that was probably finite in nature, the one-acre planting law was passed in 1830.

Private Propagation

Basically, this legislation allowed Maryland citizens to use one acre of submerged land to plant and grow oysters and other "shellfish." If you were a fortunate landowner whose property bordered a creek with a mouth less than one hundred yards wide, you had the exclusive right to use the creek for planting. The law also made it a misdemeanor to catch oysters from these private grounds without the permission of the owner. The oyster-planting law, as it came to be known, was the third such statute enacted in the United States, after New Jersey (1820) and Rhode Island (1827). The one-acre law was replaced by a five-acre amendment in 1865.

After the fourteen-million-bushel harvest of 1875, the annual catch declined, then peaked one last time at fifteen million bushels in 1885. The general assembly in Annapolis, being sensitive to the considerable political clout of the oystermen, then as now, was induced to commission the U. S. Coast and Geodetic Survey to conduct a scientific study of the extensive oyster beds in Tangier and Pocomoke sounds. The individual in charge of the study was an extremely competent man by the name of Francis Winslow, and the data presented at the conclusion of the two-year period of study (1878–1879) became known as the Winslow Report.

Winslow made many important observations about the oyster populations in the areas studied, such as the biological and physical difference between grounds that had been worked and new, unfished beds. Among other things, he noted that dredging had a beneficial rather than detrimental effect on the beds. Formerly it was believed that dredging destroyed the beds, but Winslow showed that this operation served to break up tightly consolidated "virgin" beds and spread the oysters and shell to new areas where they could grow in less crowded conditions and expand into new beds or rocks.

Winslow also found that the oyster populations had diminished dramatically during the thirty years the sounds had been fished, and he recommended the formation of an informed commission, not hampered by political influence, to oversee the entire oyster fishery. This trail-blazing oyster biologist also strongly recommended the encouragement of private oyster cultivation on bottom leased from the state in a manner already proving effective in northern states. He made his point by comparing the 40 bushels per acre taken from Maryland's public oystering grounds to the 120 bushels per acre routinely harvested from privately cultivated grounds in New England. For the most part, Winslow's recommendations were ignored.

Perhaps, however, the Winslow Report was taken seriously in some quarters; an Oyster Commission was appointed in 1882 "to examine the oyster beds within the state and to advise as to their protection and improvement." The commission was headed by the distinguished biologist Dr. W. K. Brooks of The Johns Hopkins University. There was just one small item the general assembly forgot to include when the commission was established— funding. The governor did provide a small sum from a contingency fund, and The Johns Hopkins University granted Brooks two years of paid leave to perform the work.

Professor Brooks was very knowledgeable with regard to *Crassostrea virginica*, and, in fact, a few years earlier he had discovered that the American oyster was a nonincubatory species, which, unlike the European oyster, shed its sex cells into the sea rather than retaining the eggs within the body of the female.

The Brooks Commission reaffirmed many of Winslow's discoveries and added many of its own. Included in its recommendations was a strong plea for the encouragement of private propagation far beyond what had been envisioned by the enactment of the five-acre law of 1865. Brooks also advocated such heretical propositions as closing oyster bars when necessary to permit rehabilitation and growth, and the returning of shell to the bars to serve as cultch. Though Brooks knew more about the biology and natural history of the oyster than anyone else at the time, he was attacked frequently by those who saw him as a threat to their own private interests. In 1905, Brooks reacted to the harsh criticism of his work by remarking:

> I speak on this subject with the diffidence of one who has been snubbed and repressed; for while I am myself sure of the errors of the man who loudly asserts his rights to know all about it, it is easier to acquiesce than to struggle against such overpowering ignorance, so I have learned to be submissive in the presence of the elderly gentleman who studied the embryology of the oyster when years ago

he visited his grandfather on the Eastern Shore, and to listen with deference to the shucker as he demonstrates to me at his raw-box, by the aid of his hammer and shucking knife, the fallacy of my notions of the structure of the animal.

Brooks struck back in 1905 by publishing a booklet entitled *The Oyster*. He published this classic for the general public, and it was so popular that a second edition was required. In this treatise he compiled most of the knowledge then in existence and made a strong plea for the adoption of his commission's recommendations. With illustrations seldom seen in publications of today, he depicted the early stages of the oyster (in addition to determining that *C. virginica* was a nonincubatory oyster, he was the first to successfully induce spawning in the laboratory) and discussed the biology and life cycle in a way any interested party could readily understand. He reiterated and emphasized the thesis advocated by Winslow—the oyster industry could not endure in Maryland without extensive private cultivation.

The potent recommendations of Winslow and Brooks were attacked strongly. One such condemnation came from the Nationalist Club of Baltimore City in 1891:

> It [leasing] involves the enslavement of 16,000 of the free men of Maryland; it involves the continuation of a State Oyster Police system whose inefficiency has become a matter of national comment; or the substitution of the hated Pinkerton system of police, hired by the owners or lessees of the oyster lots; it involves the employment in increased numbers of the lowest class of people, taken from the jails and penitentiaries, besides foreigners brought here to take the places at reduced pay of the American workers, and it involves the establishment, we contend, of a gigantic monopoly in the oyster business, which would control prices, charging customers what it pleases, and paying to those who do the actual work of that industry the merest pittance, which the ever increasing number of unemployed will enable it to dictate.

It is interesting to note that this ideological attack on the leasing of bottom for oyster cultivation embodied the themes of class distinction and anti-immigration, both of which were gaining in popularity in the United States at that time.

The Oyster

Up to this time, all legislation concerning the private leasing of bottom for cultivation had been shaped by three fundamental attitudes of the oystermen:

The natural oyster beds belong to the citizens of Maryland and they have the sole right to work them.

If leasing is encouraged, large corporations will take over the oyster industry and eventually control pricing and working conditions.

Oysters cannot be grown except on naturally occurring oyster bars or rocks. A new oyster rock cannot be created by man by shelling the bottom and planting seed. Any successful cultivation operation must have taken place on a natural rock, not previously recognized as such.

Unfortunately, these same attitudes are held by many today and are influential in shaping the rules and regulations of the oyster industry in Maryland.

Although the legislative body chose to ignore most of the recommendations of the Brooks Commission, for some reason it did pass the very unpopular Cull Law of 1890. This law, relating to one of the most important methods of protecting the fecundity of a natural bar, required that shells with spat and young oysters adhering to them must be thrown back on the bar from which they were taken. A minimum size of 2½ inches in height was set for oysters intended for the market.

Oystermen, however, largely ignored the new law, as small oysters (soup oysters) provided a source of income when sold to steam canners or to out-of-state cultivators to be used as seed for their private beds.

After many years of biological research and political maneuvering, Dr. R. V. Truitt, the founder of the Chesapeake Biological Laboratory at Solomons Island, Maryland, was able to persuade the legislature in 1927 to replace the 2½-inch limit with a 3-inch minimum. In a personal conversation with me in 1984, Dr. Truitt indicated to me that he considers the passage of the 3-inch cull law one of the most (if not the most) important accomplishment of his long and distinguished career as an oyster biologist. The difficulties he encountered as he championed the 3-inch minimum were many, and, like Winslow, Brooks, and others, he was ridiculed and scorned. Of course, Truitt had one advantage the others lacked: he had married the daughter of a former governor of Maryland and had certain political advantages, perhaps, that made his quest easier.

As the oyster industry entered the twentieth century the harvests continued to decline, but the progressive depletion of the mollusks caused little concern among the men who went to the water to catch them. The prevailing attitude was one of optimism; that next year would be better. This head-in-the-sand point of view, unfortunately, remains today among the watermen of the Chesapeake when they talk about declining populations of rockfish, shad, crabs, oysters, and other species. Facing reality and farsightedness are not common characteristics of the waterman. "Get it today and to hell with tommar," was the answer I received when I asked a waterman what he was going to do to make a living when the oysters were gone.

In 1906, the Haman Oyster Bill was passed after considerable political gerrymandering. B. H. Haman was a Baltimore attorney who fought tooth and nail, over a fifteen-year period, to secure legislation that would enhance private planting operations throughout the state. Haman believed what Brooks had written in the preface to *The Oyster*: ". . . the oyster grounds of Virginia and North Carolina, and those of Georgia and Louisiana, are increasing in value, and many of our packing houses are being moved to the south, but there is no oyster farming in Maryland, and our oyster beds are still in a state of nature, affording a scanty and precarious livelihood to those who depend on them."

The Haman Bill, passed over the strong objections of legislators representing the Eastern Shore, provided for the leasing of up to thirty acres of barren bottom in county waters or up to one hundred acres in the Bay outside the jurisdiction of the county lines. Natural oyster rocks were not to be leased but retained in the public domain to be fished by any citizen of the state. The question was, of course, Exactly where were the natural rocks?

In 1906 an ambitious survey of the Chesapeake system was undertaken to determine the location and extent of the natural oyster beds. The previous work of Winslow, Brooks, and others was helpful, but many additional surveys had to be performed. A State Shellfish Commission was created by the Haman Bill, and this group, in conjunction with the U. S. Coast and Geodetic Survey, performed this vital work over a period of six years. It is comforting to note that the Shellfish Commission included a biologist named Caswell Grave who had been a student of Dr. Brooks at Johns Hopkins and shared his views and opinions.

By 1912 the survey had been completed at a cost of only two hundred thousand dollars, roughly equivalent to about four cents for each bushel of oysters caught during the survey period. Forty-three large-scale maps, twenty-four hundred printed pages, and four hundred square feet of charts were produced and became available for use in 1912. These basic charts are used today in defining the locations of the natural beds, though they have been amended extensively.

C. C. Yates was in charge of the oyster survey and responsible for the publication of the findings. Yates was so elated with the state of affairs in 1913 that he optimistically wrote:

> It now seems not only reasonable but probable that within the next generation the citizens of Maryland will be leasing and cultivating a probable 100,000 and a possible 300,000 acres of so-called "barren bottoms" where oysters do not grow in commercial quantities; that the more than 200,000 acres of natural oyster bars now reserved for the use of the oystermen as a result of the Maryland Oyster Survey will be so conserved and developed that they will produce, as they have done before, twice the amount they now yield; and that the oyster industry of Maryland will be based on an annual production of 20,000,000 bushels of oysters where now it is barely 5,000,000.

That Yates's euphoric predictions were overly optimistic is attested to by the fact that in 1984 a total of 9,000 acres of bottom were under lease from the state (with probably less than 2,500 acres actually being farmed), and the oyster production for that year was only about 800,000 bushels. In 1984 there were about 279,000 acres designated as natural, public oyster bars, which means only about 3 percent of the producing oyster beds were in the hands of the private grower. It seems to me that if I had control of 97 percent of the oyster-producing areas in Maryland I would not be overly concerned that the remaining 3 percent were in the hands of private cultivators and not available to me—unless I believed that the methods used by the 3 percent minority were so good they could outproduce me and take charge of my profession.

The fundamental reason Yates's prediction did not come true was the passage of the Shepherd Act of 1914 which, in effect, repealed the Haman Oyster Act. Goaded by representatives of the disgruntled oystermen, who still held firmly to the attitudes previously mentioned, the politically perceptive legislature virtually did away with the provisions of the earlier bill by saying that any bottom resorted to by at least one oyster catcher at least once during the preceding five years was to be classified as natural oyster rock and therefore was not available for leasing. Even though the bottom in question was not on the survey maps of 1912, if fished for oysters once during the last five years it was to be reclassified as a natural bar and added to the charts.

One can readily see how the individual wishing to start out in the oyster-farming business could be denied lease rights to a piece of bottom he had determined was barren. Then, as now, an application had to be filed with the state, and the intention to lease a designated area, along with the exact survey coordinates secured at the expense of the future oyster cultivator, were to be published several times in a newspaper of general circulation in the geographical region concerned. About the only thing an oysterman who did not want the state to approve the proposed lease had to do was to file a protest in the circuit court. In court, he had to swear under oath that he had fished the area in question at least once in the last five years, and the usually sympathetic judge would rule in his favor. The area would then be ordered reclassified as natural rock and so placed permanently on the official charts. Needless to say, almost every protest was allowed, and, between the years 1915 and 1963, some fifteen thousand acres of bottom once classified as barren were removed from consideration as sites of artificial propagation. The Shepherd Act has effectively choked off oyster farming in Maryland to this day.

A New Kind of Waterman.   The wind was blowing fiercely out of the north one June morning in 1985 as I waited on the pier at

The Oyster

Tyaskin for Ken Lappe to bring his skiff alongside to take me aboard. Looking out of the sheltered harbor to the open Nanticoke River, I could see the presence of many nurses (whitecaps), and I felt sure we would get a bath that morning when we ventured out of the relative calm of the harbor to have a look at some private beds located in the main part of the river. With the exception of a lone twenty-five- or thirty-foot workboat crabbing in the sheltered area across the river in Dorchester County, not another vessel was in sight. Few had been so bold as to leave port that morning.

I first met Ken Lappe at the harbor in Cedar Hill Park (sometimes called Jackson or Bivalve Harbor) in the spring of 1985 when we struck up a casual conversation concerning the lack of rainfall so far that year. I offered my opinion that the river was much saltier than it was at the same time the preceding year, being as much as ten to twelve parts salt per thousand parts water—according to my unscientific method of determining salinity, tasting it. Lappe retorted that the salinity was a good bit higher than my estimate, and, to prove his statement, produced an expensive refractometer (which is used to take a quick and accurate reading of salinity). After placing a drop of river water on the stage of the instrument and holding the device skyward to see the graduated scale within, he announced that the precise salinity at that time was sixteen parts per thousand. Then and there I knew I had encountered a different breed of waterman.

Lappe is a Connecticut Yankee who migrated to the Eastern Shore in the early 1950s. Having grown up on the water in his New England home, it was natural he should enter the U. S. Merchant Marine. After sixteen years of circling the globe, he found himself a second mate without a berth. As one will recall, the decline of the U. S. Merchant Marine service began after the end of World War II, with fewer and fewer of the ships transporting commercial cargo around the world flying the American flag. By the early fifties, it was very difficult for a merchant seaman, especially an officer, to find a job on an American vessel. The sailor had two choices: sign on, if possible, with a ship flying a foreign ensign or hope for a slot on one of the ships of the Military Sea Transport Service (MSTS). These latter vessels were used to

86

transport troops and supplies (as well as authorized civilians) to military operations overseas and were operated by the merchant marine, though a skeleton crew of navy personnel was aboard to attend to matters not concerned with the operation of the ship. Though the MSTS ran many vessels during the Korean War, the scope of its activities was greatly reduced with the end of that conflict.

Finding himself on the beach for longer and longer periods of time and clearly interpreting the handwriting on the wall, Ken decided to seek a new way of life, one in which he could be his own boss and decide for himself when and how much he would work. After sharing his plans with his father, who was familiar with the Eastern Shore, he decided Tyaskin, Maryland, was the place to start a new life for himself and his wife, a former member of the famous Radio City Music Hall Rockettes.

When Ken Lappe established residence in Tyaskin he fully intended to become a waterman and seek his livelihood from the oysters, crabs, and rockfish that abounded in the Nanticoke at that time. Though he was quickly informed by his new neighbors, "You got to be born on the water to do anything on the water," he persisted, and over the years developed the skills necessary to making money "the hard way."

Even in the 1950s, however, when the oysters, crabs, and fish were relatively plentiful, there was always a nagging uncertainty about depending entirely on the water. Lappe decided the prudent thing to do was to secure a job that provided a regular paycheck, and he found employment as an operating engineer at a state institution in nearby Salisbury. He did not abandon his quest for the fruits of the Nanticoke, however, and continued to tong oysters, net fish, and run trotlines for crabs.

Now that he has retired from his state position, he is free to devote all his time to the water (he says he is not as strong as he used to be; after tonging twenty or twenty-five bushels of oysters, he is tired), but the seafood harvested these days hardly warrants the effort expended to catch it. The rockfish are all but nonexistent, some say, and a new law prohibits fishing for the remaining few. The crab populations are only a shadow of what they were in bygone years. And the oysters are definitely in trouble. Today,

The Oyster

Ken spends most of his time growing oysters on a few acres of leased bottom he has recorded in his own name and supervising other leases he has in partnership with other individuals.

As we edged out of the protection of Wetipquin Creek (the entrance to Tyaskin Harbor) and entered the open river, the expected bath did not materialize. Ken's wooden skiff was built over twenty years ago by an Eastern Shore craftsman who knew how to build a boat sensitive to the needs of the waterman. The beam of the fifteen-footer is about five feet, and the bow is upturned to aid in the manipulation of fishing nets. Powered by a fifty-horsepower outboard motor, it is an ideal boat to use for net fishing, crabbing, or oyster work.

Four long stakes embedded in the bottom of the river clearly outline Lappe's leased three-acre plot a few hundred yards from the mouth of the harbor. The law is quite explicit on the subject of marking a leased area: At least four stakes, buoys, or monuments bearing the lessee's initials are required. If the markers are destroyed or in some other way removed, the marine police are obliged to prohibit the lessee from fishing for his own oysters until the situation is corrected. Though the law temporarily protects the lessee's oysters from tongers or dredgers while the plot is unmarked, it is difficult to prove in court that someone knowingly misappropriated private oysters if he was apprehended in an unmarked area. Marking devices have been known to disappear from a plot shortly before the dredge of the rustler plowed through the bed.

As we approached the lease, Ken readied a pair of fourteen-foot hand tongs, and when we drifted over the desired area within the staked boundaries, he plunged them to the bottom some eight to ten feet below. He deftly performed the characteristic scissors-like motion with the tongs to amass a pile of the oysters. Closing the sharp jaws of the instrument, and with a hand-over-hand movement, he brought the oysters to the surface and into the boat. At least three dozen living oysters were included in this first "lick," along with some of the shell cultch and a few "boxes" (dead oysters whose two valves are still adhering to each other). All the living oysters were of the same size, about 2 to 2½ inches in height. Upon examining the shells of these specimens, it was

A handtonger at work.

The Oyster

readily apparent that rapid growth had recently taken place. The
ventral lips of the valves were thin and razor-sharp, and one had to
be careful when handling them to avoid being cut. I was as-
tounded when Ken told he had planted the oysters the previous
December (a little over six months previously) as 1-inch seed. The
rate of development had been phenomenal, especially considering that little if any growth had occurred during the winter and
early spring months. One factor contributing to this extraordinary
increase in size was the high salinity of the river that year due to
lack of rainfall. High concentrations of the salts and minerals
required for the construction of the shells were available, as was
an abundant supply of plankton to feed the juvenile animals.

Ken was positive his oysters would attain the mandatory 3-
inch height by the end of the summer and be legal to catch for the
market. He was undecided, however, what course of action he
would take. If he let them grow for another year they would be
larger, naturally, and bring a better price. Undoubtedly another
year would bring sexual maturity (this could possibly occur during
the current year) and the reseeding of his bar, as well as other beds
up and down the river, would occur. But there would always be
the risk during the additional year of losing the entire crop to an
epidemic disease like MSX, siltation resulting from a storm or the
screw of an off-course tugboat, or the tongs or dredge of a thief. A
slick oyster purloiner could get most of the crop with a few passes
of the dredge during the dark of night, and in a period of about
thirty minutes, 90 percent of the Lappe oysters would be heading
downriver in a fast getaway boat. An act of oyster piracy is punish-
able as a misdemeanor, but if Ken Lappe and some other oyster
planters I know had their way the punishment would be much
more severe. He emphasized his position by saying, "If a couple of
those thieving bastards were strung up there would be no more
poaching. It worked with horse and cow thieves in the Old West,
and it would work here too." The decisions of an oyster grower are
many, and he must weigh many factors before deciding on a
course of action for the management of his crop. Any decision is a
gamble, as in more conventional types of farming.

Some of the seed oysters Lappe placed on this and other beds
were obtained from the FLOMAX hatcheries at nearby Nanticoke,

90

but most of the seed were obtained from beds in the James River in Virginia. The ecological conditions found in the James are approximately the same as those in the Nanticoke, and seed oysters obtained from that source have always done well on the Lappe farms in Maryland. Seed oysters are not always available, however, from the Virginia source. Only when the Virginia Natural Resources Commission determines that a bumper crop of oysters has been produced within its jurisdiction are seed oysters permitted to be sold outside the state.

The 1-inch seed purchased in December 1984 cost Lappe $4.50 a bushel delivered by boat to his grounds in the Nanticoke. Each bushel of seed oysters contains 800 to 1,100 individuals, depending on size, whereas a harvested bushel of 3- to 5-inch oysters will number about 175 to 200. In recent years, depending on the season and the abundance of the catch, a bushel of oysters will bring a dockside price of up to sixteen dollars or more. But in some years and at certain times of the same year this price can drop to as low as ten dollars or less. Adding up the figures and calculating an approximate average dockside price to be expected, one can estimate the profit Lappe stands to make on his oysters in the next year or so—that is, if everything goes all right.

In spite of my precautions, I managed to inflict a cut on one of my fingers while handling the quarter-bushel Ken gave me for "research" purposes. The research I had in mind for these beauties was to study the commensal organisms associated with them—worms, sea anemones, barnacles, mussels, and so on. But, after they had been shucked, I decided I might as well test their gustatory qualities; I found them to be succulent and absolutely delicious.

I thought nothing of the cut on my finger at the time it occurred and simply washed the mud from the wound with river water. But, later the same day, when the finger reddened and became hot and painful, I realized I had become a victim of an occupational hazard of the oysterman—"oyster-finger." Cuts made by oyster shells have a difficult time healing unless immediate attention is paid to them and the invading microorganisms are destroyed with a strong antiseptic. Septicemia (blood poisoning) is a definite possibility if oyster-finger is allowed to proceed pathologically without treatment. Twelve hours after the cut was made I was able to take therapeutic action. The finger was badly swollen and feverish, and I could detect the presence of pus deep within the wound. I lanced the finger, drained it of the purulence, and after soaking it in hot water for a time, flooded the cut with iodine. This treatment temporarily relieved the symptoms, but the next night the entire medical procedure had to be repeated again. Finally, after four days, the pain and swelling abated, and I decided the wound had begun a normal healing process. I was wrong in this assumption, in that the wound did not close over as is the normal case but healed by granulation of the tissues under the skin. Many months have now passed since this experience, but the site of the wound is hard to the touch from the granulated material below, and I feel quite sure I will retain a quarter-inch scar on my finger for a long time, to remind me of the day I spent with Ken Lappe.

One sure way to identify an oysterman encountered out of his natural environment is to look at his hands, paying particular attention to the fingers. If he has been at his profession for any extended length of time, the telltale scars of past bouts with oyster-finger will be obvious.

As Ken and I were returning to the calm of Tyaskin Harbor after inspecting two other leases, we made good time riding the incoming flood tide. Over the hum of the outboard motor and the whistling of the wind, he explained to me how a knowledgeable sailor could make better time going up a tidal river than coming down it. As a young man growing up along the Connecticut River, he deduced that if he started up the river from its mouth at Saybrook, about two hours behind the incoming flood tide, he could run the tide most of the way to Hartford, forty miles up the river. Care had to be taken not to go too fast and outrun the incoming tide, and the last part of the trip would be made in backwater, where the tidal flows were neutralized, as the tide was starting to ebb at Saybrook. Coming back down the river from Hartford, the navigator would find himself running with the ebb tide part of the way and in backwater at another time. But there was no way one could make the return journey to the mouth of the river without bucking the flood tide for a portion of the journey.

Private Propagation

They told Ken Lappe that he would never be able to do anything on the Nanticoke because he had not been born there and could never understand the secrets of the river which were revealed only to its native sons. In spite of this handicap, he has been able to develop an intimate relationship with the river and solve many of the enigmas that have been puzzling for generations.

Oysters as Bacterial Incubators.   In October 1883, an event took place at Wesleyan University in Connectict that was to affect profoundly the entire oyster industry of the United States. A group of students was stricken with typhoid fever, and the disease organisms were traced to a batch of raw oysters they had consumed. The germ theory of the cause of disease was gaining wide acceptance in the scientific community at that time, and there seemed to be little doubt the oysters were the culprits in this case. Scientists and others had long suspected oysters of being able to harbor human pathogens, but the Wesleyan University incident represented the first instance in which oysters had been incriminated beyond a shadow of a doubt. The industry was thrown into a state of chaos, and the oyster lobby, representing both watermen and packing houses, went to work to enact laws prohibiting the dumping of raw sewage into the Bay and to secure the construction of efficient sewage treatment plants both on the Western and Eastern Shores.

From 1883 onward, the oyster industry in the Chesapeake Bay region would never be the same. Public health agencies, both state and national, would come to exercise great influence on the everyday lives of the people who depended on the oyster for a living.

Inspections of oyster-production areas for bacteriological contamination became routine, and, when high counts of bacteria associated with human wastes were detected, the offending bar was officially closed. With a close system of monitoring, the disease issue was effectively quieted until 1924, when major outbreaks of typhoid occurred in Chicago, Washington, D. C., and New York City. Some 1,500 cases of the illness were diagnosed, resulting in about 150 deaths. (Typhoid fever was a very dangerous disease at that time, before an effective immunization

93

The Oyster

was developed.) Most of these cases were directly traced to contaminated oysters, and the state of Illinois imposed a ban on the importation of raw oysters. The repercussions of this bad publicity were felt immediately, and the American oyster industry ground to a virtual halt. Since that time no major epidemics of oyster-related diseases have made the headlines, and most people today do not even think about the possibility of acquiring some virulent microorganism when they down a raw oyster. A few members of the elder generation of Americans remember, however, the association of oysters with the deadly fever and refuse to eat them.

Military personnel, as well as the accompanying civilians, stationed in France during the 1950s were warned that a whole host of bad things would happen to them if they consumed the oysters of that country. Apparently the preventive medicine experts did not trust the efficiency of the French health officials who carried out routine inspections of one of their valuable crops. Most Americans, myself included, ignored the warnings of our self-appointed protectors and devoured great quantities of oysters, as well as a host of other forbidden items, and suffered no ill effects.

Over the years, sanitary inspection of oyster beds have increased in frequency and sophistication. Laboratory equipment is now available that will detect potential pathogens in a mere fraction of the concentration that was required for recognition in the past. Many private planters have had their crop of oysters declared off-limits in recent years because the lab apparatus was able to detect bacteria seeping from the pit of an outdoor privy located too close to the water's edge.

Bob Mitchell, Jr. a biology graduate of Salisbury State College, has worked with his father and grandfather, Boyd Whitney, on oyster leases the family has controlled for many years. One such lease was located in the Wicomico River at the entrance to Mount Vernon Harbor in Somerset County and had been determined to be ready for harvesting. Just as the tongers were going to work to bring up the oysters for his grandfather's packing-house, officials from the state Health Department arrived and quarantined the area. At that time, the City of Salisbury, some fifteen miles up river, was suspected of discharging unknown amounts of raw sewage into the Wicomico from time to time, and numerous outhouses and primitive septic systems along the river contributed to the high bacterial counts that led to the closing of the bar. The prohibition remained in effect for several years until it was finally lifted and Mitchell and other oystermen could legally catch their oysters for the market. Bob describes what he found when he put his tongs over and brought up the first batch: "They came up as big as shoe soles and laughing at me." By "laughing" he meant the oysters were dead and the shells were agape—boxes, as they are called. They had died of old age.

Around the southern lip of the mouth of the Wicomico River is an excellent oyster-producing area known as Monie Bay. Official charts showing the distribution of private leases in this shallow sound indicate that a large percentage of the bottom is in the hands of private lessees. Yet today only one or two small plots are receiving any attention whatsoever from their lessees because the entire bay is under state quarantine. The lease holders, for the most part, continue to pay the annual rental to the state in the hope that the ban will eventually be lifted, but there is no such event in sight. Understandably, many of the propagators are bitter toward the state. Not so much because the sanitarians find high bacterial counts each time they sample the area, but because the state apparently does nothing to eliminate the sources of pollution. The proprietors are not going to spend additional funds to rehabilitate and seed the bottom when state officials can give them no indication when they might be able to retrieve their crop.

Acts of God.   Bacteria have not always been the number one enemy of the oysters of Monie Bay. In 1972, many of the leased grounds were ready to harvest; surveys had shown the oysters were plentiful, legal, and fat. Mitchell relates that his family had a twenty-acre plot they had shelled and seeded in 1968 at considerable cost and were just ready to reap a return on their investment when Hurricane Agnes struck. The waters flowing into Monie Bay from its principal tributary, Monie Creek, carried tons of silt into the growing areas and covered the oysters with several inches of the lethal material, which effectively smothered them. The entire crop was wiped out, as was that of other growers. Since that time, the Mitchells have faithfully paid the rent each year, but with the quarantine in effect, they see no sense at all in seeding again.

As one will recall, Agnes was a devil of a storm, creating huge deluges of fresh water that inundated the Bay as it rushed in from the many tributaries. The salinity was reduced to almost zero in many areas and remained near the fresh-water level for several weeks. Consequently, a large portion of the oysters in the entire ecosystem were killed. But the oyster has tremendous staying power, as much or more than any other animal, and some did manage to survive to repopulate the rocks. Slowly the populations recovered, but even today, the effects of Agnes are still in evidence in the oyster populations as well as in the populations of other species.

Though the Mitchell family of Mount Vernon might seem to be a victim of a run of incredibly bad luck as far as their oyster endeavors go, their experiences are typical of most of the others who try their hand at this risky business. The final blow came a few years ago, when a lease in the Wicomico they operated was declared "healthy," but, before they could instigate tonging operations, a barge, enagaged by the Army Corps of Engineers to dredge the river's channel, went off course and plowed through their lease, destroying 90 percent of the oysters. As the lease agreement with the state contained a clause declaring that the state was not responsible for accidents or acts of God that damaged a plot, they had no legal recourse.

Apparently, little animosity exists between the lease holders and the other oystermen in that part of Somerset County encompassing the mouth of the Wicomico River and Monie Bay. When the official oyster season ends, usually about April 15, the watermen gear up for the forthcoming crab season. Frequently, however, there is a period of a month or more during this time when sufficient quantities of marketable crustaceans are not available.

During this slack period, many of the watermen contract with the leaseholders to catch oysters from the private beds on a share basis (leased ground may be fished at any time of the year). Thus, many individuals who would normally face a period of several weeks in which no revenue could be generated from the water, are provided with a source of income to tide them over until the crab run starts. Unfortunately, this spirit of cooperation between the two groups does not seem to be prevalent in most other parts of the oyster-producing region.

Of course, there are many years when there are no oysters on the private beds to be harvested, and the coffers of both groups remain empty. Most people, in the face of all the adversities facing the private propagator, would have long since given up trying to raise oysters on leased bottom. But people who have been intimately associated with the water all of their lives are eternally optimistic. They will continue to pay the rent each year and hope for a time in the uncertain future when the oysters from the private beds will again come up "as big as shoe soles." I can only hope their perseverance will be eventually rewarded.

CHAPTER SIX

Life on the Oyster Bar

So, naturalists observe, a flea
Hath smaller fleas that on him prey;
And these have smaller still to bite 'em,
And so proceed ad infinitum.

Jonathan Swift

MOST people partaking of oysters in one form or another have no idea of the intricate and complex ecological community from which the succulent morsels were taken. Once in a while, however, the oyster lover may be dismayed to find a small pealike crab floating about in his oyster stew or discover one of these pale crustaceans, seemingly alive, within the body of an oyster presented on the half-shell. Those who purchase their oysters alive in the unshucked state may, if they are observant and possess acute vision, notice small, many-legged worms scrambling about in the mud adhering to the shells, but, mostly, these creatures are disregarded and washed away as the oysters are prepared for shucking. A barnacle or two might be noticed sticking tightly to the shells, as well as some other things that do not resemble animals at all. The focus of attention, however, is the oyster, and the other members of the fauna connected with it are ignored.

Biologists interested in oysters have, of course, long been aware that many different types of animals are associated with the bivalves in their natural environment, and that some of these organisms are detrimental to the oyster itself. Most of these oyster scientists were, however, shocked when they read a report issued in 1961. H. W. Wells studied the animals that make up the

99

ecological community of an oyster rock, and, when the identifica-
tions had been finally completed, he listed 303 different species
found to be sharing the bar with their oyster host. Of course, all
303 species did not occur on the same rock at any given time or
place, but a large number were found to be residents of the
community most of the time. No one had any idea the diversity of
an oyster bar was so great, and, since that time, this type of
ecological neighborhood has assumed its own individuality when
studies of marine ecology are undertaken.

In a biological community, each of the resident species must,
more or less, have its own environmental niche if it is to become a
permanent part of the ecosystem. This is because if more than one
species stakes a claim to the same piece of real estate, intense
competition will result, and one of the competitors will triumph
eventually at the expense of the other. Over time this struggle for
a place in the community has been occurring over and over again,
until a community evolved that was composed of a fauna best
suited to dwell in the various nooks and crannies of the bar. When
the best tenants are finally selected by the forces of evolution, the
community becomes stable and all the creatures, both great and
small, exist in a state of dynamic equilibrium. But if one of the
resident species is displaced by a disease epidemic, a change in
the physical conditions, or some other catastrophe, a vacancy will
exist and a new type will move in and lay claim to the uninhabited
niche.

Certainly, there are not 303 different environmental slots
available for 303 different species on an oyster bar, but the number of niches available for occupancy is large. Considering that an
oyster bed is usually made up of great numbers of oysters clus-
tered together and creating untold numbers of hills, valleys, secluded chambers, flat surfaces, and the interior of the oyster shells
themselves, it is not too surprising that so many species have been
able to establish their own individual microenvironments. It has
been estimated that the area of an oyster bar available for habita-
tion by other species is fifty times greater than that of a flat sand or
mud bottom of the same size.

Many of the animals found on an oyster rock are attached to
the shells of living and dead oysters; numerous types are found on

the surfaces of the shells in and out of the numerous tunnels and caverns; and many have adapted to life within the valves on a permanent basis. In addition, numerous species frequently spotted on oyster bars are not permanent residents but casual visitors who have dropped by to utilize some of the established guests as food. It is interesting to note that when the renowned German biologist Karl Möbius established the concept of a biological community over one hundred years ago, he used an oyster bar as the prime example. According to his definition each oyster bed is, to a certain degree

> a community of living beings, a collection of species, and a massing of individuals, which find everything necessary for their growth and continuance, such as suitable soil, sufficient food, the requisite percentage of salt, and a temperature favorable for their development. Each species which lives here is represented by the greatest number of individuals which can grow to maturity subject to the conditions which surround them, for among all species the number of individuals which arrive at maturity at each breeding period is much smaller than the number of germs [i. e., sex cells] produced at that time. The total number of mature individuals of all species living together in any region is the sum of the survivors of all the germs which have been produced at all past breeding or brood periods; and this sum of the matured germs represents a quantum of life which enters into a certain number of individuals, and which, as does all life, gains permanence by means of transmission.

Möbius also pointed out that a change in one member of the community will eventually result in changes of the entire society.

The relative abundance of life on an oyster bar is affected by many things. The turbidity of the water, direction of currents, and degree of salinity may be affected by dredging operations, the construction of inshore installations, and other harbor and waterway changes made to improve navigation or to provide boat slips for a waterfront condominium. The planting of seed oysters on an established bar increases artificially the number of oysters, which may be detrimental, and the accidental introduction of foreign species, predators, and competitors can upset the delicate balance of nature that has been perfected over an extended period of time. Any thing or event that would tend to disrupt or change the environmental equilibrium will probably be harmful to the bar.

The activities of man, perhaps the oyster's worst enemy, frequently have an adverse effect on oyster bars, and in many cases result in total destruction of the community. Möbius comments on this aspect of the ecological picture by noting that many of the rich natural oyster beds on the western coast of France have been taken over by mussels and cockles. Before man started taking great numbers of oysters from these beds the mussel and cockle populations were held in check by the dominant and flourishing oysters. When most of the oysters were removed by man more food and space were made available to the less desirable mollusks, and they quickly multiplied and assumed command of the community.

In this case, at least, the French harvested the oysters and put them to good use after disrupting the ecology of the beds. But in another instance of man playing havoc with nature that occurred on the Nanticoke River early in September 1984, the entire community was lost before the oysters could be harvested. In this example, a three-hundred-foot barge loaded with fishmeal fertilizer was headed up river to Seaford, Delaware, when it ventured off course and ran solidly aground on a shallow, public oyster bar of some 230 acres in the vicinity of Ragged Point. How the barge, with its accompanying tugboat, came to be about two miles off-course is a great mystery, as the channel is clearly marked and the accident occurred during daylight hours. Rumor along the river has it that the captain was on his first run to Seaford and inadvertently read his chart upside-down. Be that as it may, the stranded barge was drawing only eight feet of water when I inspected it, and, laden as it was with its fifteen-hundred-ton cargo, the local sailors estimated it would take a minimum of fifteen feet of water to float her free. As the tides normally do not vary more than two feet in that part of the Nanticoke, there seemed to be no way the vessel could be freed by natural processes.

Realizing this, the owners brought in tugs in an attempt to pull the stricken vessel to deeper water. With all engines going full-reverse, a great amount of silt was generated as the propellers gouged out large chunks of river bottom. Try as they did, the barge could not be freed.

As it happened, the 230-acre oyster rock had been seeded by the Maryland Department of Natural Resources some three years previously, and the untold numbers of now legal oysters were ready for catching when the season started around the middle of October. As many of the local watermen were counting heavily on working the bed that fall and could see it being destroyed by the tugs before their eyes, they raised such a brouhaha that a local state legislator quickly contacted the marine police, who in turn ordered the salvage operation to cease.

As the only apparent way to free the vessel without doing more damage to the oyster bar was to unload the cargo, smaller barges were brought in, along with a clamshell, to accomplish the actual transfer. When I inspected the situation on a Sunday afternoon, a marine policeman had anchored his patrol boat nearby and was keeping a watchful eye on the unloading procedures. At the rate the fishmeal was being transferred, I estimated it would require at least ten days before an appreciable amount of the cargo could be unloaded. An old waterman of my acquaintance was anchored nearby, taking in the proceedings, and he grunted to me that the transfer operation was "sorta like pissin' in the ocean to raise 'er up an inch."

I left the scene in late afternoon and returned to my slip in the harbor of Bivalve. Early the next morning I returned to Ragged Point to see how much progress had been made during the night, and I was astonished—not a boat in sight; no barge, no transfer lighters, no marine police; the area was deserted. In some mysterious fashion, the problem had been rectified during the hours of darkness. The only way the barge could have been freed was by the pulling power of additional tugboats. The oystermen knew this also and complained long and loud to the Department of Natural Resources to investigate the damage which had undoubtedly been done to the bar. After a time, the department reported the damage to the bar was minimal, but this report did not coincide with the observations of the watermen. Long poles were used to test the bottom, and where, before the accident, the probes had struck hard oyster shell, they now became mired in a foot or so layer of mud. Surveying the bottom with the aid of tongs also revealed that the oyster community was now buried under a blanket of smothering mud.

As the department had declared the damage to be minimal, no official action was instigated against the company for damages. An official of the state agency did, however, suggest to the owners of the barge that they "think about" sponsoring a restoration program for the bar as a voluntary goodwill gesture. At last word, the company was doing just that, thinking about it. The oystermen were dejected, as many of them had been counting on the oysters they anticipated catching from the bar that fall to see them through much of the winter. It is not too surprising to learn what the oystermen consider to be their worst enemies—the weather, thieves, and the state of Maryland, and not necessarily in that order of importance.

A year after the grounding I eased my boat over the middle of the bar and attempted to "hit a lick" with my tongs. After expending much effort to break through the mud, I was able to bring up a considerable number of shells and a few boxes (dead oysters in which the shells have not yet separated), but, as expected, I found neither living oysters nor any of the types of animals associated with them.

These two examples of how man can alter the ecology of an oyster bed are what one would term extreme cases in that the community was heavily damaged or wiped out completely. But in many instances, damage to the oyster rock is much more subtle. Even in small amounts, chemical pollution can upset the balance of the bar by selectively killing or retarding certain species, and, as Möbius so astutely perceived, if just one member of the society is changed, it is only a matter of time until the entire system is adversely effected.

In many ways, the ecological community of an oyster bar can be compared to a human (or any other multicelled organism) as it exhibits growth, specialization, interdependence of parts, characteristic form, and even development from immaturity to maturity, old age, and death. Just as environmental poisons can upset the functioning of the human body, they can disturb the homeostatic state of a living oyster bar. And, as the human environment in the vicinity of Mount Saint Helens was obliterated by countless tons of ash resulting from the recent eruptions, the oyster bar off Ragged Point was destroyed by the silt generated by the screws of the errant tugboats.

Oyster Associates and Competitors

In discussing the animals making up the dynamic community of an oyster bar, it would be impossible, of course, to consider each of the 303 species known to share the bar with the dominant oyster. Rather, we will discuss the more common types, which are fairly easy to identify and seem to make up a significant portion of the fauna of the beds found in the Chesapeake system.

One way the animals found in association with oysters may be classified is on the basis of relationship to the oyster. Thus, one broad group may be listed as commensals. *Commensalism* is the association of two organisms where one of the associates benefits and the other is neither helped nor harmed. However, certain commensals can assume the role of competitor when they become too numerous and compete with the oysters for the necessities of life or in other ways interfere with their lifestyle. Another group can be termed predators in that they actively seek out another animal upon which to feed or use otherwise for their benefit. I will use the term *parasite* sparingly, as, strictly speaking, only a few of the animals known to be associated with the oyster in its natural habitat can be considered to be parasitic in the correct definition of the term. A true parasite is intimately involved with its host for the completion of the life cycle (as a tapeworm or blood fluke), and the host animal is always harmed by the invader's presence. The relationship has been so finely honed by the processes of evolution that, though the host is definitely harmed by the parasite's presence, it is not killed. After all, if the parasite killed the host, as a predator does, it would be like killing the goose that lays the golden eggs.

In this chapter we will consider in some detail only those animals that would be classified as commensals or competitors. Predators will be mentioned, but a discussion of their activities will be reserved for the following chapter.

The Oyster

When we examine the types of commensal-competitor animals that make up an oyster bar community, we find most of the major animal phyla are represented. The list is impressive, at least from a standpoint of diversity, and is composed of two species of sponges; three nettle-bearers, or coelenterates; three types of mosslike animals; five segmented worms; two soft-bodied mollusks; three members of the great group of jointed-leg animals; and two chordates (animals with backbones).

Phylum: Porifera (The Pore-bearers, or Sponges)

The sponges are lowly multicellular animals, incapable of movement, which resemble various plants more than animals. The different types of cells found in the sponge's body are not differentiated into tissues, and the main opening to the body is excurrent, or outgoing, in function. The sponge is riddled with pores by which food-laden water carrying oxygen is circulated through the body. With the exception of a few freshwater types, the five thousand known species of sponges are marine.

Red Beard Sponge *(Microciona prolifera).*   This red-to-orange sponge varies from a thin encrusting layer of less than ⅛ inch in height and covering a few square inches on the oyster shell to 8 inches in height by 8 inches in width with many fanlike branches. This sponge is common on bivalve shells, rocks, pilings, and other hard objects in bays and estuaries along the eastern and western coasts of the United States. It is a commensal that rarely offers much competition for the oyster.

The red beard is of historical importance in that it was the first animal shown to be able to reorganize its form after its cells had been experimentally separated. In 1907, Dr. H. V. Wilson, an American biologist, placed a red beard in a finely meshed silk bag and squeezed the sponge into a finger bowl containing seawater. The meshes of the cloth were so small that each cell of the sponge's body was effectively separated. After a period of orientation, the cells formed a mass that eventually reorganized itself into a new sponge. Wilson thus demonstrated in an admirable fashion and for the first time the amazing powers of regeneration possessed by these primitive members of the animal kingdom.

The red beard sponge is a frequent inhabitant of oyster bars in most regions of the Chesapeake system. In the saltier parts of the Bay near its mouth, the volcano sponge and the so-called yellow sun sponge may be found as encrusting commensals on oyster shells. In heavy infestations, as with other animals that occupy a portion of the outer part of the shell, the oyster larvae may experience difficulty in spatting if a significant portion of the landing area is taken up by another.

Burrowing Sponges (*Cliona* spp.)   Several species of this type of sponge are found throughout the Chesapeake Bay, and they may cause severe damage to oysters as they mine their way through the shells. The burrowing sponges will be considered in more detail in the next chapter.

Phylum: Cnidaria (Nettlelike Animals)

Unlike the sponges, the cells of this group of primitive animals are organized into definite tissues. The cnidarians have only two embryonic cell layers from which the organs of the body develop, whereas all other animals, sponges excepted, of course, have three layers of developmental cells. The most distinctive feature of this group is the presence of stinging cells (nematocysts) located in structures called cnidoblasts. No other group of animals possesses these unique, nettlelike cells, which are used for protection and the securing of food. The cnidarians include such animals as hydroids, jellyfish, corals, and sea anemones.

Snail Fur (*Hydractinia echinata*).   This species is the most common hydroid (a polyplike body form as distinguished from the jellyfish or medusa type) found growing on oysters in the region of the Chesapeake. As its name implies, it is equally at home on the shells of other animals, especially the snail shells inhabited by the hermit crab. Its fuzzy body covers portions of the shell and may be recognized by its whitish or pale pink color. Nematocysts are used to secure food and may offer some degree of protection to the oyster. Snail fur and other hydroids are commensals.

Ghost Anemone *(Diadumene leucolena)*.   The sea anemones are the most advanced of all of the cnidarians and are plentiful in the warm seas of the world. Many types of anemones are colored brillantly and, in fact, resemble beautiful flowers more than animals. The ghost, or white, anemone lacks the vivid coloration of its relatives and is the most common member of this group found in the Bay. Frequently, several ghost anemones will be found attached to the surface of the oyster's shell. The ghost anemone is a smallish animal no more than 1½ inches in height, and it appears to have tremendous staying power. I have collected oysters and witheld them from water for as much as two days, and, upon placing them in an observation tank, was amazed to see numerous anemones appear in short order—as if by spontaneous generation. The anemone has the capacity to contract its sinuous body and long tentacles into a compact structure when adverse conditions are encountered. When a favorable environment is reencountered, the animal assumes its typical shape and resumes its physiological activities.

About sixty half-inch-long tentacles, loaded with stinging cells, project from the body and probably offer some protection for the oyster against potential enemies. I once observed in a laboratory tank a ghost anemone attack and devour a flatworm making its way over the surface of an oyster shell laden with spat. Flatworms are notorious predators on oysters, especially the spat, and in this case the worm ended up as food for the anemone rather than as an uninvited guest of the oyster. Ghost anemones appear to be long-lived, at least in the laboratory. In one of my oyster tanks, I have watched several of these delicate animals grow and thrive for a period of over two years, and, at the time of this writing, they appear to be in excellent physical condition.

Sea anemones are routinely studied in college zoology courses, but the pickled specimens used bear little resemblance to the living animals. The aforementioned ghost anemones in the oyster tank have afforded numerous undergraduates the opportunity to observe this type of animal in its natural state, and, therefore, have more than adequately paid for their room and board.

Striped Anemone *(Haliplanella luciae).* The striped anemone is sometimes found attached to oyster shells in company with the ghost variety. It is somewhat smaller than its cousin and is easily distinguished by its orange, yellow, or cream striping on a brown to olive-green background. This cnidarian is not found in the upper parts of the Bay region, as it prefers a saltier environment. Apparently the striped anemone is not a native species; indications are that it was introduced into this country from Japan in the late nineteenth century. It adapted to its new surroundings well and is now a cosmopolitan species found along both the Atlantic and Pacific coasts as well as the Gulf of Mexico.

Phylum: Platyhelminthes (The Flatworms)

These worms are compressed from the dorsal to the ventral side and are much more advanced than the cnidarians. They have three layers of embryonic germ cells from which the rather complex organs of the body are constructed, whereas the cnidarians have only two such layers. They are considered primitive creatures, however, because they have no body cavity. Some flatworms are free-living, but many, such as the tapeworms and flukes, are truly parasitic animals that infest many species, including man. As noted, a few types of free-living flatworms attack oysters, and serious damage can result from their presence in the community. These important predators will be considered in more detail in the following chapter.

Phylum: Bryozoa (The Moss Animals)

Many individuals have collected bryozoans during beachcombing activities and mistakenly pressed them in a book thinking they were some sort of seaweed. These animals are, in fact, rather advanced colonial animals that only superficially resemble plants, especially mosses. Most moss animals are matlike in form, forming thin incrustations on rocks, shells, or kelp. Many are widely distributed as fouling organisms, and one freshwater species sometimes finds its way into the pipes of the water-supply systems of municipalities. Superficially, each member of a bryozoan colony (there may be thousands of individual animals in a single colony) resembles a primitive cnidarian in that tentacles are present, but the tentacles surrounding the mouth of a moss animal are in reality extensions of the animal's body cavity and not simply outgrowths of the outer integument.

Sea Hair *(Anguinella palmata)*. This common bryozoan, frequently called just "hair" by watermen, also resembles seaweeds, and its outer, opaque covering is impregnated with earthy, foreign material. The branches of the sea hair usually are no more than one inch in length, but occasional specimens are seen with strands up to two inches in length.

Anyone who has ever left a crab pot in the water for any length of time during the summer months is certainly familiar with hair. It quickly catches in the wire meshes of the trap and is tedious to remove. I can see no reason why the presence of sea hair on a crab pot should be of any concern to the crabber, but some insist a crab is hesitant about entering the cage if the bryozoan growth is extensive. Being widespread in its distribution, hair is a common commensal on oyster shells.

Cushion Moss Bryozoan *(Victorella pavida)*. Cushion moss is prevalent in the middle and upper sections of the Bay and becomes rarer as the salt concentration increases. It is truly an animal of the estuary and is very familiar to anyone who has kept a boat moored in the water for any length of time during the summer months. A soft, brownish growth will cover the hull of a boat in a few weeks, and the hydrodynamics of the vessel will be adversely influenced. In addition, I can think of no messier job than attempting to remove cushion moss from the boat's bottom. I have found the best way to free the hull of this bryozoan is to anchor the boat in shallow water and scrub the surface with a stiff brush. This seems to work better than attempting to do the job with the boat out of water on a trailer.

Life on the Oyster Bar

Advanced growth of the cushion moss may measure up to half an inch or more in thickness and even obscure any barnacles that may also be attached to the hull. Usually the growth on oyster shells is not extensive, but, on other occasions, the cushion moss may become so plentiful that the filtering aspect of the oyster's physiology is impaired.

Lacy Crust Bryozoan *(Conopeum tenuissimum)*.   This is an encrusting species rather than one with an upright posture. The lacy crust is abundant in the middle portions of the Bay and its estuaries, where the salt concentration is less than eighteen parts per thousand parts of water. This commensal frequently becomes a competitor of the oyster, as it may completely encrust the outer surface of the shell and prevent normal spatting. The lacy crust bryozoan is by no means confined to oyster bars but may be found almost anywhere a suitable place for growth is found—rocks, shells, sticks, pilings, and plants.

Phylum: Annelida (The Segmented Worms)

The great phylum Annelida consists of about ten thousand described species and is the most successful of the so-called worm phyla. The annelids are abundant in marine waters, fresh waters, and terrestrial environments. Such familiar forms as the earthworm, sandworm, bloodworm, clamworm, and leech are members of this phylum, which is frequently cited as being the "typical" group of animals—not too specialized and not too advanced (a zoology professor once described the annelids to me as "wormier than other worms," and I suppose I understood his metaphor, but I am not sure). Annelids are composed of many segments, some of which may be modified to accomplish certain activities. The organs are well developed in an extensive body cavity, and the blood runs red because of the pigment hemoglobin.

The class of annelids with which we are most concerned is called the *Polychaeta* (many bristles), and members of this group are all marine. They produce the typical trochophore and veliger larvae which resemble greatly the immature forms of oysters and other mollusks. Polychaete worms are easily recognized by the fleshy, padlike appendages (parapodia) that are found on each segment of the body and bear the setae, or bristles.

Clamworm *(Nereis succinea).* Of the several species of clamworms found in the Bay system, this species is by far the most common. One has to be cautious when making absolute statements in biology, but I feel rather safe in stating there is probably no oyster bar in the Chesapeake Bay that does not contain large numbers of these worms. The common clamworms of the Bay may be as long as five inches, but usually they are much smaller. A large blood vessel runs down the dorsal part of the body and is quite obvious. Under low magnification, the blood can be seen circulating through the vessel and into the parapodia on each segment. These padlike organs have a dual function, serving both as a means of locomotion and as gaseous-exchange organs. Four small eyes are present in the head region, which also possesses four fleshy projections that function as sensory organs. Most polychaete worms have an eversible proboscis, or beak, which is normally stored in the throat or pharynx region. When disturbed or when feeding or defending itself the beak can be thrown out in the twinkling of an eye. Two vicious hooklike jaws are located at the tip of the beak and serve to effectively impale items of food or enemies. Being voracious feeders, any animal or vegetable matter within range of the beak is fair game.

Clamworms are quite hardy and can be detected scurrying over the shells of oysters that have been out of the water for a considerable period of time. On some oyster bars *Nereis* is extremely numerous, and I am convinced it is the presence of these worms that makes oyster bars preferred fishing sites for many anglers. Fish such as hardheads (croakers), spot, perch, rockfish, and trout (weakfish) gather on the bar to nip at the clamworms, and sometimes a large number of them may be taken by drifting a baited hook across the oyster community. Of course, there are other delicious tidbits of food available to the fish on an oyster bar, but, after examining the contents of the stomachs of hundreds of these fish and finding large numbers of clamworms present almost every time, I am convinced the clamworm is the item that captivates the fish.

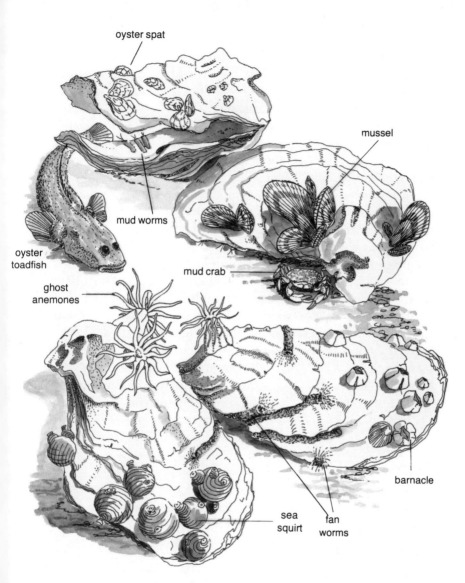

oyster spat

mussel

mud worms

oyster
toadfish

mud crab

ghost
anemones

barnacle

sea
squirt

fan
worms

Life on an oyster bar.

Bloodworm (*Glycera* spp). If a poll were taken of Chesapeake Bay fishermen as to what bait they would choose if they were restricted to just one type, I feel confident the peeler, or soft crab, would be named more often than any other. I am likewise convinced second place would go to the bloodworm. Unfortunately, the species of bloodworm, or beak thrower as it is frequently called, used for bait comes from the colder waters of New England, where it may reach a length of fifteen inches. The two species of bloodworms found in the Bay are much smaller, and the angler would experience great difficulty trying to place even a mature specimen on the smallest of hooks.

Bay bloodworms are cosmopolitan in their housing requirements and frequently establish residence on oyster bars. As in the clamworm, a dorsal blood vessel is easily detected, but the bristles on the parapodia are far less noticeable. Being tapered at both ends of the body, the worm presents a streamlined appearance; the shape helps these worms burrow into a soft bottom when threatened by enemies. A large knoblike beak bearing four sharp, dark hooks is readily extruded from the head region. Many a fisherman has had his finger pricked painfully as he attempted to insult a large New England bloodworm by weaving its body onto his fishing hook. The small species of the Bay presents no such problem to the naturalist interested in examining it because its hook-like teeth are incapable of piercing the skin of humans. Unlike other worms of this group, venom glands are associated with the hooks on the beak, and a poison is injected when the integument of another animal is pierced. Commensal bloodworms are always present in fewer numbers on an oyster bar than clamworms.

Oyster Mud Worm (*Polydora* spp.). There are several species of mud worms found in close communion with oysters, and sometimes their numbers are so great that they become deleterious to them. These worms live in soft, fragile tubes, which they construct of mud on almost any hard object found in intertidal zones or shallow water. They may become so abundant on an oyster bar that they bury the oysters in several inches of mud tubes. Some of them may actually run their tubes inside the valves of the oyster or the snail shells occupied by hermit crabs.

The worm itself is about one inch in length and has a translucent body. The reddish tinge one frequently notes is due to the red pigment, hemoglobin, of the blood showing through the body wall. The worm has two exceptionally long antennae or feelers, which are easily broken off. Four smallish eyes are arranged in the form of a rectangle.

In the case of the mud worm that actually invades the privacy of the oyster's interior (the whip mud worm), the tube is built along the inside edge of the valve rather than on top. The oyster reacts to this outrage by laying down a thin layer of nacre over the offending tubes. Dark shell "blisters" along the edge of a freshly shucked oyster shell offer conclusive evidence of the whip mud worm's presence. It is believed the whip mud worm does not appreciably affect the oyster's chances of survival.

Fan Worm *(Sabella microphthalma)*. This commensal polychaete builds a tube of a leathery consistency on the outside of the oyster shell. As the tube is frequently covered with silt and sand, this species may be easily mistaken for a mud worm. Fan worms are sometimes called "feather dusters" because the head bears numerous long, feathery gills. As the tubes have only one opening, the problem of how to dispose of fecal pellets arises. The feather duster solves this problem with the aid of a ciliated groove that runs the length of the body; the beating of the tiny, hairlike cilia carries the waste material to the top of the tube where the worm unceremoniously dumps it to the outside. Large populations of fan worms are seldom found on oyster bars, and it is believed they rarely if ever cause a problem for the oysters.

Limy Tube Worm *(Hydroides dianthus)*. Reaching a length of three inches or more, *Hydroides* is considerably longer than the other worms described here. The residence tubes are built of calcium carbonate and are very obvious on the exterior of an oyster shell. They may be solitary or occur in tangled masses resembling a colander of spaghetti. The worm within has a number of ornate tentacles attached to the head end, and one is modified as a lid to effectively close off the tube when the worm desires privacy. Once the worm is encamped within its tube, it is very difficult to extract it alive in one piece. Wishing to have complete living specimens to study, I have spent hours chipping away at the calcareous tube with a sharp-pointed needle while viewing the field of operation under the low magnification of a dissecting microscope. As this is a time-consuming and tedious task, I found out the hard way that the only effective procedure for acquiring a living, intact specimen was to chip away the entire tube. If one becomes impatient and tries to remove the worm with fine forceps when the body is only partially exposed, the result will be two pieces of polychaete. The setae, or bristles, on the parapodia are wedged into the side of the tube, making it all but impossible to extract the worm in one piece.

If one desires to study tube worms found on an oyster bed, one of the best ways to encourage the worms to expose themselves, at least partially, is to place the oyster shell bearing the tubes in a jar of seawater. In a few minutes, as the oxygen content of the water goes down and the concentration of carbon dioxide increases, the commensals will usually protrude their bodies in an attempt to satisfy their gas-exchange requirements. With the aid of a hand lens, most species may then be studied in detail. The bizarre colors and anatomical adaptations of the polychaetes make them an extremely interesting group.

Sometimes the limy tube worm, as well as other tube builders associated with oyster shells, becomes so plentiful they interfere with the spatting part of the life cycle, as is the case with other shell-inhabiting denizens.

Phylum: Mollusca (The Soft-Bodied Animals)

Oysters, of course, are included in this great group of the animal kingdom of which more than one hundred thousand different living species have been described. In addition to bivalves, the phylum includes such familiar animals as snails, chitons, squids, and octopuses. The multipurpose mantle is a common feature of this advanced group of invertebrate animals, and many of them (oysters and other bivalves excepted) possess a rasplike drill associated with the mouth, called the radula. Though from a standpoint of species numbers the mollusks represent the second most prolific group of animals found on earth today, they were the dominant group for millions of years in the distant past.

Class: Gastropoda.   The gastropods ("stomach-foot") are the snails; there are about thirty-five thousand separate species. This largest and most diverse class of mollusks includes such creatures as whelks, conchs, limpets, sea slugs, periwinkles, odostomes, and oyster drills.

These last two types of snails are important enemies of oysters and can literally destroy a bar when they are numerous. They will be considered in detail in the next chapter.

In addition to these two detrimental snails, a myriad of others live on the bar and cause the oyster little if any grief. Slipper shells and nudibranchs (snails without shells) are common residents; they use their radulae to scrape off encrusted bryozoans and sponges to be used for food. As they are motile creatures, they are unlikely to present any difficulty at spatting time.

Class: Pelecypoda.   This name literally means "hatchet-foot," which describes the shape of the foot of the clam and some other bivalves in the class. The oyster, as we know, has no foot in the adult stage and is, along with a few others, an exception to the descriptive name of the group. Some zoologists use the name Bivalvia for the members of this class, and I agree that the name is more appropriate.

Hooked Mussel *(Ishadium recurvum)*.   This bivalve is commonly found attached to oyster shells by many strong threads called byssal filaments. It will readily attach to almost any solid surface it encounters throughout the region of the Chesapeake. Hooked mussels are usually small, no more than two inches in length, and are rather nondescript in color—black to gray, tinged with dull yellow. The shell surface is strongly ribbed, like the ribbed mussel *(Geukensia demissa),* but the strongly bent shell is twisted just below the umbo. Though the exterior of the shell presents no pattern of beauty as far as coloration goes, the inside is a beautiful iridescent purple. While the ribbed mussel may be dangerous to eat because of its frequent association with species of toxic blue-green algae, the hooked type can be eaten without fear. I have eaten hooked mussels on several occasions and found them to be without any distinctive flavor or taste, however. The blue or edible mussels *(Mytilus edulis)*, which a few people put in the same class as the oyster as far as gustatory qualities go, have only rarely been found attached to oysters. In France, blue mussels are plentiful along the western coast and are eaten more often than oysters because of their abundance and low price. Though some seafood gourmets in this country swear by them, the oyster is in no danger of being displaced as the number one bivalve.

Phylum: Arthropoda (Jointed-Leg Animals)

This group represents the culmination of the animal evolutionary process. Included in this expansive group are such familiar types as insects, spiders, ticks, mites, scorpions, horseshoe crabs, and the crustaceans. Well over one million species of living insects are known to science, and almost every nook and cranny on, above, and below the surface of the earth is occupied by some arthropod species. As the phylum is so diversified, about the only general characteristic of the group that can be given is the fact the legs are jointed. But there are a few arthropods that do not have any legs at all in the adult stage.

As far as oysters are concerned, the class Crustacea is the group of arthropods of most importance. Crustaceans include crabs, crayfish, lobsters, pill bugs, shrimp, and many minute members of the group that make up a very important segment of the plankton of any body of water—marine or fresh. Crustaceans in general may be distinguished by the presence of two pair of antennae or feelers and two general divisions of the body—a cephalothorax and an abdomen.

Pea or Oyster Crab *(Pinnotheres ostreum)*. Every year, at least a few oyster fanciers in the mid-Atlantic and Chesapeake Bay regions are in for a surprise. Just at the moment when a human is removing an oyster from the half-shell to place it in the mouth, a small, spidery-looking creature may wander out from the oyster's gills. The first reaction of the ordinary person encountering one of these small rose-pink or whitish crustaceans is to get rid of it immediately. But if he does he will be missing a real treat as well as a tasty oyster.

Pea crabs are in demand as a *bon vivant*'s delight—in fact they are far more valuable than the oyster in which they live. A pint of pea crabs will bring about twice as much on the market as will a pint of shucked oysters. Usually only 1 or 2 of these creatures will be found inside a single oyster, but one investigator found 262 pea crabs living within one oyster.

The larvae, or immature forms, of these crabs invade the oyster and set up housekeeping in the gills, where usually they do no harm. If a portion of the delicate gill is destroyed, the oyster's cells quickly proliferate into the damaged area and form new gill tissue. If, however, large numbers of the crabs are present, the vital functions of the gills may be hampered. The young crabs are less than one millimeter in size and frequently enter young oyster spat. Female oyster crabs live permanently within the oyster, but the smaller males soon depart to seek mates in other oysters. Consequently, any pea crab found in an oyster is apt to be a female.

Though the nutritional value of oyster crabs has not been studied in detail, it is well known that they are prized as an exotic seafood. Some watermen attribute aphrodisiacal properties to the small crabs (as well as to the oysters), but such claims have never been substantiated. Aphrodisiacal or not, watermen of the Chesapeake have long recognized the distinct flavor of these tiny crustaceans, and many stories describe the consumption of great numbers of pea crabs. When asked how he liked pea crabs, a waterman replied to me, "They take considerable tongue and cheek twistin' to get the little buggers down, and when you do they causes a ticklin' of the throat, too."

A Sea Grant Program bulletin issued by the University of Delaware extolls the value of the pea crab as a valuable economic species and even lists a series of recipes for preparing these tiny beasts for the table. Two of these recipes intrigue me:

The Oyster

Fried Oyster Crabs

½ pint oyster crabs
¼ cup pancake flour
deep fat
1 egg
1 tablespoon milk
salt and pepper

> Wash and drain oyster crabs.
> Dip crabs in beaten egg mixed with milk.
> Shake crabs in seasoned pancake flour.
> Fry till crisp in deep fat.

Oyster Crab Hors d' Oeuvres

1 pint oyster crabs
¼ cup butter
¼ teaspoon garlic salt

> Wash and drain crabs.
> Sauté in butter and garlic salt for 3 to 7 minutes
>   or until brown.
> Serve individually on toothpicks.

Pea crabs are not confined to oysters alone but may also be found in other bivalves such as scallops and mussels. The oysters and mussels I devoured in great numbers while living in France were frequently infested with a small crab that I ignored at the time. I doubt, however, if it was the same species we encounter in the Chesapeake, because the French, as far as I know, did not eat them.

The pea crab's adaptations for life within the bivalve have caused it to lose many of the characteristics normally associated with crabs. Pea crabs are flattened, pale in color, and, as they have no need to move about, the legs are poorly developed. Some biologists regard the oyster crab as a true parasite, but, in my opinion, commensalism more accurately describes its relationship with the oyster.

Life on the Oyster Bar

Mud Crabs.   Whereas the pea crab usually does little or no permanent damage to the oyster, the five species of so-called mud crabs are definite predators. They will, consequently, be considered in the chapter on enemies and disease.

Barnacles *(Balanus improvisus* and *Balanus eburneus). Improvisus* is the bay barnacle most common in the northern parts of the system; *eburneus* is called the ivory barnacle and dominates in the southern and saltier portions of the estuary. Both are equally at home attached to the shells of oysters, boat hulls, pilings, or almost any other solid object found in the water.

To the uninitiated, barnacles superficially resemble mollusks more than crustaceans, and the newcomer to the study of marine biology is to be excused for confusing the two. Barnacles are authentic crustaceans who have found their place in nature by secreting a protective shell of calcium carbonate for themselves. Each conical shell consists of a series of six overlapping plates, with two plates serving as lids and guarding the opening to the interior. A round base is firmly attached to the substratum. When the barnacle feeds, the lids swing open and two long, feathered appendages protrude and wave about, collecting tiny bits of food, which are transferred to the animal's mouth.

It is advantageous for barnacles to occur in clusters because, though they are hermaphroditic, cross-fertilization must occur to perpetuate the species. The male portion of the barnacle's anatomy includes a long penis, or sperm tube, which is thrust into the shell of a neighbor to transfer sperm for egg fertilization. Two types of larvae are produced in succession: the nauplius swims around, serving to disperse the species, and then changes into the cypris, which seeks out a place to attach permanently. Apparently chemical messengers, or pheromones, are generated by older, attached barnacles, and the powerful attractant guides the cypris to a point of attachment within the cluster. Consequently, great numbers of these crustaceans may build up in a given area.

Almost every oyster brought up from the bottom will have barnacles attached. If, for some reason, the barnacles have died— they have many enemies—the plates of the shell will eventually fall away, leaving only the circular base to indicate the animal's former presence. As anyone who has ever had the unpleasant task of removing barnacles from the hull of a boat (their presence and that of other fouling organisms adversely affect the boat's operation) knows, the cementum used for attachment is very strong—stronger perhaps than the superglues touted as being able to withstand the pull of two-and-a-half-ton truck. I have heard it debated whether the stickum secreted by oyster spat when attaching is more powerful than that manufactured by the barnacle, with opinion being divided more or less down the middle. Offhand, I would vote for the adhesive of the barnacle.

Antifouling paints containing a copper base may be effective in repelling barnacles, but they do not always work. A paint dealer in Salisbury told me the results of an experiment he conducted with a new, "wonder" antifouling paint his company placed on the market. Living in Bivalve on the Nanticoke, he asked three of his waterman neighbors to paint the hulls of their workboats with the paint he provided. This material costs more than twenty dollars a quart, so the watermen were eager to participate in the test. Each boat was moored in a different part of the harbor and subjected to different tidal flows, and the effectiveness of the paint varied from place to place. One boat was subjected to the full current at each changing of the tide; the other two were berthed in more secluded areas of the harbor. Only a few barnacles attached to the boat subjected to the forces of the tide, whereas large numbers of the crustaceans established residence on the hulls of the craft in more secluded waters. The paint vendor told me of his experiment after I had purchased a quart of his material, but I must add the magic in the paint worked very well to keep the hull of my boat free of barnacles and bryozoans that one year.

Years ago, a waterman suggested a way to facilitate the removal of barnacles after they are established. He had learned that hydrochloric acid (a 1 or 2 percent solution) effectively reacted with the calcium carbonate of the shell to dissolve it. If the shells are bathed with the acid, they may be easily removed with a scraper after a few minutes.

Barnacles are true oyster commensals, and, as with others previously mentioned, may be detrimental to the oyster when they become plentiful and reduce the spatting area.

122

Other Crustacea.   A variety of other types of crustaceans may be observed as more or less casual visitors to an oyster bar, not being semipermanent or permanent residents. Various species of iso-pods (aquatic pill bugs), amphipods (scuds), and the common grass shrimp frequently sojourn at the bar to feed on the many organisms available. None of these incidental crustaceans is clas-sified as either commensals, competitors, or predators.

Phylum: Echinodermata (Spiny-Skin Animals)

This phylum of invertebrates, on the same line of evolution that leads to the chordates and man, consists of such diverse forms as the sea star, sea urchin, brittle stars, and sea cucumbers. They are the most advanced of the true invertebrate animals and possess, in addition to a spiny integument, complex organ systems. One class, the Asteroidea, includes an archenemy of the oyster, the sea star or starfish. Fortunately for oysters, the sea star is found only in marine waters of high salinity and, consequently, present a prob-lem only in the region encompassing the mouth of the Bay. Their destructiveness of oyster beds will be documented in the next chapter.

Phylum: Chordata (Animals with Backbones)

The chordates represent the highest group of animals on the tree of evolution. All chordates, during at least a portion of their life, have the following salient characteristics:

A notochord stiffens and gives support to the body. In more ad-vanced chordates, the vertebrates, the notochord develops into the spinal column, consisting of individual bones called vertebrae.

A dorsal hollow nerve cord is always present. Some nonchordates have a ventral nerve cord and some have a solid cord more or less dorsal in position, but these do not satisfy the requirements for membership in the chordate phylum.

Pharyngeal gill clefts are present at one time or another during the life of the true chordate. During man's early embryological stages, when it would take an expert to distinguish a human from a fish,

The Oyster

toad, turtle, or bird, definite cleftlike structures occur in the region of the developing pharynx or throat. As the embryo is destined to become a human and breathe by means of lungs, these clefts disappear as development proceeds. If, however, the chordate is destined to become a fish and accomplish gas exchange by the use of gills, the clefts break through to the pharynx and become the typical organs of respiration of fish.

A postanal tail is present in some stage of the chordate's development. Just as with the gill clefts, humans, in their early embryological stages, possess a taillike appendage that projects backward from the anal opening of the body. But as the genes of the embryo dictate the development of a human, the tail is gradually resorbed as development continues. It is not uncommon, however, for a human baby to be born with a portion of its embryonic tail still persisting. Instant surgery corrects this.

The Sea Squirt (*Mogula manhattensis*). The sea squirts are members of a primitive group of chordates called the Urochordata. These animals lack a cranium, or brain case, and other advanced characteristics of vertebrate animals. They are, however, bona fide chordates—at one time or another in their life cycle they exhibit all four of the requisites just described.

A person untrained in biology, if shown a sea squirt, will probably have no idea at all what the object is. He may think it is some kind of fungus or guess it is some type of egg. The neophyte might even suggest that the object is a grape cast overboard by some passing boat, but the chances are slim that it will ever enter his mind that this non-animal-appearing blob of tissue is a chordate animal—relatively close to humans in the evolutionary scale.

Sea grapes, as these squirts are frequently called, are extremely common in all parts of the Chesapeake. They may be found attached singly or in groups to pilings, sticks, rocks, shells, or numerous other items. Oysters taken from the Bay are rarely without at least a few of these globose, greenish-white animals attached.

Adult sea squirts possess only one of the anatomical features required of chordates—the pharyngeal gill slits. These urochordates are sometimes called tunicates because the body is covered by a nonliving, tuniclike envelope made up of the complex carbo-hydrate cellulose. (Cellulose is the principal constituent of the nonliving wall of the cells of plants and is rarely encountered in any form in the animal world.)

When we look at the larval form of the sea squirt we find the three missing chordate features. The larval tunicate bears a great resemblance to the tadpole, or frog larva, and clearly shows an upstanding notochord, postanal tail, and a dorsal hollow nerve cord that terminates anteriorly in a well-developed brain. Here we seem at first to have a case of retrograde evolution, where the larval form is more advanced and complex than the adult. Dollo's Law in biology states that once a major step is taken in evolution, it is never reversed, and the situation with the sea squirts appears to be a clear exception to this principle. When we consider the case at hand, however, it becomes apparent that Dollo's Law has not been violated. Many times during the long history of life, advanced organisms have returned to ancestral habitats and modes of life in order to survive in a hostile environment—to occupy the niche that is available to accommodate them. With the return to the old way of life, structural adaptations arise that enable the pioneer to exist in the new habitat. Thus many reptiles and mammals have reverted to an aquatic mode of life, and in doing this they have assumed a generally streamlined, fishlike form, and the limbs have become shortened, webbed, and finlike. The same thing happened to the sea squirt.

Sea squirts are amusing little animals in that they may easily be induced to forcibly eject a thin jet of water out of one of the siphons that circulate water through the body. Watermen of the Chesapeake, and elsewhere I imagine, are generally unaware of what sea squirts really are. Most men who make their living from the water believe these blobs of protoplasm adhering to the oysters they catch are eggs of the well-known toadfish (oyster toad, or oyster cracker). A few oystermen I have encountered simply call the sea squirts "blisters" and have no idea what causes the appearance of these seemingly anomalous structures on the surface of the shell. As these "toad eggs" or blisters" do not seem to harm the "arster" in any way and are quite easily removed, most watermen pay them little heed.

The Oyster

The Oyster Toad *(Opsanus tau).* The most advanced group of chordates are called the vertebrates; they have the four chordate basic characteristics as well as a brain case or skull, and many other advanced features. The classes of vertebrates include the lampreys, bony fish, cartilagenous fish, the amphibian toads, frogs and salamanders, reptiles, birds, and mammals. The oyster toad is a bony fish that is intimately associated with the oyster bar. The many caverns and crevices of the bar afford this fish a perfect place to nest and propagate the species, as well as providing a source of immediately available food.

Contrary to popular folklore, the oyster toad does not crack the shells of oysters to get at the meat inside. It is certainly true that this fish, which has been called "The Champion of Ugliness," has a large grotesque head with powerful jaws, but as far as is known the jaws are not used to destroy oysters.

Everyone who has fished in any part of the Bay has caught a toadfish—usually to his chagrin. The hook is usually swallowed deep into the animal's body and presents the angler with a challenge when he tries to remove it. A special "toadfish hook disengorger" made of a coat hanger bent into the shape of a J is usually standard equipment in the tackle boxes of Bay fishermen, but a slimy coat of mucus covers the toad's body, making it difficult to grasp securely, even with a gloved hand. My advice to anyone hooking one of these fish is to cut the line at the fish's mouth and affix new terminal tackle.

Numerous short teeth line the mouth of the oyster toad, and the base of the dorsal fin is guarded by two hollow spines connected to venom glands. In addition, there is a small poisonous spine on each of the gill covers. The events surrounding the catching of my first oyster toad in Tangier Sound many years ago are indelibly fixed in my mind. Of course, the fish had swallowed the hook, and when I tried to pry open its viselike jaws, they snapped shut on my thumb. Instantly, I jerked the thumb free, but in doing so the teeth severely abraded the skin. I was confronted with a bloody mess that turned out to be not nearly so serious as I had first supposed. During the process of extracting my thumb, however, the palm of the hand was pierced by one of

Life on the Oyster Bar

the poisonous spines. Within a short time a burning, painful reaction set in and persisted for more than an hour despite my attempts to alleviate the discomfort by applying ice to the puncture. The wound refused to heal properly and caused me concern for at least two weeks.

The male toadfish establishes the nesting area in the oyster bar or some other secluded place such as a can, and, with a series of explosive, foghornlike blasts of sound, summons the female to the nest. The bridal toadfish responds to the love call, enters the chamber in an upside-down position, and deposits her eggs on the ceiling. Having fulfilled her biological obligation, she departs and goes on to other activities. The male immediately fertilizes the eggs and will remain in the nest to watch over them until they hatch in a month or so.

The eggs of toadfish are large as fish eggs go, up to one-quarter inch in diameter, but they are considerably smaller than the sea squirt with which they are sometimes confused. After the eggs hatch, the larval toadlets are not yet ready to venture out of the nest on their own, as they are attached to a large sac of yolk material which nourishes them as they continue to develop. All the while, the male keeps a watchful eye on his offspring and will become quite aggressive in the face of a possible predator.

Mike Manning of Salisbury is a diver who applies his submarine skills to harvesting oysters from time to time. He tells of observing a large toadfish guarding his nest on an oyster bar in the Wye River. The water was clear, so Manning could see the toad without difficulty and was able to swim within a few feet of the nest. In a playful manner he extended his gloved hand toward the alert sentry and was stunned when the fish darted out in a flash and bit down on one of his fingers, refusing to let go. Manning was able to shake the enraged toad free of his hand without too much difficulty and was amazed that the fish nonchalantly returned to the nest and resumed its guard posture.

Many other species of fish frequent oyster beds to feed on the variety of life that abounds there, and this tends to prevent an overabundance of the commensals. These fish, like many species of crustaceans and others, are transient visitors and are not to be considered typical residents.

The Oyster

To the random observer of an oyster bar at low tide, the community presents an appearance of nothing more than an irregular pile of mollusks casually basking in the sun waiting for the tide to come in and envelope them in its protective embrace. Nothing, of course, could be further from the truth. The oyster bar is a vigorous, pulsating, dynamic collection of life, living in equilibrium in a special part of the environment. The next time you have the opportunity to observe an oyster community, or acquire some recently harvested unshucked oysters, take a closer look at one of the more fascinating aspects of the natural world.

CHAPTER SEVEN

Diseases, Parasites, and Predators

*Oysters have more to worry about than we have
and less to worry with.*

Anonymous

I N spite of the fact that a single female may produce several
million eggs during the course of one reproductive season, I
have always considered it nothing short of a miracle that even one
oyster could survive and reach a height at which it may be caught
legally. During the course of its precarious existence it constantly
runs the risk of being smothered, crushed, eaten, castrated,
drilled, excavated, choked, infected, or dislodged.

But this is the way the forces of nature work. Those animals
which cast their sex cells into the cruel and merciless sea and
forget about them must produce stupendous numbers if a few are
to unite, develop, and eventually produce sexually mature offspring to perpetuate the species. Of the huge number of oyster
larvae resulting from a single spawning session, one can be sure
only three or four will be able to survive the hostile environment
and reach maturity. This is the way it must be. If as few as 1
percent survived to reproduce, and another 1 percent did the
same, and so on, it would not be very long before the oysters
would fill up the seas of the world and spill out to cover the land.
All this relates directly to the first salient point in Darwin's theory
of evolution of species by means of natural selection. Namely, all
species overproduce themselves and there are not enough of the
essentials of life to go around. Consequently, only the strongest or
best adapted will survive.

129

The Oyster

On the other side of the coin, we recognize that animals producing only a few offspring do not scatter their precious gametes haphazardly about the land or sea scape but preserve and protect and take every recourse to insure that at least some of them unite. Many of those practicing frugal reproductive procedures also have adaptations for the protection of the developing embryos and the infants after they are born. The females of many advanced animals, such as mammals, retain the embryos within the body until they are born in an advanced state of development. In mammals the mother has a self-made supply of food (milk) available immediately after birth.

While an oyster produces untold numbers of young during the annual spawning period, the elephant produces a single offspring once every twenty to twenty-three months. The populations of both oysters and elephants will remain stable in a natural environment if man does not interfere with natural processes.

The greatest enemy of both oysters and elephants, of course, is man, as he constantly seeks to gratify his insatiable appetite for so-called technological advances and personal ease. The major reasons that the oyster populations of the Chesapeake are growing smaller each year are directly related to man's activities. Overfishing to satisfy market demands and the pollution of the water with chemicals and silt have combined to upset the delicate balance of nature and prevent the three or four oysters out of every five million generated from growing to maturity and fulfilling their biological destiny.

Diseases, predators, and parasites of oysters are natural phenomena and serve to carry out the natural order indicated in Darwin's theory. The ill-adapted and the weak are eliminated so that only the strongest and best adapted will survive. This is natural selection, which results in stable populations able to adjust to changing environmental conditions. But to expect creatures like oysters to withstand the onslaughts of human progress, in addition to coping with natural adversities, is asking too much.

No one is prepared at this time to suggest that *Crassostrea virginica* is on the verge of becoming extinct, but the same cannot be said for the elephant in certain parts of the world. The destruction of the pachyderm's habitat in various parts of its range and the outrageous, wanton killing of these animals for their ivory or legs to be made into quaint umbrella holders have reduced their numbers to dangerously low levels. With a species producing only one descendant every two years or so, abnormal pressures on the breeding population can be devastating in a relatively short period of time. When man in his infinite "wisdom" defies the basic laws of nature to satisfy his materialistic and selfish desires, ecological disaster always ensues.

Diseases

A disease may be defined as anything causing a deviation in the state of health of an organism, and just like humans, oysters are susceptible to both noncontagious and infectious diseases. In the first category of ills that affect the oyster we are dealing with the improper function of physiological systems and organs due to an unfavorable environment. When chemical impurities are present due to industrial pollution or effluent from malfunctioning sewage-treatment facilities, the oyster's state of homeostasis, or health, is disrupted. Likewise, excessive siltation or unsuitable salinities and temperatures can result in organ dysfunction. In the second category, infectious diseases are those pathological conditions that are caused directly by pathogenic organisms, such as microbes and parasites. The two classes of diseases are closely related, and frequently it is impossible to draw a line of clear demarcation between the two. The oyster normally resistant to a disease organism may succumb to it if it is in a weakened state due to an unfavorable environment.

In the past, the science of bivalve pathology has been much neglected, and it has been only in recent years that detailed and intense studies of the ailments of oysters—as well as clams, mussels, and scallops—have been undertaken. Still, a great deal more needs to be learned, as only a few of the microorganisms causing disease in shellfish are known with certainty. In some cases, though the scientist is able to identify the culprit, the life cycle of the microbe is unknown or the mode of transmission is obscure. Oyster populations in many parts of the world frequently suffer catastrophic mortalities that are presumed to be associated with some infectious agent, but usually there is no way to prove definitely the cause. These devastating epidemics are rarely attributable to a single factor, but rather to a combination of conditions occurring at a given time, including the involvement of an infectious organism.

Through the years, however, a few infectious diseases of oysters have been studied, and the etiology of them is well documented. Fortunately for the oysters of the Chesapeake system, only two of these maladies are known to exist in the Bay and cause trouble from time to time.

MSX.   This mysterious disease was first recognized in 1957 when it wiped out most of the oysters in Delaware Bay. As investigators were unable to pinpoint the exact identity of the causative organism, it was given the acronym MSX, for "Multinucleate Sphere Unknown," which describes the appearance of the microbe within the oyster's cells. Prior to the ravaging attack by MSX, over seven million pounds of oyster meat were routinely harvested from Delaware Bay each year, but in a few years after infection this figure shrank to less than one hundred thousand pounds. The oyster industry in Delaware was dealt a crippling blow from which it has not managed to recover fully.

By 1959, MSX had made its way down the coast and entered the mouth of the Chesapeake Bay, where it produced a serious impact on the oysters of the Virginia portion of the estuary. Production in the lower part of the Bay dropped dramatically, and it was at this time that Maryland took over the leadership in oyster production from its rival, Virginia.

Soon it was learned that MSX was actually a single-celled protozoan belonging to a group known as the haplosporidians. In 1966 it was crowned with the scientific name *Minchinia nelsoni* in dubious honor of Dr. Thurlow Nelson, who has been called the grandfather of Chesapeake Bay research. It was quickly determined that this protozoan pathogen thrived only in water with a salinity of fifteen parts salt per thousand parts water or higher, which explains why the organism was originally confined to the Virginia portion of the Bay. But a few years later a lack of rainfall served to increase the salinity of the upper parts of the estuary, and the organism spread as far north as the mouth of the Choptank River, where it has continued to attack oysters without quarter in the years when the salinity reaches the proper level. The last attack in the mid-Bay regions occurred in 1983 when fully half of the oysters caught in the Nanticoke River were affected by this pathogen.

An oyster infected with MSX is a pitiful sight to behold. The visceral mass is wasted and reduced in size to the point where the oyster occupies only a portion of the shell. Instead of the thick mucus that forms the so-called liquor of the oyster, the mantle cavity is filled with a thin, watery liquid.

Though it should be emphasized that oysters suffering from MSX disease are perfectly safe for a human to eat, few would care to make a meal out of such unfortunate specimens. During the 1983 epidemic in the Nanticoke, I ate several oysters that had been determined to be infected with MSX. In appearance they had nothing to be proud of, and even less to brag about as far as their gustatory qualities were concerned. They were tasteless, and the quality of the meat was very poor—stringy and tough.

Minchinia nelsoni enters the oyster's body via the outer coverings of the gills and palps, and, having established itself, rapidly proliferates as the disease advances. The oyster's cells try to stem the tide of infection by secreting protective cysts around the invading microorganisms, but this therapeutic action only serves to cause severe congestion within the organs affected. The testis or ovary is a favorite organ of attack, and, even if the oyster is able to muster enough stamina to spawn, the production of sperm or eggs is greatly curtailed.

Epidemics of MSX disease do not occur in waters of low salinity, but the organism is present and lying more or less dormant in a significant number of oysters residing in water of low salt content. When the salt concentration is elevated, the hibernating *Minchinia* are stimulated into physiological activity and resumption of their destructive ways.

As MSX appears to prefer to attack gonadal tissue, a rough estimate of the level of infection of an oyster population may be made by examining microscope slides of the testes and ovaries of a selected number of oysters from a given bar. Past surveys of this

type have shown that about 8 percent of the oysters in the Nanticoke and Manokin rivers act as reservoirs for the sleeping pathogens, which can awaken quickly and develop into epidemic numbers if the environment changes.

In spite of the pillage MSX can inflict on an oyster bar, not all
the shellfish will be eliminated. As with many other disease
agents—in oysters as well as other animals—a few members of the
population will possess an inherent resistance to the pathogenic
organism. These surviving few will become the progenitors of the
next generation, and, hopefully, a significant number of the offspring of the resistant oysters will inherit their parents' ability to
withstand the ravages of MSX. This second generation of resistant
oysters will in turn pass this quality on to their descendents.
Again, Darwinian principles of evolution come into play; only the
fittest survive, and they pass on their favorable characteristics to the next generation.

Research is now underway to determine the nature of the
inherent resistance some oysters have to MSX. If this advantageous quality can be determined, the forces of natural evolution
can be accelerated. Oysters possessing this trait can be used in
artificial propagation procedures to produce large numbers of
resistant forms. These superoysters could be planted on natural
rocks, and the dissemination of the genetic factors for resistance
would spread rapidly throughout the natural populations of the
area.

Initial research studies concerning the resistance of oysters to
MSX and other infectious agents are encouraging in that they
indicate considerable genetic variability between oyster populations (future breeding programs will require such variability). The
early investigations have also shown that there is an apparent
rapid response to artificial selection for resistance. Previously,
oyster geneticists (what few of them there are) had suspected that
disease resistance was of low heritability and would require a long
time to occur in natural populations. The rapid response to selection for MSX resistance would seem to indicate the gene (or
probably the genes) that confer immunity are dominant in action.
Recessive genetic factors require a much longer time before the
characteristic they determine will appear in significant numbers

in a population. It is hoped the oyster will respond as rapidly and vigorously to other selective breeding experiments, such as efforts to enhance resistance to adverse environmental factors.

Dermo.   This disease of oysters is caused by a fungus of unde-termined origin which was recognized by oyster workers a few years before the MSX organism was identified. Originally the fungus was named *Dermocystidium marinum* (hence the nick-name Dermo), but later it was found that the correct appellation was *Labyrinthomyxa marinum*. Recently it has been suggested that even *L. marinum* is not the right name for this secretive fungus. Enough is enough, so let's just call it Dermo and let the confused marine mycologists try to figure out what to call it.

Dermo infects *Crassostrea virginica* from Delaware Bay to Mexico and requires a high temperature and salinity to flourish. In addition, it has been determined that overcrowding of oysters on a rock will encourage the spread of the fungus. In the Chesa-peake Bay the distribution of Dermo roughly parallels that of MSX, though it does not reach quite so far north as the haplospo-ridian. When conditions are optimal and both MSX and Dermo attack oyster bars simultaneously, the consequences are usually calamitous.

Dermo is probably not as important as MSX in the Chesa-peake system, but in other parts of its range it appears to be more devastating. In our region, young oysters seem to have an ac-quired immunity to the fungus, but in other areas (Louisiana, for example) it has been reported on occasion to be responsible for the almost total annihilation of seed oysters.

The fungus's method of entrance into the body of the oyster is a matter for speculation, but once inside, it ferociously attacks the gonads and connective tissue. Like MSX, Dermo is not harmful to humans, but few oyster lovers will want to devour their favorite shellfish if it is dying from the fungal disease. In the southern part of its range, Dermo will attack at any time, but in the Chesapeake it is not apparent in winter. It is not clear, however, if the pathogen is eliminated during the colder months or is lying dor-mant. It seems likely that it does have a dormant state during periods of declining temperatures and is not reintroduced to the Bay each year from an outside source.

The survey methods used to determine the prevalence of Dermo in a given area are more complicated than those used to detect MSX, but governmental agencies routinely run checks of natural oyster beds to determine the presence of this pathogen. Various other bivalves have been found to be susceptible to Dermo infection, and though the fungus appears to be identical with *D. marinum* (or whatever its correct scientific name is eventually determined to be), it is likely that the forms found attacking soft, hard, and razor clams are physiological and perhaps genetic variants of the oyster type.

Much additional research is needed to elucidate the biology and life history of Dermo, and many important aspects of its life are unknown. Particularly, we need to know more about the transport of the reproductive spores in the water and how they actually penetrate the oyster's tissues, details of the reproductive cycles, and the relationship between environmental factors and the distribution and virulence of the disease.

Miscellaneous Knowns and Unknowns.   On a worldwide basis, if we could pick the best environment to grow oysters, the Maryland portion of the Chesapeake Bay would receive more votes than any other region. Though diseases, parasites, and predators certainly take their toll of the Bay bivalves, it is far healthier for oysters than any other place.

Many diseases of oysters prevalent in other areas do not exist as far as is known in the Chesapeake. For example, foot disease, *maladie du pied*, as the French call it, is a fungus that has periodically ravaged the French beds since 1877, and is known to occur in *C. virginica* living in muddy southern waters of the United States. But it has never been found in the Chesapeake Bay. (Actually, "foot disease" is a misnomer, as the adult oyster has no foot. The fungus causing *maladie du pied* primarily attacks the area of attachment of the large adductor muscle, which functions to hold the valves together.)

But, as the study of oyster diseases expands, more and more pathological conditions are being recognized and reported. The following list of such entities represents a few of the rarer diseases recognized in Chesapeake oysters.

Neoplasia. This literally means "the development of new tissues," or tumors. Studies in recent years clearly indicate that oysters develop cancers just like other animals, but the prevalence of this condition in bivalves is not known at this time.

Ovacystis. This disease is caused by a virus similar to the papilloma virus that is responsible for benign tumors of the outer layer of epithelial cells of an animal's organs. The microorganism has been isolated from gonadal tissue, where apparently it causes cystlike structures to form. Its importance in the life of the oyster has not yet been properly assessed.

Physiological Stress Syndrome. In the 1930s the scientist Hans Selye demonstrated the effects of prolonged stress on both rats and humans. Prior to Selye's work it was believed that stress affected only the psychological well-being of an organism, but in a series of brilliant experiments, Selye was able to show that prolonged stress caused pathological changes in the cells of certain important organs of the body. As a result of these changes, physiological dysfunction occurred, along with a deterioration of the immune system, which protects the body against foreign invaders. By all indications, Selye's work with mice and men now seems applicable to oysters.

Cellular changes have been noted in oysters that have been subjected to the extended stress of severe winter weather, inadequate food supply, and polluted water. The syndrome has been observed among oysters on several different beds during the mid-1970s and seems to appear more frequently in samples collected in late winter or early spring. Just how important physiological stress syndrome is to the well-being of oysters has not been determined, but I suspect its significance is great. If the immune system of the bivalve is affected as it is in higher animals, the oyster would certainly be more susceptible to disease agents and other trauma-causing entities.

Parasites

As noted previously, the line of demarcation between a parasite and a predator is frequently indistinct. In general, a parasite is an organism that lives at the complete expense of another, offers the host animal no benefits from its presence, definitely harms the host, and depends on the host to provide it with a residential site during at least a portion of its life cycle. The relationship between a predator and its prey is not as intimate or as ironclad. Some biologists will argue that a flea on a dog is an example of parasitism, but most consider this type of association to be predator-prey in nature.

Based on this personal interpretation of parasitism, only a few organisms known to be associated with oysters will be classified here as parasites. These are as follows:

Bucephalus cuculus. This is a primitive flatworm belonging to the class Trematoda, all members of which are true parasites in a variety of animals; many species cause serious conditions in man. The life cycle of this trematode was first described in 1906, and it was noted at the time that the worm did best in brackish water, gradually disappearing as greater salinities were reached.

The immature stages penetrate the oyster's tissues and become lodged in the ramifications of the digestive system and gonads. When development in the oyster is completed, the young worms bore out of the oyster and take up residence in the tissues of a variety of small fish. Destruction of the oyster's sex organ is the most obvious pathological effect of the worm's sojourn. During routine surveys of oyster bars in the Chesapeake, biologists have found as many as 22 percent of the oysters on a given bar to be infected with this worm. Though it is not clear whether *Bucephalus* is responsible for any oyster mortality or not, it is assuredly of importance, as heavy infestation of the gonads will effectively sterilize the oyster.

Hyperparasites of Bucephalus. *Hyperparasitism* is when a parasite is parasitized by another parasite (I think Jonathan Swift had this in mind when he penned the bit about "big fleas have little fleas"). During the course of study of *Bucephalus* it was observed that the trematode played host to its own unwelcome guests. The identity of the extra freeloaders is in question, but it seems probable they belong to the same group of protozoan parasites

that cause malaria in man and many other animals. These hyperparasites have rarely been found in Chesapeake waters, and the
effects they may have on the trematode host or the oyster are
unknown. It may well be that the population of oyster-sterilizing
trematodes is kept in check by the presence of their own detrimental parasites.

Though a few other true parasites have been described, *Bucephalus* and its hyperparasites seem to be the only ones of
importance to *Crassostrea* of the Chesapeake. It could very well
be, however, that new species of previously unknown parasites
will be discovered and related to oyster mortality. And, of course,
ecological conditions of the Bay may change to a point where
previously known parasites will be afforded the opportunity of
invading the Bay, an area previously off-limits to them from an
environmental standpoint.

Predators

The list of animals that prey on the oyster is large and contains the
name of species representing several animal phyla. Not all predators are equally destructive to oyster populations, but the most
dangerous ones are those that have developed a preference for
oyster meat over other types of food and invade oyster beds in
search of it.

Boring Sponges. Anyone who has ever strolled the beach,
combing for interesting shells, has almost certainly picked up an
oyster valve and noticed it was riddled with numerous small,
round holes. If these holes go more or less straight through the
shell, expanding as they emerge on the inside, they were made by
oyster drills, but if the small perforations on the outside cannot be
correlated with an opening inside, the presence of a boring
sponge is indicated. The boring sponge may be the most common
animal associated with oysters, either while they are alive or after
they have died.

Sponge specialists have identified seven species of the genus
Cliona, the boring sponge, along the Atlantic Coast of the United
States; several other species of the genus are known to occur in

other parts of the world. These primitive animals settle on the oyster's shell and certain filamentous processes give off a minute amount of acid, which eats its way into the calcite of the valve. The sponge continues to etch and mine its way into the substance of the shell, where cavities and tunnels are created for the animal to occupy. Eventually, the shell is honeycombed with the infiltrating sponge and is weakened to the point where it is apt to break. French oystermen are familiar with boring sponges and call the condition of a sponge-infested oyster *la maladie du pain épices,* "the gingerbread disease."

Sometimes the ambitious sponge will "eat" its way through the shell to the interior, but the oyster is usually not damaged as it quickly shores up the internal opening by secreting conchiolin (a shell component) over the aperture. As a matter of fact, some scientists believe the sponge actually feeds on the conchiolin in the shell as it constructs its tunnels, as it is apparent that it does not draw nourishment from the oyster's body.

The race between the oyster and the sponge is an ongoing affair, with the oyster usually managing to plug up the inner holes before the body of the sponge can make contact with the mantle. Should something occur, however, which would slow down the process of shell production, such as a sudden drop in salinity, the sponge may succeed in breaching the oyster's defensive wall and make direct contact with the tissues. If this occurs, dark, pigmented pustules form on the mantle just opposite the inner perforation of the shell. The tissues of such an oyster become flaccid, and the mantle appears to lose some of its inherent elasticity. An oyster in such a weakened condition is obviously quite vulnerable to other types of predators and disease agents.

Cliona is found in the middle and lower Bay and the Atlantic Coast; none of the seven species is able to tolerate salinities of less than ten parts per thousand.

Jellyfish and Comb Jellies. Comb jellies are very similar to true jellyfish except that they lack the powerful stinging cells (nematocysts) that characterize jellyfish and their kin. Both these groups of primitive animals feed on oyster larvae. Numerous studies have documented the fact that the sea nettle, *Chrysaora quinquecir-*

Diseases, Parasites, and Predators

rah, and the common moon jellyfish, *Aurelia aurita,* entangle oyster larvae in their tentacles, sting them to death with their nematocysts, and eventually stuff them down their nonselective, primitive gullets. Other studies have revealed that several types of comb jellies (also called sea walnuts, sea gooseberries, and jug stoppers) seem to relish young oysters even more than their jellyfish cousins do.

In 1925, after years of research in Barnegat Bay, New Jersey, Thurlow Nelson postulated that the comb jelly, *Mnemiosis leidyi,* exerted considerable influence over populations of *Crassostrea* through its predatory habits. On one occasion, Nelson counted 125 oyster veliger-type larvae in the digestive system of one of these comb jellies. Nelson attempted to correlate the comb jelly numbers with the number of oyster larvae that successfully spatted during the same year. In 1921 and 1922, large numbers of spat were produced in Barnegat Bay, while few comb jellies were present. Conversely, in 1923, the comb jellies were very numerous and the oyster set extremely poor.

As with any theory in science, one must not jump to conclusions prematurely. Rather, the hypothesis must be tested with controlled experimental procedures and as many additional observations of natural phenomena as possible should be made. Nelson was dejected when he could find no connection between the spat set and the number of comb jellies when he conducted additional experiments in Long Island Sound in 1944. He dutifully reported this as an example of a year when both the comb jelly and the spatting rate were very high.

There seems to be no doubt, however, that various species of comb jellies (also called ctenophores), including the genera *Pleurobrachia* (sea gooseberry) and *Beroe* (jug stopper), will seriously damage oyster communities when they occur in large numbers during the oyster's spawning season.

Frequently I am asked what biological good is accomplished by the infamous sea nettle of the Chesapeake, and I have usually been at a loss in providing a definitive answer. Now we know that sea nettles are especially fond of ctenophores and will seek them out and devour them in great numbers. Years ago, the founder of the Chesapeake Biological Research Station, Dr. Reginald V.

The Oyster

Truitt, discovered an interesting and important relationship between sea nettles, comb jellies, and oysters.

Dr. Truitt found that populations of sea nettles varied greatly from year to year. In some years when the salinity of the Bay is high, the population of nettles is said to be 100 percent—meaning there is a 100 percent chance you will be stung at least once if you enter the water clad only in bathing attire. Similarly, in a 50 percent year you have a fifty/fifty chance of avoiding the dynamite contained in the long, trailing filaments characteristic of this beast. In 100 percent years Truitt found the oyster spatting rate to be very high. Knowing that the sea nettle routinely feasted on large numbers of ctenophores, he postulated that the jellyfish effectively reduced the ctenophore population numbers to a point where they were no longer predators of the juvenile oysters looking for a place to set.

In more recent times, sea nettles were noted to be very abundant off the pier at the Chesapeake Lab at Solomons Island during the years 1962 to 1966. These years also had relatively high rates of spat setting, but the numbers of comb jellies were not measured. The relationship between jellyfish, ctenophores, and oysters needs further careful investigation.

Sea Anemones.   In the chapter concerning life on the oyster bar, we mentioned the presence of the so-called ghost anemone, *Diadumene leucolena,* which is usually considered a regular commensal guest on the oyster's shell. Recent studies have shown, however, that this graceful and eerie creature is very destructive of veliger larvae settling down on the shell to start the process of spatting. One investigator reported that an anemone can capture and consume all the larvae encountering its nematocyst-laden tentacles at a rate of more than one a minute. If this practice is routine procedure, and there is no reason to believe it is not, it should be obvious that the anemone is a much more important predator and enemy of the oyster than had been formerly supposed. The investigator who reported the fondness of anemones for oyster larvae went so far as to suggest that quicklime (calcium oxide) be broadcast over oyster bars to kill these predators. Though quicklime is sometimes used to control starfish dining on clam and oyster bars in the ocean, its use over oyster beds in the Bay cannot be condoned. The ecological consequences are unknown and disaster could result from any wholesale disruption of the natural biota associated with the bar.

Turbellarian Flatworms.   These free-living worms belong to the same phylum as the flukes and tapeworms, but, as indicated, they have not adopted the parasitic mode of life. *Stylochus ellipticus* is the free-living flatworm we encounter in Chesapeake Bay oysters and is frequently referred to as the oyster leech or zebra worm (there are alternating light and dark bands on the body). Make no mistake about it, this flatworm is an extremely important predator of oyster spat and, to a lesser extent, of mature oysters. It is a physiologically adaptable worm in that it can readily adjust its body functions to salinities ranging from twenty-nine to about three parts per thousand. Consequently, it is prevalent throughout the Bay, from its salty mouth to almost fresh upper regions.

If the oyster leech were able to express a preference for food, it would probably select barnacles, but when oysters are present in large numbers, the worm quickly learns to dine on them. Young spat are attacked without mercy when the large flatworms (*Stylochus* may reach a length of fifty millimeters [two inches], which qualifies it as the largest of the known turbellarians) slither into the mantle cavity when the valves are slightly ajar during feeding. Once inside the spat or mature oyster, the predator emits powerful enzymes manufactured by the digestive system. These enzymes go to work and partially digest any oyster tissue with which they come in contact. After a time, the worm uses its muscular pharynx like a straw and sucks the partially digested oyster juice into its body. Final digestive processes are completed in the many recesses of the worm's saclike digestive system.

An oyster attacked by a flatworm will defend itself by secreting a partition around the invader to seal it off, but when the worms are numerous, the retaliatory activities of the oyster cannot keep pace. No one really knows how many oysters are destroyed in the Chesapeake each year by flatworms, but my guess is the worms take a terrific toll. Max Chambers reports considerable spat mortality due to the activities of flatworms. Chambers's spat, as you will recall from "The Ostraculturist of the Nanticoke," are placed in bags after they have set on the cultch, and the containers are located on pallets in the shallow water of the river so they will grow to marketable size. It is while they are in this important stage of production that they are especially vulnerable to the ravages of the flatworms, and Chambers reports that in some years a significant percentage of the young oysters are destroyed.

Few studies on the effects of flatworms on oyster populations have been accomplished in the past, but during 1916 and 1917 in Cedar Keys on the west coast of Florida it was noted that flatworms killed up to 90 percent of the adult oysters. It has been suggested that this predator can be eliminated by dipping the young oyster seed in a saturated salt solution for a short period of time. Apparently the high concentration of salt upsets the osmotic balance of the worm but does not adversely affect the oyster. Of course, reinfestation of the seed oysters cannot be prevented by this treatment.

Carnivorous Snails.   The deadliest enemies of oysters are various species of marine snails inhabiting coastal waters, and the worst of the lot is a demon called *Urosalpinx cinerea,* the common oyster drill, which ranges along the entire Atlantic coast from Canada to Florida. When *Crassostrea* was first shipped to the Pacific coast (sometime around 1870), this oyster drill hitched a ride and became established in that ocean. Likewise, *Urosalpinx* tagged along as excess baggage in lots of Virginia oysters destined for Great Britain around 1920. Finding the meat of the European oyster, *O. edulis,* just as tasty as that of *Crassostrea* and the waters of England to its liking, the drill quickly ensconced itself and became very abundant along the coast of Essex and across the Thames estuary. From the British Isles, it was a short hop to the Continent, where today it is regarded as the most widely distributed and dangerous of all the oyster predators in Europe.

Fortunately, brackish water serves as an effective barrier to the drills if they try to invade the upper parts of estuaries or tidal rivers. In the Chesapeake system *U. cinerea* and its close relative *Eupleura caudata* are found only at the mouth of the Bay and in the saltier portions of Tangier and Pocomoke sounds. The distribution of *Urosalpinx* extends up the Bay to where a mean salinity of about eighteen parts per thousand exists, and *Eupleura* is not found in areas of less than twenty parts per thousand. Surveys have shown that where the two species overlap, the former is more prevalent than the latter. The habits of the two species are essentially the same.

The maxim "handsome is as handsome does" is not recognized by the oyster drill, since it looks like an ordinary snail but has developed perfectly atrocious habits. Although less than one inch in length, it does not hesitate to attack oysters and clams many times its size. Early studies into the mechanism for boring through the shell suggested that the snail simply used its characteristic rasplike tongue, the radula, to bore through the oyster's valve in much the same way a dentist uses his drill. Later it was discovered that the mechanical process was greatly facilitated by a chemical action. Secretions from the accessory boring organ (ABO for short) soften the shell, probably by enzymatic activity on the conchiolin component, with the decalcified material being removed from the excavation by the rotating motion of the radula. When the drill decides to attack its prey, the chemical phase of the penetration process precedes the mechanical. The shell is weakened or softened by the enzymes in preparation for the actual drilling process. When unsoftened shell is encountered the chemical phase takes over again, lasting for more than an hour, with the ABO in contact with the shell and pumping out the dissolving agents. One biologist reports an oyster drill can penetrate one-fiftieth of an inch of shell during a twenty-four-hour period.

When the shell has been penetrated, the oyster is a goner. The hapless bivalve cannot effectively seal off the tiny hole in its shell as it frequently can do with the aperture of the boring sponge; it is at the mercy of the snail. Some have suggested that a paralyzing poison is injected into the oyster's tissues, but this has not been proven in the case of the oyster drill.

The snail's long tongue penetrates the oyster's mantle, and, like the flatworm, gives off powerful digestive ferments. The oyster's tissues are rapidly broken down and are withdrawn by a sucking action to the stomach of the gastropod. Many drills are usually working on an oyster at the same time, and once the shell has been penetrated, the prey can survive for only a short time. Perhaps we wouldn't feel so sympathetic toward the oyster if we didn't want him for our own use.

Oyster drills are indiscriminate in their selection of a victim; clams, mussels, and barnacles are attacked with equal vigor. In fact, in some situations oyster drills seem to exhibit a preference for barnacles over oysters, and they will usually stop drilling oysters and move to a cluster of barnacles if the latter are placed nearby. Some drills, if given the chance, will consume three times as many mussels as oysters, but, in other situations, just the reverse is true. A possible explanation of these deviant dietary patterns involves the concept of "ingestive conditioning." One worker found that the drill tends to prefer food on which it had fed previously, so the relative abundance of prey seems to affect prey selection. Apparently a well-developed chemical sense also permits the drill to be discriminating in the food it selects. If young and adult oysters are placed in a tank with running seawater along with a batch of hungry drills, the gastropods will invariably opt to dine on the juveniles, whose shells are easier to penetrate.

The distinctive egg cases deposited by oyster drills are frequently found adhering to oyster shells, and the resulting young snails remain in the vicinity of their birth for a considerable time. One can only imagine the numbers of spat destroyed shortly after they have completed the laborious task of affixing themselves to the cultch when they are immediately set upon by the ferocious young drills waiting in ambush.

Two other gastropod predators of oysters, perhaps occurring only in the lower part of the Bay, are the giant whelk or conch, *Busycon carica*, and the oyster snail, *Odostomia impressa*. The conch, which is a species much sought after by shell-collecting beachcombers and gastropod epicures, occurs along the Atlantic coast from New England to the Gulf of Mexico and may destroy a few oysters from time to time. Evidently, the conch is attracted to an oyster by the chemical scents of the bivalve's effluent and chips away with its radula at the edges of the shell until it is able to force it open partially, exposing the meat within.

Diseases, Parasites, and Predators

Odostomia, like the conch, does not actually drill the oyster's shell but attaches itself along the outside margin of the valves. There it patiently bides its time until the oyster opens up voluntarily to feed. When a slight gap occurs between the valves, the snail deftly inserts its proboscis into the mantle cavity and, with the aid of sharp, needlelike stylets, pierces the tissues and proceeds to nourish itself on the rich blood. Research has shown that oysters smaller than ½ inch in height are usually killed as a result of the sanguinary activities of the snail. Larger oysters may be able to withstand the attack and survive, but they usually develop deformed shells and have abnormal growth rates. The so-called oyster snail is found in the Atlantic from Massachusetts to the Gulf of Mexico and sometimes is present in great numbers. In the spring of 1985 I noticed that the bottom of the shallow beach waters near Lewes, Delaware, at the mouth of the Bay was literally covered with *Odostomia*. Countless horseshoe crabs, *Limulus polyphemus*, were coming ashore to engage in their ageless reproductive routine, and their bodies were covered with the snails. I could not determine, however, if the gastropods were attacking the large arthropods—I doubt if they were—or merely using them as a convenient means of conveyance. As the horseshoes migrate considerable distances during the course of a year, any snail hitchhikers would be widely distributed.

Control of Gastropod Predators.   Almost ever since man recognized the damage predatory gastropods inflicted on oyster bars, he has been devising means to eliminate them. Handpicking, with bounties paid per gallon of snails collected, has been employed in the past with limited success (as one can imagine), but this primitive method of population regulation is useless in water deeper than a few feet. Modified dredges and plows have been used to turn over layers of bottom sediments to bury the drills under a lethal depth, and success rates for this method of extermination have been reported to be as high as 90 percent. Unfortunately, as we known, silt and smothering bottom sediments are dangerous enemies of the filter-feeding oysters, and many of them will also be dispatched along with the snails.

The Oyster

The use of snail traps placed on oyster beds was evaluated in the gastropod-infested waters of Virginia, and it was found that large numbers of drills could be caught if the traps were serviced and rebaited weekly. Various types of barriers placed around oyster beds have also been tried with varying success. Bands of chemically impregnated grease are known to block the passage of drills, but no one can be sure the addition of these volatile compounds to an oyster bar will not harm the creatures the chemicals were designed to protect. Likewise, contact with pesticides such as Polystream and Sevin will incapacitate oyster drills and eventually do them in, but again extreme caution must be employed. It is well documented that Sevin (carbaryl) is extremely toxic in minute concentrations to all stages of the blue crab, so, if for no other reason, the use of this chemical should be banned from use anywhere in the Chesapeake Bay.

Recent studies have shown that drills are extremely sensitive to the electrically charged copper ion and will avoid contact with metallic copper. Strips of copper incorporated into bottom-mounted fences may prove to be an effective repellent (ions are released as the metal reacts with the sea water), but the biological and economic ramifications of such a procedure have not been properly evaluated. Snails attached to animals such as the horseshoe crab, as previously mentioned, or to bits of floating debris, could readily pass the copper barrier and infiltrate the bar.

Crustaceans. Over one hundred years ago the blue crab, *Callinectes sapidus*, the so-called beautiful swimmer, was listed as an enemy of the oyster. An ostraculturist reported the complaints of oystermen working in the Great South Bay, Long Island, New York; they stated that the crabs were feasting on small oysters up to the size of a "twenty-five-cent piece." Over the years, it has been learned that the blue crab, and a few other species as well, will in fact invade oyster beds and crack the shells of young oysters to obtain the delicious meat inside. The famous crustacean will also smash the thin valves of "snap" oysters—elongated, older oysters living in very crowded conditions.

Most biologists believe that the blue crab, so abundant in the Chesapeake Bay, is only an insignificant foe of the oyster. The

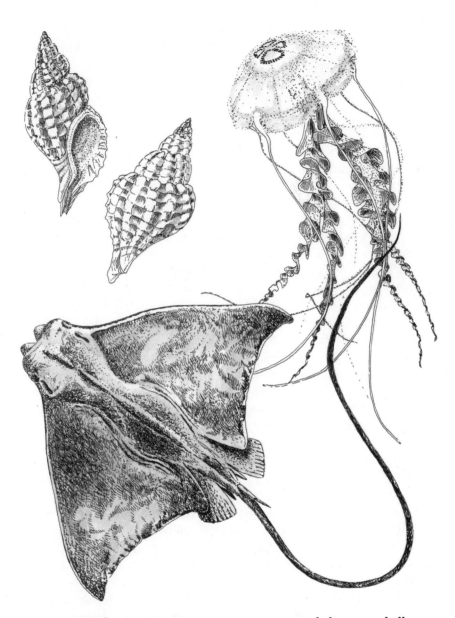

Oyster predators. *Bottom:* cownose ray; *upper left:* oyster drills;
upper right: sea nettle. To show detail, the drills,
relative to the others, are drawn considerably larger than scale.

The Oyster

crab will feed on almost anything of an organic nature, living or dead, and, as there is no evidence it is attracted to oysters or shows any preference for them, it poses no threat.

Other ocean-dwelling species, such as the rock crab, *Cancer irroratus*, and the green crab, *Carcinus maenas*, which possess lobsterlike pincers, are perfectly capable of crushing the shells of mature oysters, but these crabs are among the least of the problems the oyster who finds itself trying to make a living in the ocean has to contend with.

Starfish.   This highly advanced invertebrate animal is among the most devastating of the predators of oysters, clams, scallops, and other bivalves living in waters with salinities in excess of fifteen parts per thousand. This member of the phylum Echinodermata has long been recognized by the men who make their livelihood from the sea as a mortal enemy to be combatted with every means available.

One of the most distinctive features of starfish, and most other members of this group, is a highly developed water vascular system, which hydraulically operates the countless tube-feet used in locomotion and food gathering. A starfish preys on bivalves and opens the shells of its victims in a remarkable manner. Draping its tube-foot-laden arms around the oyster or clam, it applies suction to each of the shells. Each tube-foot is equipped with an adhesive sucking disc, so considerable pressure can be exerted in an attempt to force the shells to part. At first, the strong adductor muscle of the oyster resists the relentless force, but sooner or later, as with any muscle that is overused, it suffers fatigue and weakens. Eventually, a slight gap between the valves is produced, and through this slit the stomach of the starfish slithers.

Once the stomach has gained access to the mantle cavity, powerful digestive enzymes, secreted by the digestive gland, flow profusely to the walls of the stomach. These oyster-digesting substances immediately attack the adductor muscle, destroying whatever retracting capacity it may still have. With the muscle rendered useless, the valves gape widely, and the starfish goes to work in earnest to digest its meal. Later, the starfish retracts its stomach back to its normal position within the body, bringing with

150

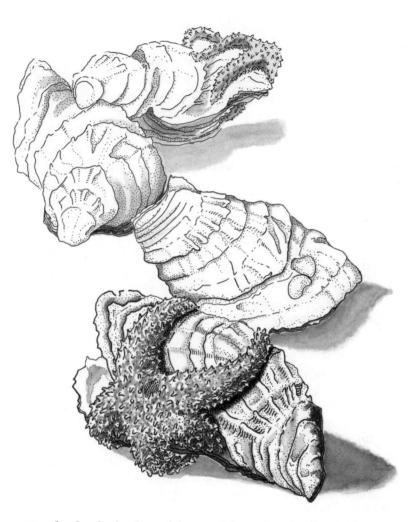

Hundreds of tube feet of the starfish apply relentless pressure
to the valves of the oyster.

it the partially digested oyster. I have often wondered what an embarrassed starfish would do if the oyster was able to muster additional strength in its adductor and manage to close its valves, entrapping the echinoderm's stomach. I have never seen an account of such a scenario in the literature concerning invertebrate zoology, but I feel sure it must have happened at some time.

Oystermen and clammers long ago devised a simple and effective method of controlling starfish numbers on oyster and clam beds by dragging special filamentous mops across their fishing grounds. Another unique organ possessed by starfish is a minute, pincerlike structure called the pedicellaria. Thousands of pedicellariae occur over the surface of the starfish and are used primarily to clean the thin-walled gills that project from the outer covering. As the mop is dragged over the animal, the pedicellariae snap shut and hold on with bulldoglike tenacity, allowing it to be dragged to the surface.

Previously, watermen would attempt to "kill" the starfish by chopping them up with a knife or axe or by simply crushing them with a mallet or heel. Unfortunately, they did not realize the starfish has tremendous powers of regeneration, and, by cutting one into four or five pieces, they were not killing one predator but creating four or five new ones. The common starfish preying on oysters in the Atlantic has five arms or rays, each of which is capable of growing into a completely new star. Later, when this ability to regenerate was recognized, starfish captured from the depths were executed in a bucket of lime or other such caustic material before being dumped back overboard.

Starfish-mopping or drill-trapping must be undertaken on a widespread basis if the predator's numbers are to be significantly reduced. Mechanical control measures are labor-intensive activities, and, although such efforts may be worthwhile on a private oyster lease, how many oystermen are willing to put forth the effort on a public bar to have the protected oysters harvested by another individual? And, since oyster predators do not read lease survey plats, it does little good for the propagator of a private lease to take action against predators unless his neighbor who operates the adjacent bit of leased bottom does likewise.

Diseases, Parasites, and Predators

Fish.   Many species of fish have been accused of raiding oyster beds and feeding on both young and adult oysters, but the incriminating evidence against most of them is flimsy at best. An exception to this is the cownose ray (sometimes called batwing ray) *Rhinoptera bonasus,* which is a serious predator.

This species of stingray is light to dark brown on the topside and white below. The head is slightly protruded and blunt, somewhat resembling the muzzle of a cow. It is highly migratory and occurs in the Bay from May to October, following the North Carolina coastline south during the colder months. Reaching forty-five inches across and weighing in excess of fifty pounds, these dangerous fish travel in schools of five or ten to several hundred. Often the tips of their "wings" break the surface of the water, resulting in cries of "Sharks!" from apprehensive swimmers and boaters.

A mature oyster or clam is a pretty tough nut to crack, but the cownose accomplishes this feat easily with its very hard teeth and powerful jaws. The terrible teeth are used to bite off the top few inches of the shell, and, with the aid of suction created by the beating of the wings, the oyster is extracted from the shell. At certain times of the year the cownose's diet is composed almost entirely of oysters, clams, and other shellfish. One private lease propagator in Virginia is reported to have lost $40,000 in planted oysters to the appetites of the rays in a single year's time. Another planter, when asked how much damage the rays had done to his bar, replied, "I don't know for sure, but those bastards slurped their way through so many of my arsters my next stop is going to be the poorhouse." There seems to be no doubt about it—a school of rays can inflict heavy damage on an oyster bed in a very short time.

In recent years the numbers of cownoses have increased, and outraged oystermen and clammers have tried everything from cherry bombs to barbed-wire entanglements to keep them away from their fishing grounds. Wire fences and explosive charges fail to deter the rays once they have decided to dine on oysters or clams, however. The oysterman can take a bit of solace from the fact these fish definitely prefer clams, but once a clam population is decimated, the rays will turn to oysters with undiminished zeal.

In an attempt to reduce the numbers of rays, federal and state agencies have tried to influence people to fish for them, either for sport or for food. Unlike their relative the shark, the ray maintains a very high level of the nitrogenous waste product urea in its bloodstream to effect an osmotic balance between itself and the salty sea. Urea is a bitter, foul-tasting substance that few if any diners care to tolerate. To make the flesh of a cownose halfway palatable, it must be soaked in fresh water for a number of days. The sporting aspect of ray fishing leaves a lot to be desired by anglers interested in taking fighting fish. Once a ray is hooked with rod and reel, the only way it seems to know to escape the hook is to dive and pull steadily against the line—no zigzagging or aerial acrobatics. I hooked a big one in Tangier Sound several years ago and was utterly bored for the hour it took to bring the fish to the gaff. In view of its inability to endear itself to sport fishermen and its unacceptability for the frying pan, it seems hardly likely that humans will be attracted to the ray with sufficient enthusiasm to reduce its numbers appreciably.

Several other species of fish inhabiting the Chesapeake have been accused of eating oysters from time to time, including the spot, drum, croaker (hardhead), and oyster toad. There is no way any of these finny creatures can destroy a healthy adult oyster, but it is possible they may occasionally destroy young spat. As noted in the previous chapter, the oyster toad *(Opsanus tau)* has long been charged with cracking the shells of adult oysters with its powerful jaws, but all evidence is to the contrary. Toadfish are frequently caught from the oyster bars they inhabit, and this is the reason many assume they are feasting on the bivalves. Rather, as mentioned previously, they are feeding on the many species of worms and other invertebrates who also call the oyster bed home. In New Jersey waters, at least, the toadfish seems to be a benefactor of oysters, as it is known to consume great quantities of mud crabs which destroy some juvenile stages.

Birds.   Certain species of ducks are credited with being enemies of the Pacific coast oyster *(Ostrea lurida)* on beds that are periodically inundated by the tides in the Puget Sound area, but no species of waterfowl, or any other type of bird for that matter, known to inhabit the Chesapeake region makes a habit of consuming oysters. I imagine old fishing-long-legs, the great blue heron, with its long, sharp bill will occasionally partake of an oyster in shallow water, but the heron or any other bird cannot inflict any harm on oyster populations.

Some people believe the oystercatcher, *Haematoptus palliatus*, is a definite threat to its namesake, but such is not the case. This bird is rather rare in the region of the Chesapeake, but is common south of Virginia to the Gulf of Mexico. This long-legged creature has the interesting habit of constructing several dummy or decoy nests in the vicinity of the real one. In each of the bogus nests, the resourceful oystercatcher places a number of sun-bleached oyster shells to simulate eggs. Any would-be predator is supposedly thrown off the track in its search for a meal of oyster-catcher eggs. This practice of utilizing shells in the dummy nests is responsible for the erroneous idea that these birds have a taste for oysters.

Mammals.   Though the sea otter of the West Coast is credited with eating an oyster, clam, or abalone every now and then, I know of no mammal (other than man, of course) of the Chesapeake that does this. Incidentally, it is interesting to note the method used by the sea otter to acquire its shellfish victuals. Swimming on its back, the agile creature places a shellfish on its chest, and, with the aid of a rock, smashes the shells and extracts the meat. Thus, the sea otter is one of the very few animals, other than man and higher primates such as chimpanzees and monkeys, known to use a tool in its day-to-day life.

After the foregoing discussion of the various and sundry enemies of oysters, one might legitimately wonder how any at all manage to survive. The oysters survive because the ecological community they evolved into has its own system of checks and balances for all the creatures that are part of it. It is a finely tuned system where all the residents live in a state of dependency and tolerance. And, it has been like this for at least fifteen thousand years, since the

Bay was formed by the flooding of the lower valley of the greatest river on the East Coast, the Susquehanna.

Everything was going along just fine, according to the laws of nature, in this giant estuary until the Europeans arrived on its shores some 350 years ago. From the very beginning, man's activities have tended to disrupt the delicate balance of nature enjoyed by the Bay's organisms, and in the last few decades man's detrimental activities have been accelerated.

Occasionally I am asked, "What is the most important enemy of the oyster we have to contend with? MSX, toadfish, oyster drills?" The answer to this one is easy—it's man.

CHAPTER EIGHT

Tonging, Dredging, and Diving

It's hard to get oysters out of your system
once you are clogged up with them.
                              Dr. Reginald V. Truitt

THE four main methods of taking oysters from the Chesapeake Bay are hand tonging, dredging, patent tonging, and diving. The extensive set of laws are frequently ambiguous and confusing, but if one perseveres and is alert to almost yearly changes in the regulations, it is possible to find a method and location suited to one's needs and talents.

With the exception of diving, which is a fairly recent innovation, the methods of catching oysters have been used for many years and have continued relatively unchanged since the earliest days of the oyster fishery in the state. The design of any one harvesting implement varies in different localities, but its principle is essentially the same throughout the Bay area. In fact, all of the methods of capture, again with the exception of diving, are based on the same idea, that of a bar with attached teeth that project downward into the bottom. This bar is so operated that the teeth move along the bottom and slightly penetrate it. In this manner, oysters are dislodged or broken loose from clumps and pushed into a bag or basket that is brought to the surface either by hand or by power equipment. Some of these devices are much more efficient than others and tend to remove oysters more effectively from the bottom, thus causing depletion. In an attempt to retard some of the effectiveness of these items of oyster-catching equipment, much of the law concerning the taking of oysters deals with the construction of these mechanisms, and where, when, and how they can be legally employed.

Hand Tonging

Of all the enigmatic practices of the native North Americans observed by the first white settlers, I imagine the use of primitive, scissorslike tonging devices to retrieve oysters was one of the most puzzling. In Europe someone wanting to gather a batch of oysters from the nearby seacoast simply waited for the tide to ebb, exposing the oyster bed for a period of several hours. Then it was only a matter of wading out through the mud, selecting the oysters, and picking them up by hand. With the American oyster it was a different story, as the beds of this species are almost always inundated by anywhere from three to forty or more feet of water.

No one knows for sure when the Indians invented the first set of hand tongs, but we can be sure they had been using them for hundreds of years prior to the invasion of the white man. As noted earlier, the campsites of the Indians inhabiting the Atlantic coast are characterized by the presence of heaps of discarded shells, or middens, that mutely testify to the Indians' fondness for the abundant and nutritious mollusk. In all probability, the ever-present oyster saved numerous native settlements from death by starvation during periods when crops failed and hunting was poor.

The first tongs employed by an Indian in the distant past were probably simple machines consisting of two small-diameter, straight trees lashed together a few feet from one end to form a scissorslike apparatus. The branches of each tree were carefully trimmed to form a sort of crude basket or rake when closed, or bits of wood were attached to a bar to form the basket. I can envision some early colonial blacksmith taking stock of the situation and deciding that toothed, basketlike rakes fashioned from iron and attached to the ends of the poles or shafts would be more efficient, and a reasonable facsimile of a set of oyster tongs used today was created. By 1793 the use of wooden tongs with heads made of iron were in common use. In that year, Moreau de St. Mery, a visitor from France, wrote at Norfolk: "Many boats engage in oyster fishing, using a scissorslike instrument ending in two iron rakes to scrape the oysters from the bottom of the river. The oysters are large but have little taste because the water is not sufficiently salty."

The use of hand tongs, or hand shafts or shaft tongs as they are sometimes called, to catch oysters is about the most demanding type of physical labor in which man has ever chosen to engage. A pair of twenty-four-foot tongs will have a dry weight of about thirty-five pounds, and when a third of a bushel of oysters (that is about the maximum number of oysters an experienced tonger can retrieve with one "lick") is added, a considerable amount of strength is required to raise the cumbersome tongs from the depths and deposit the catch in the boat. Though recently a power-lifting device has been perfected to raise the tongs, the mechanism is rather expensive to fabricate and only a few oyster-men have them on their workboats at this time. It seems only a matter of time, however, until the power lifting device or auto-matic winder becomes an item of standard equipment on the hand tonger's boat.

The power winder to the hand tonger is the equivalent of the Designated Hitter rule to the baseball player; it prolongs the career of each.

The oysterman must construct his own power lifting device from odds and ends. Some. sort of small power winch must be obtained and modified for attachment to the boat's battery. A nylon line is secured to the basket of the hand tongs and attached to the winch, and a foot-operated switch is wired into the ap-paratus. After the oysters have been gathered into the basket, the lifter efficiently brings the load to the surface, and considerable wear and tear on the oysterman's body is avoided. Recently the use of the power lifting device has come under fire by an official of the Maryland Department of Natural Resources—supposedly its use will permit the tonger to catch more oysters and thereby threaten the already dwindling population. Hand tongers and other watermen consider such a viewpoint ridiculous. They point to the legal use of power dredges and patent tongs to catch oysters and laugh at the idea that a power lifting device on hand tongs will deplete the Bay of its oysters.

During the course of a day's work, the oysterman may em-ploy his tongs one hundred or more times while trying to maintain his balance standing on the gunwale of the boat, which is probably

The Oyster

pitching in a rolling sea. Add to this a wind-chill factor of 10 degrees Fahrenheit or less, and you will probably decide that a man must be out of his mind to subject himself to that sort of physical torture and danger to catch a few bushels of oysters. Only a waterman knows why he is compelled to earn his living this way, and has difficulty explaining his reasoning to an outsider. I once asked an oysterman who had been hand-tonging for over thirty years the intimidating question, "Why?" The irony in his reply surprised me when he answered, "Soon or late a man tells himself he's crazy to go tong for arsters; go tongin' fer em just the same."

The oysterman is a breed unto himself. He knows this and is proud of his ability to challenge the forces of nature and other sources of adversity to make a living by his individual skill and physical prowess. I think this pride in himself and in his ability to do something few others have the skill or courage to attempt is a major reason they "go tongin' fer em just the same." William Warner, the noted chronicler of the blue crab in the Chesapeake Bay and of the fishing industry of the North Atlantic, once asked a waterman on Maryland's Eastern Shore and a commercial fisherman in England the same question: "Why do you do it?" The men replied with the identical answers: "Because, that's what I do best." This poignant answer given by two men of seemingly very different backgrounds pretty well sums it up.

If he has been engaged in his profession for any length of time, certain physical traits will be manifested, and a man can be readily identified as a tonger. A tonger's upper body muscles, especially those in the chest and shoulders, will be developed enormously, and his hands will be covered with scars that have resulted from numerous bouts of oyster finger and oyster hand infections. His leathery face will be deeply lined and weathered from exposure to the elements, and there may be a few scars to indicate where skin cancers resulting from overexposure to the damaging rays of the sun have been excised. Arthritis seems to strike oystermen more frequently than members of the general population, bending and crippling their bones. But more than any of these telltale signs, the somber, forlorn look in the eyes betrays, at least to me, the identity of the hand-tonger.

Tonging, Dredging, and Diving

The oysterman's eyes are but windows to his inner self which reflect his emotions and perceptions as well as a constant, nagging fear of the forces of nature. He knows nature has control of his life and there is little if anything he can do to change this; just live with things the way they are. Is it little wonder that the oysterman rebels when those whom he perceives as governmental bureaucrats place innumerable additional obstacles in the path of his already precarious existence?

Lou Griffin of Tyaskin, a neighbor of mine on the Nanticoke River, believes a person must be born with the correct body chemistry to be an oyster tonger. According to Griffin, those who possess this right combination of protoplasmic ingredients are able to function as tongers, and those who lack "the right stuff" can never successfully operate in this capacity. Forty years ago Griffin came to the conclusion that his body was not suitable for hand-tonging. As a young man he followed the water, crabbing, fishing, and for a time oystering. Though he was very successful as a crabber and fisherman, he was unable to cope with the physical demands made by the tongs. Make no mistake about it, crabbing with either trotline or pots and fishing with several miles of netting are physically demanding jobs that quickly eliminate the weak of back or heart. Lou relates that after a day of tonging in Tangier or Pocomoke sound he would return home exhausted and find the muscles in the upper part of his body refused to relax. After crabbing or fishing ventures he would also be fatigued and his muscles tense, but after a period of rest his body could relax and accommodate itself to a period of inactivity. Not so after tonging. The muscles he had used so extensively in bringing oysters to the culling board refused to relax and would remain in a state of painful tetany for several hours. Eventually, the chemical reactions that cause muscles to contract would be reversed, and he would be able to sleep for a few hours. But the next day when he returned to the oyster bars and subjected his body to the unique strain of tonging, his muscles would tighten up again, and the same pattern would be repeated. Wisely, Griffin deduced oyster tonging was not for him, and he has not hit a lick with the tongs since 1943.

The Oyster

Almost all longtime oystermen suffer, to a greater or lesser extent, from what is termed "tonger's disease." This malady involves numbness and soreness in the arms, hands, and fingers but it usually is not disabling enough to keep a man off the water. When asked how prevalent this condition was among oystermen, a veteran of many years with the tongs replied, "All of em's got it, but none'll admit it."

JR and Jane.   The wind was whistling out of the west at about fifteen miles per hour one April morning in 1984 as I waited on the shore for the boat to arrive. I knew that this would be the last chance for several months I would have to experience what tonging for oysters was really like. I had, of course, read descriptions of the process, had the procedure explained to me, and spent countless hours in my boat watching the tongers work on the various beds found throughout the lower Nanticoke River. I thought I knew all about the operation, but the nagging feeling persisted that until I had actually worked the tongs and culling board over an oyster rock, some important phase of tonging—perhaps we could say the feel for it—would not be understood. I felt I had to do it myself; to actually raise the oyster-filled tongs from the depths and swing them onto the boat. Then, perhaps, I could understand in a small way what it is like to tong for oysters to sell for money.

As I nervously bided my time on the shore near Ragged Point, I wondered if the whitecapped river would permit us to scrape its bottom for oysters that day. There was only one day left in the tonging season for that year. Because January and February had been severe months and the boats were iced in their slips for several weeks, the Department of Natural Resources had extended the hand-tonging season on public grounds a month, until April 15, but after that date there would be no more compromise with the law, and the season would end.

Suddenly I recognized a boat heading into shore. As the craft neared the beach, Jane Insley waved from the bow, and I returned the greeting with enthusiasm. Jane's husband, Don Insley, Jr., whom everyone simply calls by his initials JR (though pronounced more like Jar), skillfully guided the boat to the shore, and when the hull hit the bottom I was surprised when Jane sprang overboard in about a foot of water with a line to hold the craft steady while I clumsily clambered aboard. Having successfully loaded his passenger, JR put the outboard in reverse and slowly backed into deeper water.

"Yes, it is going to be rough today, but I think we will be able to hit a lick or two," JR replied when I asked him if we were going to be able to catch some oysters. With that, he gunned the motor, and we sped off into the wind toward a distant bar.

JR and Jane represent a new concept in oyster people. In their twenties, they have a varied lifestyle, in that part of the year they farm a few acres and raise some chickens. Crabbing has its place during certain periods, and "arstering" is undertaken in turn. It is from the latter endeavor, however, that they hope to make most of the money they will need to pay the bills. Both are part-time students at nearby Salisbury State College—JR working toward a degree in business administration and Jane well into studies that will eventually lead to a bachelor's degree in nursing. It was my pleasure to have had both Jane and JR as students in my classes at the college, and I clearly recall the first time I met Jane. She was enrolled in a course entitled "Human Anatomy and Physiology," which is required of nursing majors, but at first she was only a name on a roster of over one hundred students whose faces I saw massed together three times a week in a large lecture hall. One day when I had just finished grading the papers from an important examination she appeared at my office door to tell me that she had missed the exam. Expecting the usual excuse of a grandmother's unexpected death or a vehicular breakdown, I was stunned when Jane told me why she had been unable to take the test at the appointed hour. She explained that JR had proposed marriage the night before and "I was so excited I just couldn't make any sense out of anatomy and physiology!" In deference to such a unique situation, I permitted her to take a makeup exam, on which she scored very well.

The Insleys' boat is typical of the type used by the new breed of watermen. Instead of the individually constructed thirty- to thirty-five-foot wooden so-called workboat powered by an inboard engine (usually pirated from a junk automobile) theirs is a sleek twenty-two-footer of molded fiberglass, with a wide beam and powered by a 115-horsepower outboard motor. The boat, motor, and trailer on which the rig may be easily transported cost about seven thousand dollars when purchased new in 1982. More and more watermen are acquiring the new type of boat and motor, and in the various harbors around the Bay the "For Sale" signs posted on many of the older craft are harbingers of their ultimate demise.

The traditional workboat is a cumbersomely slow vessel that literally sucks the expensive gasoline from its large tanks. Once one of these boats is "put over" for the season, it usually stays in the water until it has to be removed for repair or barnacle removal. An oysterman hearing of a bar in another part of the Bay or its tributaries where oysters (or crabs) are being caught in large numbers usually cannot take advantage of the situation if he operates one of the older workboats. Frequently, a voyage of a day or two is required to get to the new location, and the logistical problems of docking and housing are always present. With a boat capable of being easily trailered, the oysterman can transport his craft to the desired area in a matter of hours. Or, if the new bed is not too far away, the run to it can be made by water in a relatively short period of time. The outboard-powered craft is much lighter and much more efficient, so the all important matter of economics comes into play. JR estimates that his boat requires five to six gallons of gasoline during a day's tonging operation, whereas one of the older boats would consume about twenty-five gallons for the same amount of running time. With gasoline being sold around docking areas for about $1.40 a gallon, the owner of the outboard-powered craft is two to three bushels of oysters ahead of his counterparts before the tonging day even starts.

Just prior to our expedition on the Nanticoke, JR had been working some oyster beds in the Choptank River near the city of Cambridge. About an hour and a half trailering time was required to reach this productive area, and, at the end of the day he simply hauled his boat onto the trailer, sold his oysters, and returned home to Tyaskin. To reach the oyster beds on the Choptank from our area of the Nanticoke at Tyaskin would have required at least six hours running the outboard at full throttle, and a day or more would have been needed to reach the beds if a slower, older boat had been used. For example, Quincey Blevins of Nanticoke needed twelve hours to guide his wooden boat through stormy seas to Oxford, Maryland, on the Tred Avon River, when he heard oysters were plentiful in the vicinity. Blevins recalls the trip as a demanding one, with the Bay being so rough he was required to grip the wheel with both hands for most of the tedious journey, afraid even to let go for the moment needed to brew a cup of coffee. Arriving on the beds off Oxford, he found that the word had spread, and boats from up and down the Bay had converged on the area; in a few days, the beds had been depleted of oysters.

When we arrived over the public bed JR had decided was worth a try that morning, the wind seemed to intensify, and I wondered again how we would be able to tong in the face of the disrupted and threatening river. Noting, however, that other boats were, indeed, in the area and the tongs were going up and down with monotonous regularity, I realized that where there is a will, there is a way.

Upon JR's order, Jane cast the killick (a sort of anchor designed to deter a boat's drift but not station it in one place) overboard and delicately fingered the line attached to it. She was feeling the vibrations sent back from the bottom by the killick (in this case a piece of heavy chain) to determine if it was being dragged over oyster shells. When she announced that oysters were below, JR swung into action. After selecting a pair of sixteen-foot tongs (he always carries a spare set in case one breaks), he leaped onto the wide gunwale of the boat and plunged the tongs to the bottom. I noticed that he placed himself in front of a small cabin he had constructed in the middle of the boat for protection from the elements. He explained that this position was necessary in case he lost his balance. The outer edge of the gunwale was raised slightly, so that when tonging his body was tilted backward, and, he hoped to direct a fall backward and into the cabin's wall instead of going forward and falling into the river or bottom of the boat.

Using the tongs like scissors, he alternately opened and closed them, explaining that he was amassing a pile of oysters on the bottom. He added that when the shafts come together in your hands you know the pile on the bottom has been properly positioned. After a few such movements, he spread the shafts widely and then closed the heads around his pile of oysters. With a hand-over-hand movement he brought the heads of the tongs containing the oysters to the surface, and with a mighty heave of his upper body he skillfully guided the heads over the side of the boat and released the contents onto the culling board.

My first job that morning was to assist Jane in the important culling of the catch. The culling board reaches from one gunwale of the boat to the other, and has three-inch notches cut into it at various locations to assist in the sizing operation. The unique culling hammer, which is used to break up clusters of oysters so that the small ones may be returned to the bar, also has a three-inch gauge incorporated into its handle. All undersized oysters as well as boxes (dead oysters in which the two valves have not separated) and individual shells and bits of slag or other types of cultch must be returned to the immediate area from which they were taken. Care must be taken to insure that each bushel of oysters harvested contains no more than 5 percent undersized oysters or cultch. Smaller oysters adhering to legal specimens must be broken loose and returned to the bar unless it is obvious that to do so would destroy them. This is a judgment call on the part of the marine policeman who might inspect the catch either on the water or at dockside, but JR says he has had no trouble with the authorities on this point of the law.

If a policeman decides to check an oysterman's catch he will personally cull a bushel of oysters retained on the boat. The law states that all undersized oysters and cultch must be returned to the bar immediately, and the presence of undersized specimens on a boat is considered to be evidence of one's intent to retain them. During the inspection the officer will use a special cup that measures exactly one-twentieth of a bushel. When the inspector finds oysters less than 3 inches, boxes, shells, and slag in the batch he is culling, they are placed in the cup. If the cup "runneth over" before the bushel is worked over, the oysterman is in trouble.

I noticed that Jane, after explaining all of this to me, kept a watchful eye on my work as I helped her cull the oysters JR continued to dump unceremoniously before us. She wanted to make sure my inexperience at culling oysters did not result in

166

their getting a ticket if "The Man" (as a marine policeman is called) chose to inspect our catch that morning. If the marine cop finds you in violation, he will probably require you to recull all the oysters caught that day and return the small ones to the nearest natural bed. In addition, a fine of from twenty-five to one hundred dollars may be levied if you are a tonger; if you are a dredger the amount rises to fifty to two hundred dollars. If the violation occurs in the Potomac River, *all* oysters caught that day must be returned to a natural rock. These penalties are greatly magnified if the illegal oysters or cultch are found at the end of a day's work. It is important for a skipper to have a trustworthy culler working with him, as a careless one can create all sorts of trouble. Quincey Blevins thought he had found a reliable culler to work with him when his daughter Beth volunteered for the job. After checking her work on the first bushel or so of oysters tonged the first day they worked together, Blevins immediately returned to the harbor and discharged his culler.

After I had served my apprenticeship on the culling board and we had caught two or three bushels of keepers, it was time for me to take my turn with the tongs. JR carefully placed me in position on the gunwale and reiterated that if I was going to fall, "be sure and fall backward." After a minute or two of swaying several degrees to both port and starboard, I felt I was adjusted to the movements of the boat and was ready to proceed. I plunged the tongs to the bottom but quickly realized the heads were too far out from the side of the boat. To be manipulated properly, the tongs have to be in a perpendicular position no farther away from the boat than an arm's length. Trying again, I managed to submerse the tongs in the correct position, and, feeling the oysters beneath the heads, I pushed them to the bottom. After I had imitated JR's scissorslike movements and had raked a few oysters into a pile, I closed the jaws and proceeded to bring my prizes to the surface. As the head of the tongs containing a couple of dozen oysters broke the surface of the water, I attempted to lift it free and dump the contents on board. Unfortunately, something went wrong. The boat pitched one way and I lurched the other, losing my balance in the process. I managed to hang onto the tongs as I fell backward, but the contents of the heads spilled back into the river. JR didn't say anything, but Jane eased my embarrassment by commenting, "It takes a little practice to get it right."

After a few more mistakes in my technique were rectified, I experienced a feeling of great satisfaction when at last I managed to hit a lick and successfully deposit a dozen or so oysters on the culling board. I went on to hit several more licks before lunch.

Jane apologized for the fare she served, which consisted of bologna on white bread and Kool-aid. She explained that in the fall when the oysters were plentiful and they were making a lot of money the menu would have consisted of sliced roast beef and canned soft drinks. The bologna and Kool-aid were fine with me; the crisp April air and exercise had whetted my appetite to a fine edge, and I can't remember a lunch I have enjoyed more than the one I shared that day with my young friends on the beautiful Nanticoke.

After lunch the velocity of the wind had increased to such an extent that it was obvious our oystering was over for the day. All in all we had caught about four bushels that morning, and at a dockside price of fourteen dollars per bushel, expenses had been met with enough left over to cover the bologna and Kool-aid. On the way back to the harbor, JR selected a bushel of the largest oysters to be taken home that night and shucked out to be sold by the pint or quart. A little more revenue from the day's labor would be realized by this endeavor.

We encountered the local marine police boat on our way in, but the officer merely waved to us as we passed. The Insleys said they had not been checked in over a year. Apparently their reputation for following the law was established with the enforcement agency. Sometimes, however, they admit taunting "The Man" by taking their small dog along on the boat. They know that Title 4, Subtitle 741 of the Maryland Annotated Code strictly forbids carrying domestic animals of any species on a boat transporting shellfish, and if the pooch is detected a ticket may be issued. In general, their opinion of marine policemen is favorable. They understand that the cull law must be rigidly enforced if the oyster populations are to survive, and the catch limits must be observed for the same reason But, as JR put it, "I'll be damned if I can see why taking my dog along with me for company should be against the law."

That evening I sensed a tightness and soreness in the muscles of my upper torso, but after a hot shower and two aspirins the discomfort abated. Whether I have the right type of body chemistry to do this sort of work on a regular basis is yet to be determined.

The Messick Brothers. Nestled on a rural lane in the small hamlet of Bivalve (a most appropriate name), Maryland, on the Nanticoke River is a unique business enterprise. Located in an ancient two-story barn and operated by the Messick brothers, Cornelius and Wilbur, this shop fabricates oyster-tong shafts, which are utilized by a majority of the oystermen who hand-tong along the eastern seaboard. At the present time, the Messick workshop is probably the only establishment in the country that turns out tong shafts in any appreciable numbers, and their manufactory is operated only part-time.

Cornelius's primary occupation is proprietor of the local funeral home, which members of his family have operated since the 1860s; Wilbur is the postmaster of Bivalve. Like the funeral business, the shaft-making enterprise was started by the great-grandfather of the brothers in 1859. Just how much longer Corney and Wibbie, as the brothers are always called, will be able to meet the demands of the oystermen is not known, because the supply of the basic type of wood used in making the shafts is very limited.

The shafts (or shaves, rakes, stales, ignorant sticks, or widow-makers, as they are also called) made by the Messicks are constructed from the heartwood of the long-leaf pine, which today is almost an endangered species, at least in the size required to make tong shafts. Some 15 years ago, in a book about watermen, the author mentioned the work of the Messick brothers and sadly reported they were no longer in business because their supply of wood had been exhausted. When I mentioned this to Corney, he laughed and paraphased Mark Twain, saying, "The reports of our demise are greatly exaggerated." Actually, some years ago the business was in danger of being closed because an adequate supply of the necessary heartwood could not be located. Supplies

169

The Oyster

from Florida, New Jersey, and Virginia were unreliable and dwindling with each passing year, and, rather than compromise the quality of their product by using fir or loblolly pine, they seriously considered terminating the business.

Long ago the Messicks learned that the heartwood of the long-leaf pine was by far the best type of wood they could use to fashion the shafts to which the metal rakes or baskets would be attached. The wood used in making the shafts must possess certain important qualities if it is to withstand the rigorous use to which it will be put. It must be strong, densely grained, flexible, waterproof to a certain extent, and not splinter easily. To the brothers, only the long-leaf pine fulfills these requirements.

A loblolly pine grows rapidly and is ready to harvest for lumber about twenty-five years after a seedling is planted, but the long-leaf pine requires two hundred to three hundred years to match the same growth of the loblolly. This slow rate of growth is responsible for the dense grain and inherent tensile strength found in the wood, especially the heartwood. The growth rings in this tree reveal that the diameter of the trunk increases only about one thirty-second of an inch a year, and this accounts for the denseness of the grain. Also, the sap or resin of the long-leaf is such that the pores in the wood are effectively sealed, and the wood is rendered more or less water resistant, even many years after the tree has been harvested.

If the face of a stump of a loblolly pine is examined, one will note that the most of it is composed of an outer type of wood, the sapwood, whereas the inner or heartwood forms a much smaller fraction of the entire tree. With the long-leaf pine, just the reverse is true: The heartwood makes up about 80 percent of the trunk. The heartwood of all pines is much stronger and more resilient than the sapwood.

In colonial times, a significant part of eastern North America was covered with forests of long-leaf pine, and it did not take the early pioneers long to find out that lumber from this beautiful tree made excellent building material. Consequently, most of the native stands of long-leaf pine have long been harvested, and, because it grows so slowly, no one bothers to replant it. The

170

long-leaf pine in harvestable numbers exists primarily today in national parks and forests and on a few old plantations in the South.

Several years ago when the Messicks' supply of long-leaf was all but exhausted, Wibbie and Corney made an expedition to the rural South in an attempt to locate a new supply of long-leaf heartwood. They were not too optimistic about their chances of success, and consequently were elated when they discovered, quite by accident, a considerable stand of the desired pine on a private plantation in Georgia. After explaining to the owner why they had to have some of his trees, a simple handshake sealed the deal with the gentleman, who supplies their needs today.

Each year, Corney and Wilbur make a trip to the plantation, taking precautions, I imagine, to assure they are not followed. They inspect the wood after it has been processed in a primitive sawmill; there, they have the prerogative of rejecting any piece of heartwood that has passed through the saw but does not meet their specifications—the grain might not be straight or a small knot might be present in the wood. Of course, they pay a premium price for the wood they finally select as being suitable for tong shafts. After the wood is chosen it is loaded on a tractor-trailer truck and transported to the Bivalve area, where it is stored in a barn and air-dried for one year.

When I visited the factory in the summer of 1985, Corney greeted me as I entered the door and said, "You chose a historic day to visit us, because we are finishing up the last pair of twenty-eight-foot tong shafts we will probably ever make." He went on to explain that, as far as they could determine, there were no more long-leafs remaining on the plantation in Georgia that were of sufficient size to yield shafts of that length. They had constructed six pairs of twenty-eight-footers for the 1985 season, and after these were gone, there would be no more. They can provide shafts from twelve feet in length to twenty-six, and in two-foot increments anywhere between. Most oystermen in the immediate area use shafts in the sixteen- to twenty-foot range, but those from the upper Bay, where the oysters are located in deeper water, need the longer shafts. There is a report of an oysterman near Rock Hall, Maryland, who tonged for years with a set of thirty-five-footers, but he did not acquire these huge sticks from the Messicks.

At the time of my visit, the brothers were putting as much time as possible into their shaft-making operation in preparation for the upcoming oyster season. Wilbur had taken his annual leave from the post office and Corney was devoting as much of his time as possible, between services at the funeral home, to establishing an inventory.

For the 1985-1986 oyster season the brothers charged the same for their implements as they had for the past several years— $6.50 a foot up to twenty feet and $7.00 a foot for those over twenty feet in length. Most oystermen coming to the Messicks for a set of shafts also want the head to go with them. The heads are made solely for the Messicks by a master blacksmith who lives in Pennsylvania but who was born in Bivalve and grew up with the brothers. Making the heads is also a part-time occupation for this craftsman, who manages to produce enough of the rakes to match the production numbers of the shafts. Each of the heads is an individual creation—in my opinion, a work of art—and was sold to the shaft makers for eighty dollars each in 1985. Corney explained that their friend had to raise his price from the previous year by five dollars because the price of the teeth he expertly welds on each side of the tooth bar had increased. The teeth, which are made of a specially hardened steel, cost more than all the rest of the metal he uses to make the head.

Two types of heads are available for attachment to the shafts. The so-called eelpot head is somewhat curved and, as the name implies, bears a superficial resemblance to a common type of trap used to catch eels. The other type of head an oysterman might request to have attached to his newly purchased shafts is called the "straight" or "Cambridge" variety. The eelpot type is slightly more curved on the bottom than the straight type and is preferred by oystermen working on hard bottoms. The straight head is said to be better for working on muddy bottoms. The cost of attaching a straight head to the shafts is ten dollars; it costs only eight dollars to affix the eelpot type. So, a twenty-foot set of Messick Brothers oyster-tong shafts (complete) cost the waterman $220 dollars dur-

The tong shaft factory in Bivalve. The structure is more than
a hundred years old and has been used by earlier generations of
Messicks as a funeral parlor, casket factory, and hat shop.

ing the 1985-1986 season ($130.00 for the twenty-foot shafts; $80.00 for the head; $10.00 for attachment of the head). Some oystermen buy new tongs each year whether they need them or not, but the majority of the watermen use their Messick shaft tongs for several years—five, ten, even fifteen years of hard use. The demand for these shaft tongs is great and almost always exceeds production. Smart watermen know it is wise to get their equipment from the Messicks early in the year, lest they be disappointed later on.

The demand for the Messick product grows each year as more and more oystermen come to realize that the brothers make the best shaft tongs available. Corney also relates that in the last few years he has seen their business grow because of first-timers entering the field. If a man loses his job and has difficulty finding another, it does not take too much of a capital outlay to go into the oyster-tonging business, providing he has access to some sort of suitable boat. Corney notes with a bit of amusement, however, that he rarely sells a second set of tongs to the neophyte oyster tonger. One season (or less) tonging is usually enough for those trying it for the first time.

Only Wilbur has ever tonged oysters for a living, and that was during the 1949 season when he "had nothing else to do." After thirty-six years, he fondly remembered his year of work on the water. Using only a small skiff, he was able to bring up about ten bushels a day. At the start of the 1949 season he recalls, the dockside price was $1.25 a bushel but rose to a top of $1.75 as the holiday season approached; $17.50 wasn't bad money in those days when, according to Wilbur, $10.00 would buy your week's groceries. After tonging for one season, he "took up carpentering" at $1.00 an hour and, at the end of a forty-hour week, he remembers he had more money than he has ever had since.

The late Ed Bedsworth of Nanticoke related to me once that in 1939 he tonged oysters for 25¢ a bushel, when he could sell them. When he was able to find a buyer, he made out all right as he claimed, "It wasn' no task atall to catch fifty or so bushel a day." And $12.50 cash money was certainly excellent wages for the depression year of 1939—many workers took a week to earn that much in other lines of endeavor. Bedsworth went on to tell of his experience in 1940. During the late summer of that year the oystermen became very excited when the word was passed along the river that oysters would bring 75¢ a bushel at the start of the season—maybe even going to $1.00 by Thanksgiving. New markets had opened up, and the buyers were willing to pay the unheard-of price to get the quantity of oysters they wanted. Ed was ecstatic when he dreamed of how he was going to spend all the money he would make that fall. But the first peace-time draft took place in September of 1940, and the first quota for Wicomico County, Maryland, was one able-bodied man. As luck would have it, Ed's number was drawn from the fishbowl, and he was duly inducted into the army just before the start of the oyster season. Years later, he told me that he was proud to have served his country for five years, "but I sure as hell hated to lose out on them 75-cent arsters while I was gone."

Corney and Wilbur worry a little bit about who will carry on the family business when they are gone. They recall that as young teenagers the responsibility was thrust into their hands when their father suffered a paralyzing stroke while in his early forties. By necessity, they took over the operation of the business and, aided by the experience they had gained working at their father's side, have continued it ever since. Corney has two sons and Wilbur one, but, according to the brothers, "The boys haven't shown too much interest in the business." They rationalize the situation, however, by remembering that the supply of long-leaf pine will probably be gone anyway by the time the boys would have to take over.

In the small hamlets of Bivalve, Tyaskin, Nanticoke, and Waterview the locals are fond of saying, "The Messicks will take care of all your needs. First they will sell you the widow-makers and, when you kill yourself tonging, they will see to it you are put away in the proper manner. Why, they will even sell you a tombstone to put on your grave to keep you from coming back to get them for selling you the tongs in the first place."

Dredging

By far the most efficient way to harvest oysters is to dredge them up from the bottom ("drudge," as every waterman I have ever known pronounces the word). The type of dredge most often used is a simple, triangular metal frame with teeth in the bottom to pry the oysters loose from the bottom, and a rope and chain net attached between the sides to retain them. Though there are many variations on the construction of the device, all "drudges" include the following parts: teeth, side bars, formers, whittlerrod, braces, and brail. At the point where the formers and side bars come together to form the nose, or nozzle, there is an opening called the eye. The eye serves as the point of attachment for the dredge line, or cable, from which the dredge is operated from the boat. As commonly used, the length of this line is about six times the depth of the water in which harvesting operations are being conducted.

The feature of the dredge that breaks up and gathers oysters from the bed is the bar or plate, which is equipped with the teeth on the front or attaching edge. Bolted to each bar are two rods, which give form, shape, and strength to the apparatus. Two of these are known as formers, and the others are side bars. The formers bend upward and forward, and are joined to the side bars to make the nose or nozzle. Parallel to the tooth bar is the brail, a small steel rod fastened at each end to the formers at points near the tooth bar, which it parallels, and to which it is attached in one or more places by metal links.

The whittlerrod connects the formers at the points where they straighten out and from which they run to the nose. Attached to the brail, whittlerrod, and the curved portions of the former is the bag, which catches the oysters as they are dislodged from the bar. The bag is typically constructed of chain and rope of about equal parts. A large link is attached to the upper and outer edges of the chain part of the bag to facilitate the dumping of the catch, which is done by hand.

The teeth are often modified to suit the type of bottom on which the dredge operates. The mud-bottom dredge usually has teeth about four inches long and set on a flat bar. If the bottom is hard—consisting of shell or rock—the teeth are about three inches long and set on a round-shaped bar. The so-called stone dredge has a flat metal plate affixed to the bar instead of teeth and is used in areas where there are large stones that would break the teeth of an ordinary dredge. Oystermen sometimes call this type of dredge a gummer because of its toothless condition. All of the variations of the dredge used in the Chesapeake region are characterized by the basic design shown in the illustration.

No one knows when the first dredge was invented, but it certainly was used in the eighteenth century and immediately became the cause of hostilities between hand-tongers and dredgers. Dredgers raked over beds usually reserved for hand-tongers, who couldn't retaliate because rocks reserved for dredgers were too deep for the tongs. Bloody battles between the tongers and dredgers were an accepted way of life for many years on and about the waters of the Bay (and still are to a limited extent). Eventually, the carnage led to the formation of the infamous "Oyster Navy" by the state of Maryland. This scandal-ridden organization eventually was abolished and replaced by the modern marine police force operating under the jurisdiction of the Department of Natural Resources.

Boats that dredge on public beds, by far the main source of the oyster supply in Maryland and Virginia, are required by law to be driven most of the time only by wind and sail power. The boats that dredge the public rocks are, for the most part, the famous skipjacks of the Chesapeake, of which only about thirty-two remain today. These vessels, most of which are quite old now, are wooden, rakish sloops which carry a small powerboat or yawl on the davits. The yawl is used to push the boat when power is needed to reach the oyster beds and the wind is not cooperative. However, as the law now stands, the yawl boat may be used to propel the dredge boat when it is actually catching oysters on Monday and Tuesday of each week during the season in most parts of the Chesapeake Bay system. The yawl is also used as a lifeboat in case of an emergency at sea in which the ancient skipjack must be abandoned.

The dredges are usually operated on both sides of the boat and are attached by cable to a power winder on the deck. Cables rather than chain or rope are used in this operation because their weight, strength, and low resistance to the water make it possible for them to take the dredge quickly to the bottom. The winders used in this activity are operated by a small gasoline-driven donkey engine located on the deck. Oystermen dredging their own

The Oyster

leased beds generally employ a power take-off from the engine of the boat to operate their winders. Dredge boats used on public rocks may not, of course, have an engine incorporated into their structure, so the cumbersome dredges must be raised by hand or by the auxiliary donkey engines.

The dredges used in the Chesapeake Bay are not allowed by law to measure more than forty-two inches between the outside teeth or weigh more than 200 pounds, except for the type used on mud bottoms, which may be forty-four inches between the teeth. In certain county or tributary waters open to dredging, the weight of the dredge is limited to 135 pounds. In no case, however, can there be a "diving device" attached to the dredge to take it down faster. Such devices cause the dredge to bite deeply into the bottom, disrupting the oyster community. The capacity, or gross tonnage, of the dredge boats also is regulated, with those in certain tributaries differing in size from those of other localities and of the Bay itself. Small dredge boats, however, are permitted to operate in the territory of bigger craft.

Oystermen learn to operate dredges by experience that is gained by an apprentice system; there is no formal school of oystering. The usual pattern is for the young, aspiring dredger to work for an experienced captain until he gains sufficient experience and knowledge to qualify as a captain for an owner or of his own ship. The crew of a skipjack generally consists of a captain, mate, cook, and three or four deckhands who do the dirty work of operating the dredges, two to a gear.

While the dredges are being pulled over the bottom, the crew culls the material brought up previously. The legal oysters are thrown into a pile on the side of the deck, and the culled material (undersized oysters, boxes, shells, and other items of bottom cultch) is unceremoniously dumped back on the bar from which it was originally taken. The mate and cook, by tradition, take turns at relieving the deck hands of this hard work, in addition to carrying out their special duties. The captain, of course, is in charge of navigating the boat and has the final say on which area is to be dredged and what method is to be used. In directing the overall operation, the captain's word is law, and if a crewman disagrees with a command decision, his only recourse is to seek a berth on another vessel.

Obviously, the financial success of the operation depends in large part on the decisions made by the captain, and skippers who have developed a reputation for finding and bringing home the "arsters" have a waiting list of individuals who want to sail with them. Typically, no salaries are paid to crew members; rather, the profits from the operations are divided on a predetermined percentage or share basis. The "boat" usually receives one share of what the oysters are sold for, and the remaining money is evenly divided among the members of the crew, including the captain. Crew members normally sign on with a given skipjack for the entire oystering season and are expected to be ready to go to sea whenever the captain decides the time is right—regardless of the weather or the area he has decided they will fish.

In bygone days, certain nefarious captains were known for their habit of paying off crew members "with the boom," but in all probability the number of such men was small indeed, and the stories of shanghaiing crew members, after plying them with alcohol and opiates in waterfront dens of iniquity, are also greatly exaggerated.

As previously mentioned, the number of skipjacks plying the waters of the Chesapeake has been greatly reduced. In fact, the youngest of these unique vessels, which represent America's last commercial fleet powered by sail, was built over forty years ago. In 1985, a majority of the vessels (seventeen) were berthed at Tilghman Island, and the remaining fourteen or fifteen called Chance or Wenona, on Deal Island, their home port. One cannot help but wonder how much longer these relict and sometimes derelict ships can continue to dredge for oysters. Sooner or later they will pass from the scene, and a unique chapter in the history of the Chesapeake Bay will be closed.

Dredging with a boat powered by means other than sail is, of course, permitted at any time on leased bottom. Power dredging is much more efficient than sail operations, as the operator who has complete control of his boat may systematically take all the oysters from a bed in a fairly short amount of time. The sailboat is

The Oyster

at the mercy of the wind, tide, and waves and is, in reality, no match for the powerboat.

When dredging on private beds, care must be taken to assure that the dredge not only scoops up the oysters efficiently but also that it not jump from one clump of oysters to another and break off the oyster's bills, or growing edges. Also, the operator on leased grounds cautiously avoids having a full dredge drag on the bottom, as the extra weight tends to disturb the oysters left there and press them into the muddy bottom. If too great a length of line is used, a dredge digs into the bottom and loosens up the surface, creating silt. When the cable is too short, the opposite effect is experienced in that the dredge slides over the tops of the oysters and none are taken. Experience is required to get the job done in a way that produces oysters and does not damage the bottom, but, under typical conditions, the rule of thumb is that the length of the dredge cable should be six times that of the depth of the water being worked.

Dredging for Seed Oysters. In Maryland, certain highly productive public oyster rocks are designated by the state as seed oyster areas and may be dredged for a short time during the regular season. Seed oysters are spat usually less than 1 inch in length and are harvested to be sold to lessees of private grounds or transferred, under state supervision, to public bars. The law says the state of Maryland may sell no more than 50 percent of seed oysters in excess of one million bushels produced annually in seed areas to citizens who hold valid leases of bottom. No less than the prevailing price for seed oysters of comparable quality in nearby states is to be charged. The "catch" in all of this is that one million bushels of seed oysters have not been harvested in Maryland for as long as almost anyone can recall. Consequently, all the young oysters taken up for transplanting have been placed on public beds. Individual ostraculturists, like Ken Lappe, must obtain seed oysters for their leased bottoms from Virginia or from individuals like Max Chambers at FLOMAX hatcheries.

Dredging for seed oysters is strictly controlled by the Department of Natural Resources, and the actual operations are closely supervised. Reseeding operations normally take place near the end of the regular oyster season and provide employment for the dredger who is about to put his boat and equipment away for the season. In some seed areas the spat are very numerous, yielding up to eight thousand per bushel, but in other areas the young bivalves are not as numerous due to decreased reproduction. Nevertheless, the oysterman usually makes good dredging for seed, as the areas designated for harvesting are frequently prehistoric oyster rocks with the shells of countless generations of oysters piled up to a depth of many feet. With several boats working the rock at the same time, the dredges break up the clusters of shells, making for easy pickings. The first oyster biologist of the Chesapeake, Francis Winslow, in the 1870s advocated the use of dredges on the large rocks to give the oysters room to grow. Oysters crowded together tightly have no room literally to "spread out" as their shells calcify and grow. These oysters develop into "snaps," which bring low prices at dockside.

All in all, most knowledgeable people believe the Maryland Department of Natural Resources's Tidal Fisheries Division is doing a fairly good job of managing the seed beds. They are responsible for building up the oyster bars with new shell as the old cultch material with the attached oysters is removed, as well as for picking up and distributing the young oysters as they develop. Most private propagators, however, would like to buy some of the seed from the state to plant on their leased bottoms. This has not been permitted in many years and the way things are going at present offers no change in policy in the foreseeable future.

Patent Tongs

Though no one knows when the first dredge was invented and used to catch oysters, the record clearly shows that patent tongs first came on the market in 1887. Essentially patent tongs are a larger version of the rakelike heads of the hand tongs but lacking the shafts. Patent-tonging is another method of taking oysters from water too deep for hand-tonging operations, and it is frequently practiced in areas where dredging activities are illegal, though it is not as efficient as the dredge.

Patent tongs consist of two opposed rakes, about forty inches between the outside teeth, fastened to iron handles or shafts as shown in the illustration. The line by which the tongs are lowered to the oyster bar below is attached to a bridle, some six feet in length, which runs to the eyes and is made fast to them. When the rakes on the bottom are in an open position, the line by which the apparatus is lowered is pulled by a series of sharp jerks. These yanks on the line force the rakes to scrape the oysters between them into the basket made by the two heads. The tongs are then raised to the deck of the boat by means of a power winder attached to a donkey engine, or by hand, and the contents are dumped on the culling board to be sorted.

To accomplish all of this, the line from the winder passes through a pulley at the end of a boom, which is connected to a short mast and around which it swings freely for a positioning effect. This type of rig makes it possible to swing the tongs out over the side of the boat as they are raised from or lowered into the water.

The crew of a patent-tong boat usually is made up of two men, one to handle the tongs and the other to cull the catch and operate the winder. A third crew member may be added if necessary. Patent-tong boats may be used in any depth of water but are most efficient in water twenty to forty feet deep. When used properly, patent-tonging is a very effective way to catch oysters, and the crew that knows what it is doing can easily take up to fifty bushels a day. For this reason, the areas in which patent tongs may be used are greatly limited by law. In general, patent tongs may be used legally in the Bay itself, in certain deep-water sections of the Patuxent River, and in a few other deep tributaries to the Bay. Patent tongs, however, are rarely used on the Chesapeake Bay itself because the boats used are generally too light for operations on open water.

Diving

Undoubtedly, diving for oysters has been a method of retrieving them from the bottom for a long period of time. In all probability, the Indians and some of the long-breathed early colonists found they could collect a considerable number of oysters in shallow water by diving beneath the surface and simply picking them up with their bare hands. But for some unexplained reason, the

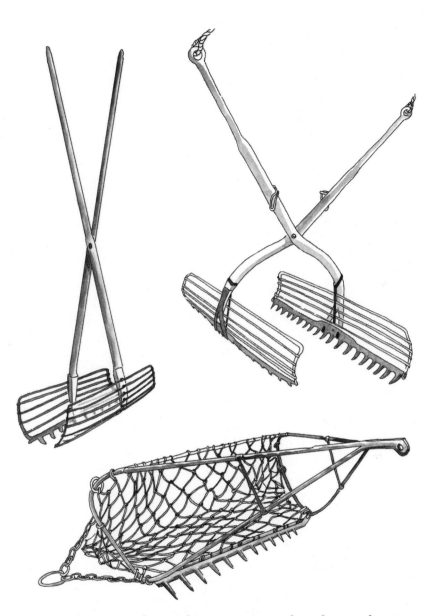

Basic equipment for catching oysters in the Chesapeake Bay.
Bottom: dredge; *left:* hand tongs; *right:* patent tongs.

The Oyster

practice of diving for oysters in earnest with scuba (self-contained underwater breathing apparatus) gear or surface-supplied air sources did not become popular until the 1970s. In 1981, it was estimated that at least forty full-time divers were engaged in harvesting oysters from the Bay without benefit of mechanical devices such as tongs and dredges.

As with anything that differs from established and traditional ways of doing things on the water, diving was regarded with suspicion by the tongers and dredgers when the first submariners appeared on the oyster beds. Afraid that this new method of catching oysters would somehow interfere with their method of making a living, the conventional oystermen did not exactly welcome the divers to the public rocks. Rumors to the effect that the divers would soon remove all the oysters from the public beds circulated widely, and open hostility between the two groups resulted, especially if the diving crew was not from the immediate area and was not known to the old-timers.

When underwater conditions are such that the diver can see exactly what he is doing, he naturally is going to collect the largest oysters he encounters. Tongers, noting the high percentage of big oysters in the basket bringing the diver's oysters to the surface, became more resentful of this new type of oysterman, who seemed to be able to catch the biggest and most valuable oysters from "their" beds.

As in the past when something seemed to threaten their way of life, the watermen turned to the Maryland legislature, and, with the considerable political clout they still manage to retain, secured the passage of certain laws and regulations that made it more difficult for divers to operate and make a profit. A law was soon put in force that set a 4-inch limit on any oyster taken by a diver (recall, a 3-inch minimum applies to all other operations), and a boat from which a diver worked was limited to a total catch of 30 bushels a day. A hand-tong boat, in contrast, is limited to 75 bushels a day, and a dredge boat may take as many as 150 bushels. The new regulations also decreed that each diver have at least one personal attendant on deck, and this individual also must have a license to catch oysters. No more than two divers are permitted to work from a single vessel, no matter how large the craft is.

184

Tonging, Dredging, and Diving

Power-assisted lifting devices used to haul the oysters to the surface are permitted, however, provided the total length of the cable or rope attached to the container does not exceed one hundred feet. In addition, the diver working on the bottom must only use his hands to gather the oysters. Rakes, scoops, shovels, and scrapes of any kind, which would facilitate the taking of oysters, are not permitted. Sometimes the marine police employ their own diver to check the procedures being used on the bottom to collect the oysters.

Mike Manning of Salisbury, Maryland, is a master diver and over the years has gained a vast amount of experience working on a variety of underwater projects in Ocean City. He and Captain Eddie Fooks of Talbot County decided in 1981 to try their hands at diving for oysters for profit. To Manning, this sort of diving in relatively shallow water to pick up oysters and place them in a basket seemed like an easy way to make a living. Usually, he was engaged in more exacting work in much deeper water, though he was employed occasionally by charter fishing boats. In this capacity, he would take the angler's line down, perhaps seventy-five feet to the bottom of the Atlantic, and dangle the bait in front of a prize bluefish or sea bass until the fish snapped up the bait to the delight of the fisherman on the boat above.

Though Manning is proficient with both scuba and surface-supplied air apparatuses, he chose to dive for oysters using the latter type of gear. Scuba divers must have six to eight tanks of air available when diving (each tank costs about two hundred dollars), and they must surface at least every hour and a half to exchange tanks. A surface-supplied air system can be completely assembled for about three hundred dollars, and the diver can remain submerged and working for several hours. Of course, the disadvantage of the surface-supplied system is the danger of fouling or cutting the air line with the propeller of the boat as the skipper moves the craft from spot to spot on the bar.

The captain and the diver obviously must work as a close team, and the man who goes under must have every confidence in the one who stays on the surface. Manning tells of the time he signed on with a captain who was known to "take a little nip now and then." On the first day of operations, Mike began to feel a little

185

The Oyster

uneasy when an empty pint whiskey bottle came down through the water to land near where he was gathering oysters into the basket. Shortly thereafter, the skipper severed the life-sustaining air line with the boat's screw as he was attempting to manuever to another location. Fortunately Mike was working in only twenty feet of water and was able to surface before his air supply was completely exhausted. The partnership was dissolved on the spot. No matter how trustworthy the man on top is, however, the diver must be prepared to take care of himself and to cope with any emergencies that may arise.

Working in warm water when the season first opens in September, Manning prefers to wear a 3/16-inch wetsuit with a full face mask. Later in the season, when the water temperature drops into the 50s, he switches to 1/4-inch wetsuit, again with a full face mask. The face mask is an absolute necessity to protect the diver from the stings of sea nettles. Mike relates the story of a young diver from Baltimore who submerged in the Wye River for the first time in quest of oysters, and, because he knew nothing about sea nettles, did not wear a protective face mask. In a short time he surfaced, writhing in agony from countless stings to the face. Temporarily blinded by the numerous nematocysts (stinging cells) embedded in his eyes, he was rushed to a local hospital, where he recovered in a few days.

As the oyster season progresses into winter and the water temperature dips into the 40s or 30s, Mike changes to a drysuit of neoprene rubber worn over a pair or two of thermal underwear. Even with this type of protection against the bone-biting cold of the water, the diver is uncomfortable when he first submerges. After going to work gathering oysters, however, he usually finds himself perspiring. There is no way around it—diving for oysters is hard work, in no way related to the romantic image projected by old movies about pearl divers in the South Pacific.

Under certain conditions, diving for oysters is a much more efficient way of catching them than tonging. In other circumstances, however, the tonger has the advantage. When oysters are concentrated in a relatively small area, or when the water is clouded with silt to the extent a diver must work more or less in the dark, the hand tonger can easily catch more oysters than a diver. But when the oysters are scattered over a relatively wide area and the water is clear enough for visual operations, the diver in the wet suit can do much better than his counterpart with the tongs.

As far as being able to make a living diving for oysters, Mike and his partner made good money during the fall of 1982, grossing up to a thousand dollars a week for an extended period of time. These wages did not continue, however, because after the densely populated rock they had been working in the Wye River had been depleted of its oysters, they experienced difficulty making five hundred dollars a week diving on bars with fewer oysters. In the usual diving operation, the income is divided equally between the captain and the diver, the boat receiving no share. Of course the man working under water does the lion's share of the work and takes most of the chances, but the re-sponsibilities of the man on top are many. He must cull the oysters sent up from the bottom and make sure none are kept that do not meet the minimum size requirement. He must also maneuver the boat systematically so the man below can cover every square foot of the area being fished, and he is, of course, charged with the responsibility of keeping the air supply flowing when surface-supplied air is used in the operation.

Most divers engaging in the oyster-catching business are, like Mike Manning, certified in their profession by either the National Association of Underwater Instruction (NAUI) or the Professional Association of Diving Instructors (PADI). Maryland law, how-ever, does not require a diver to be certified if he wants to go down for oysters. Requiring certification seems to me to be an absolute necessity, and I am frankly surprised that the state does not insist on at least some minimum amount of demonstrable skill on the part of the diver. Most dive shops that refill scuba tanks, in an attempt to protect themselves from lawsuits, will not perform this service for a noncertified diver.

Mike Manning can recall only one instance of an accident related to oyster diving in the Bay area. In 1982, a relatively inexperienced diver was working in the Wye River at a depth of about twenty-five feet when some difficulty with his air supply arose. After surfacing to rectify the situation, he resubmerged immediately and presumably resumed operations. About a half hour passed, and the man on top had received no indication of activity from below since the diver had gone under, so he decided to pull him up with the air hose. The diver was brought to the surface with his face mask missing and was determined to be dead. The autopsy results were inconclusive, and to this day no one really knows what happened. Mike speculates that the diver's air-intake apparatus may have been contaminated in some way with carbon monoxide gas from the fumes emitted by the engine of the air compressor, but others suggest that the diver lapsed into a state of unconsciousness after surfacing and then submerging almost immediately. A marine policeman I talked to regarding this tragedy reports that he had heard the carbon monoxide theory was proably correct.

In any event, divers being the special individuals that they are, Mike is ready to don the wetsuit again and resume oyster operations whenever a reliable captain with a boat and a proposition comes along.

A member of the new breed of oystermen at work.

CHAPTER NINE

Oyster Gallimaufry

Let us royster with the oyster—
in the shorter days and moister,
They are brought by brown September,
with its roguish final R;
For breakfast or for supper,
on the under shell or upper,
Of dishes he's the daisy,
and of shell-fish he's the star.
So welcome with September
to the knife and glowing ember,
Juicy darling of our dainties,
dispossessor of the clam!

Detroit Free Press
12 October 1889

DOWN through the ages, no animal as much as the oyster has piqued man's imagination and inspired the fascination and respect of naturalists, philosophers, artists, writers, and laymen alike. Because of the attraction oysters have for most people, it seems appropriate to consider some of the more common questions I am frequently asked about them and to review some of the facts and fallacies one frequently encounters as one—as the ditty goes—roysters with the oyster.

How Nutritious Are Oysters?

In addition to their delightful taste, the oyster is the most nutritious seafood eaten by man. In fact, few foods are better-balanced nutritionally than the oyster. Looking at a raw oyster, however, many may be inclined to dismiss its food value as minimal.

The Oyster

A general idea of the composition of the meat of *Crassostrea virginica* can be deduced from tables published by the United States Department of Agriculture for use by dieticians, physicians, nutritionists, and others involved in planning diets. These tables show, in spite of variations in the composition of oyster meat taken at different times from different locations, the order of magnitude of the three common foodstuffs (protein, carbohydrate, and lipids) is constant. The all-important proteins make up 50 percent or more of the meat, carbohydrates are less than 25 percent, and lipids (including fats) constitute less than 20 percent. In addition, all of the essential amino acids used by the body to construct human proteins are provided by the oyster.

Vitamins are various organic substances that are essential in minute quantities to the nutrition of most animals and some plants. Some vitamins are produced within the body, but the majority of them must be obtained from food. It has long been known that oysters are excellent sources of the following vitamins essential for good health in humans: A, B_1 (thiamine), B_2 (riboflavin), B_3 (niacin), C (ascorbic acid), and D (calciferol).

Proteins, carbohydrates, lipids, and vitamins are all organic substances required in the diet, but certain inorganic elements or minerals are also required for good human metabolism and overall physiology. Iron, copper, iodine, magnesium, calcium, manganese, phosphorus, and zinc are present in relatively large amounts in oyster meat. To secure the recommended daily allowance (RDA) of all of these substances, one has only to eat four or five medium-size oysters each day.

In addition to satisfying our nutritional requirements by eating oysters, we may be protecting ourselves from several bacterial organisms that, after gaining access to our bodies, may cause certain pathological conditions. Research in recent years has shown that some antibacterial agents are found in oysters and other shellfish such as the abalone, but the exact nature of these agents has not yet been determined. They have, however, been found to inhibit the growth of such pathogenic bacteria as *Staphylococcus*, *Streptococcus*, *Salmonella*, and *Shigella*. This discovery is of great potential importance, and, in fact, opens a new chapter of research into the role of naturally occurring antibacterial and antiviral agents.

Why Is There a Taboo against Eating Oysters in Months without an R?

Before the days of rapid transportation and refrigeration, oysters frequently spoiled before they were brought to market, and it is likely that people who ate them became ill and thought themselves poisoned. With modern transportation and refrigeration facilities, spoilage has been virtually eliminated and oysters may be consumed in relative safety during even the hottest months.

A still-valid reason oysters are not consumed in large quantities during the *r*-less months is because of their poor quality. As we have seen, the *r*-less months of the year correspond to the spawning period. Spawning is a massive physiological experience for an oyster, whether it be playing the role of male or female, and almost every iota of food taken in must be metabolized and used in the production of the great numbers of sperm and eggs generated by the reproductive process. After the gametes are discharged into the water, the oyster is a mere shadow of its former self—thin, watery, almost transparent, with nothing really to be proud of. When spawning ends in the fall, food material is directed to storage in the various organs of the body, and the oyster becomes plump and fat and ready for the market. There is no health reason why oysters cannot be eaten during the *r*-less months, but they are really not very appetizing at that time.

Oyster season in Maryland usually starts on or about September 15, and many oystermen and biologists firmly believe the opening day of the season should be delayed until the middle of October or the first of November. By then the oysters would have had a chance to get their metabolic process more in balance and bring a much better dockside price. If the opening date were delayed, oystermen, of course, would want the season for catching them extended a comparable amount of time in the spring.

During September and October of 1985 I frequently tonged my "free bushel" of oysters from the public rocks located in the

The Oyster

lower Nanticoke River (a citizen is permitted to take one bushel a day from the public rocks for his own use without purchasing a license), and I was disappointed with the quality of the specimens I caught. Oystermen were having trouble disposing of their catch taken during this period, and, when they were lucky enough to find a buyer, the dockside price was only eight or nine dollars a bushel.

Will Eating Oysters Enhance Your Love Life?

For as long as oyster lore has been recorded, the oyster's value as an aphrodisiac has been debated. Casanova supposedly gulped down several dozen raw oysters each time he embarked on one of his famous boudoir escapades, and Don Juan is reported to have relied heavily on the oyster to sustain the strength required by his amorous adventures. The ancient Romans firmly believed that if you ate oysters in great numbers you would live and love longer, and Galen (130–200), the noted Greek physician who was recognized as the "authority" on medicine until the Middle Ages, prescribed the use of oysters by both men and women whose interest in the opposite sex had waned.

As civilization advanced into modern times, scientists sought to establish some link between the oyster and human sexual potency. Whenever a myth or folk story or remedy has persisted for as long a time as this one has, there is usually a grain of truth in it, however small. In fact, many of the present-day remedies and therapeutic agents used in the practice of medicine are products of folk medicine used for hundreds of years.

Not so long ago biochemical researchers announced the "discovery" that oysters were rich in the essential component of protoplasm, cholesterol. This important lipidlike compound provides structural material for a variety of cell parts and furnishes the molecular building blocks for the manufacture of various hormones, including testosterone, the primary male sex hormone. At last, it was thought the answer to how the "magical powers" of the oyster worked was known. But alas, additional studies revealed that the data collected in the first analyses were incorrect. The truth is that the oyster possesses only a trace of cholesterol. As a

194

matter of fact, oysters are now suggested by the National Heart and Lung Institute as an ideal food to be included in low-cholesterol diets.

Zinc, one of the minerals associated with oysters, appears to have a special affinity for them and is taken up from the seawater in great quantities and stored primarily in the mantle and gills. Under certain circumstances, the meat of an oyster may contain more than twenty times more zinc than it does iron and copper combined. Zinc, in the opinion of many physicians and nutritionists, is the most important mineral in human physiology to come forward in recent years. The benefits of this element are too numerous to mention and many are still, apparently, unknown. Zinc appears to be essential for the metabolism of testosterone. Without enough of this powerful hormone sex cannot get into gear, and, when the supply of zinc is deficient, the hormone level is low. Other studies indicate that zinc is necessary for a healthy prostate gland in the male. This gland, closely associated with the male reproductive system, is responsible for secreting most of the seminal fluid that carries the sperm out of the body during ejaculation. When this gland is malfunctioning, sex is difficult. Urological investigations indicate that the prostate gland contains and requires more zinc than any other organ in the body if it is to function properly.

So it appears that at last the mythological and traditional aphrodisiacal properties of oysters have been affirmed, but controlled experiments designed to test the relationship of oysters and zinc to the love lives of humans have failed to reveal any clear-cut connection between the two, at least on a biochemical-physiological basis.

This is exactly what psychologists, sex therapists, and physiologists have been maintaining for decades—it's all in one's mind. If you think something works, then you can "work" yourself into a mental state where the involuntary nervous system takes over and directs certain physiological functions to occur. There seems to be no question about the matter of oysters extending and enhancing one's sex life, however, as far as many people are concerned. An eighty-one-year-old oysterman from near Crisfield, Maryland, with whom I am acquainted, married a woman fifty years younger than himself a few years ago. This man vehemently proclaims and insists that his ability to father three children with this spouse during a six-year period was due to the fact that he has eaten at least three dozen oysters each week during the entire period of his marriage.

Are Oysters Used for the Treatment of Other Disorders?

In ancient times, physicians recommended oysters for the treatment of almost any human malfunction from gout to kidney failure to indigestion. Anyone deficient in iron, which is essential for the production of hemoglobin, a shortage of which may cause a type of anemia, would do well to include oysters as a regular item of his diet. After all, oysters are better tasting than most of the iron-enriched pills or elixirs sold in drugstores. Some iron-fortified tonics, however, are formulated from a base of about 30 percent ethyl alcohol, and the regular user of such concoctions forgets to worry about his anemia because he feels so good after taking his medicine.

Another type of anemia, as well as other maladies such as goiter, is caused by an iodine deficiency. Seafood, especially oysters and other shellfish, is an excellent source of this important element. French ostraculturists learned more than fifty years ago that the iodine content of oyster meat can be artificially increased by placing living oysters in seawater to which free iodine has been added. In experiments in the great oyster-producing region of Arcachon on the southwestern coast of France in 1931 it was shown that the concentration of iodine could be increased to seven hundred times more than its normal value after live oysters were maintained for a day or two in water containing three milligrams of free iodine per liter of water.

In 1932 a commercial company in Bordeaux, France (just north of Arcachon), artificially produced what were termed "superiodized" oysters and advertised their beneficial effects in treating cases of anemia, goiter, and other disorders related to an insufficient amount of iodine in the diet. During the 1950s, when I lived in that region of France, an elderly gentleman who was my neighbor and friend routinely ate these iodine-loaded oysters on the advice of his doctor. Once he offered me one; I managed to swallow it only with great difficulty, because of the strong taste and smell of iodine. This type of therapeutic oyster may help build up the concentration of iodine in one's body, but it certainly will win no prize for its taste.

Because of the oysters' ability to amass certain minerals and chemicals in their tissues, this method of treating certain diseases and conditions of man might gain favor in this country, especially among the practitioners of naturopathic medicine.

What Are Some Other Nonfood Uses for Oysters?

Oyster shells have been used for many purposes in addition to providing the preferred type of cultch for the spatting of the juveniles.

In many parts of the South (especially in eastern Texas), back roads are paved with oyster shells, and Crisfield, Maryland, is said to be built on a foundation of untold numbers of shells. "Tabby," which consists of a mixture of ground-up oyster shells and cement, was a favorite building material in parts of the South for decades.

A Baltimore company uses oyster shells in the production of chicken feed. The finely pulverized shells are added to the regular food and provide an excellent source of calcium of which the birds require large amounts for manufacturing eggshell. Several other companies in the United States market finely ground oyster shell for human consumption for the same purpose, calcium being needed by humans for bone and tooth maintenance.

Oyster shells have long been used in the rubber industry as an "extender" in industrial rubber and roofing materials. The fine powder to which the shells are reduced leaves the finished product with a unique ability to maintain its elasticity and flexibility.

Lime, which is an infusible solid consisting of calcium oxide with magnesium, is extracted by burning from the calcium carbonate in the shells of oysters. The process is called "calcining" and is used with either oyster shell or quarried limestone. When the shells are burned at high temperatures, the resulting ash is lime and is used industrially in the manufacture of steel and other products such as plaster wallboard. Lime is also used to maintain the proper acid-alkaline balance of farmlands and gardens.

In Maryland, burning oyster shell for use as an agricultural fertilizer (that is, lime) has been prohibited by a series of laws dating back to 1836.

Is It Dangerous to Eat Oysters and Partake of Alcoholic Beverages at the Same Time?

Many people believe it is dangerous to one's health to eat oysters, especially while they are alive in the raw state, and imbibe fermented beverages at the same time. Supposedly, however, gin, white wine, and champagne are compatible with oysters, quickly dissolving them and assisting in their digestion. On the other hand, whiskey, red wine, vodka, cognac, and schnapps are thought to fossilize oysters, turning them to stone instantaneously. Such a digestive malfunction would certainly be injurious to the alimentary system and most assuredly result in a bad case of indigestion.

Apparently this myth became so prevalent in England some years ago that the ancient, respected committee charged with maintaining the quality of Scotch whiskey and prompting its use decided to conduct an investigation of the matter. After considerable research, the committee issued a report stating that there was no truth to the superstition that Scotch whiskey turned oysters to stone.

Feeling that the report of the Scotch committee might be somewhat prejudiced, I decided to conduct my own investigation of this phenomenon. Into a shot glass of each of several beverages (gin, Scotch, bourbon, blended whiskey, white wine, and vodka), I dropped a large *Crassostrea virginica* that I had shucked from its shell only moments before. Nothing unusual happened to the test specimens, even after three hours in the various liquids; neither did they dissolve in the gin or white wine nor did they petrify in the whiskeys or vodka. There was really no point in my making the test with the white wine or cognac as I had performed this "experiment" countless times during the period I resided in France and already knew what the results of the test would be.

It should be reported, however, that the ethyl alcohol, which is the same chemical in all alcoholic drinks, did preserve the tissues of the test specimen in all but the wine experiment. The "hard liquors" contained about 40 percent alcohol, which is just a little less than the concentration of the material used by museum preparators to preserve zoological specimens. Though the oyster's tissues were fixed (meaning the water in the cells was replaced by the alcohol), they certainly did not turn to stone. One can see, however, how the myths originated. Hard liquors with their high concentration of alcohol preserved the oysters indefinitely while wine with a much lower concentration of the preservative failed to fix the tissues. Eventually, the oysters dissolved away through bacterial decomposition. All of this does not, however, explain the belief that oysters dissolve in gin.

Opening, or Shucking, Oysters

For as long as man has been eating oysters he has been devising new and better ways to pry open the shell. It is a difficult task at best, and it is not surprising that not one person in a thousand knows how to open an oyster. The skilled shucker who performs this arduous task with speed and skill is a constant source of amazement and admiration to the uninitiated.

The professional shucker is a vanishing breed, and the proprietors of packinghouses are concerned about where the next generation of shuckers will come from to replace the present aging work force. As a rule of thumb, about 250 medium-size oysters measure a gallon in volume, and some professional shuckers are capable of producing as many as ten gallons of oyster meat during an eight-hour period. Looking at these figures another way, we find the talented shucker can open 2,500 oysters during the work day, or a little over 300 per hour—truly amazing figures, especially for those of us who struggle to shuck three or four dozen in an hour's time.

The Oyster

The preferred method of opening oysters often depends on the geographical location, with each oyster-producing area developing its own technique as well as the shucking implements to do the job. In the region of the Chesapeake Bay, three methods are generally employed in this tedious process.

Stabbing Method.   In any type of procedure used to open oysters, the hands must be protected from both the ragged (and often razor-sharp) edges of the shells as well as from the blade of the shucking knife itself. Thick rubber gloves are usually worn by any shucker who is opening more than a few oysters. Though care must be taken with any method to prevent piercing the palm or wrist or the hand, the stabbing technique offers the greatest danger in this regard.

1. Brace the oyster with your gloved left hand on a nonslip surface such as a wooden board, with the flat side of the oyster up. The widest part of the oyster faces the shucker, and the hinged end is wedged against a cleat of some sort to prevent slipping. Sometimes a depression is gouged out of the holding board into which the enlarged, bottom shell is nestled.

2. With a series of clockwise and counterclockwise twists of the wrist, the point of the knife is worked between the edges of the two shells until slight penetration is accomplished.

3. After the seal is broken, the blade is inserted fully into the oyster, and the left hand moves it sideways until the adductor muscle (sometimes called the "eye" of the oyster) is severed. A release of tension will be felt when the muscle has been cut.

4. Turn the oyster over in the same motion of the left hand and cut the muscle as close as possible to its point of attachment on the remaining half-shell.

The Chesapeake Stabber knife is used for this type of operation.

Cracker Method (Billing or Breaking).   This method is far less dangerous to the shucker than the stabbing technique, and is the one I use. Its major disadvantage is that bits of shell frequently

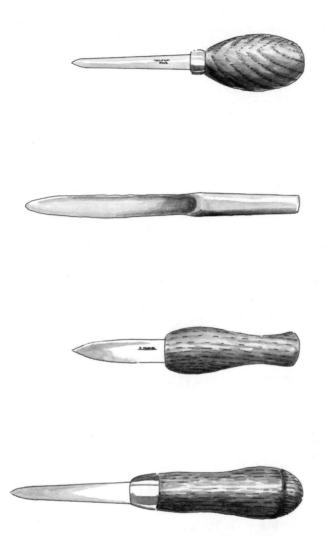

Various types of shucking implements.
From top: Chesapeake stabber; Crack knife; New Haven blade;
Southern or Galveston knife.

The Oyster

find their way into the shucked oysters and may play havoc with the teeth.

1. Grasp the oyster in your left hand (deep shell down and flat shell up) and place it on a block of wood or iron rail with the bill or edge of the shell protruding slightly over the edge of the block.

2. With a small hammer break off the edge of the bill (some individuals prefer not to employ a block and hammer but simply break off the bill with a pair of pliers while holding the oyster in the left hand).

3. With the edge of the shells broken off, the insertion of the knife into the interior is accomplished more easily than in the stabbing technique.

4. Work the knife back and forth to sever the adductor muscle on one valve. Flip the oyster over and repeat the procedure to cut the muscle attachment on the other shell. Using the knife as a lever, pry the shells apart.

The stabbing knife, or the Southern or Galveston knife, is used in the cracker method. Remember, be careful to remove bits of shell and other detritus that may make their way inside during the cracking operation.

Hinge Method. This means of opening the shells requires a significant amount of pressure and is generally not used in shucking houses or restaurants. The short, stubby New Haven knife is best suited to the process of hingeing an oyster.

1. Grasp the wider end of the oyster in the palm of the left hand after providing extra protection for the hand with a towel.

2. Break the hinge, or ligament, of the oyster's shells by pressing the point of the knife into the center of the dark material located between the two shells.

3. With considerable force, press down on the blade of the knife; the lid (the upper shell) should pop open.

4. Sever the adductor muscle attachment on the upper shell, which should be apparent. Working under the oyster, the muscle is cut from the lower shell.

Oyster Gallimaufry

For over one hundred years, men have been trying to devise machines or other apparatus to overcome the tremendous strength in the oyster's adductor muscle—to avoid using a knife in one of the methods just described. To date, however, I know of no oyster-shucking machine ever devised that has gained acceptance, even on a limited basis. This may change, however, in the near future.

When I arrived on the Eastern Shore of Maryland in 1971 to teach at Salisbury State, I soon met a biologist stationed at the Seafood Laboratory of the Maryland Department of Natural Resources in Crisfield. He quickly informed me that he had been working on an oyster-shucking device (using laser rays) for the last five years and was very close to achieving success. In 1977, he was still working on his machine when he was transferred by the department to another project at a different location. While looking through the extensive newspaper files of the library of Salisbury State, I noticed a series of articles from the 1960s concerning the invention of an oyster-opening machine by an individual on the upper Eastern Shore. One item carried a series of photographs depicting the inventor proudly showing off his brainchild to some state and local politicians, but as far as can be determined this "Super-Dooper-Oyster-Shucker," as the infernal machine was called in the newspaper, was never put to successful commercial use.

Apparently the use of lasers to shuck oysters has not been abandoned; in April 1984 an article appeared in a Salisbury newspaper describing the efforts of a physics professor at the University of Maryland Eastern Shore to achieve with these rays what his predecessor at Crisfield had failed to do. The physicist described his research on oysters and lasers: "Laser heating of the shell from the outside detaches the adductor muscle from the inside. Once the adductor muscle is detached, the upper half shell springs open leaving the raw oyster alive in the lower half." All of this sounds wonderful, but to date no commercial application of the professor's method has been forthcoming.

Seemingly, faculty members of the University of Maryland have become quite interested in the process of oyster shucking

203

The Oyster

the easy way. In the April 1984 issue of *Science Digest* magazine an electrical engineer at the College Park campus of the university announced that he had invented a way to open oyster shells by the use of microwaves. In fact, it was stated that a patent for a microwave oyster burster had been granted to the university. Using electromagnetic impulses to penetrate the tissues, water molecules are set in violent motion. The device is a hand-held apparatus and has a small loop antenna. When properly positioned against the shell, microwaves bombard the adductor muscle which, in a matter of seconds, heats up and literally explodes in a cloud of steam. The remainder of the oyster remains cold and raw, but the inventor cautions that if you gobble up the oyster immediately you may sense a warm spot or two. The device is designed for use of the individual, shucking houses, and taverns and should be on the market sometime in 1986.

Oysters as Pets

Oysters may be brought into the home and easily established in a salt-water aquarium. Along with the commensal animals living on their shells, they make an interesting exhibit for study or display and are guaranteed to be quite useful in stimulating conversation with uncommunicative visitors and guests.

To establish your artificial oyster rock you will need:

1. Five-gallon fish tank

2. Eight pounds of limestone or calcite chips

3. Sixty-watt aquarium illuminator or gooseneck lamp

4. Four gallons of water from the source of your oysters, or a package of sea salts (available at fish shops) sufficient to prepare four or five gallons of salt water. Try to have the salt concentration of the tank approximately the same as the water from which your oysters were taken.

5. Two oysters with unwashed shells. A ten-gallon tank will support four oysters, and a twenty-gallon aquarium will hold six.

Wash the limestone or calcite thoroughly in plain water (no soap or detergent should be used) to remove the fine dust usually adhering to it, and, after thorough cleaning, arrange it in the tank to create a slight slope from rear to front. After the salt water is added, let the setup stand for two days before introducing the oysters; this permits the water to clear.

The oysters you select as your pets should be obtained from an oysterman as soon as possible after he has tonged them from the bottom. They should not be washed off or scrubbed with a brush—the muddier the better—as the natural algae they will use as food and many of the commensals residing on the shells will be destroyed by cleaning. After the oysters are placed in the tank, cover the tank with a sheet of window glass to protect it from pollutants.

Use the light for a minimum of twelve hours each day during the first two weeks of operation of the tank to promote the growth of the all-important algae. (An inexpensive timer is useful in this respect.) After the algae have established themselves, the light may be operated for a period of only eight hours a day, but make sure that the tank receives light every day.

An artificial filtering system such as recommended for most aquariums should not be used. Remember, your oysters are natural filters and secure their food by trapping the tiny plants on their gills. A small aerator may or may not be used. If algae accumulate on the walls of the tank (this is a healthy sign) they should be scraped free with a razor blade and allowed to float about within the tank to be ingested by the oysters and some of the commensals.

A week or so after the tank has been established your oysters will become adapted to their new surroundings and begin to feel at home. They will begin to entertain you with their feeding process when the valves open slightly, and a distinct stream of water will be observed passing through their bodies. Occasionally, they will snap the valves shut to expel any accumulated waste material or fecal matter. A gentle tap on the side of the aquarium with the finger will result in the oysters quickly closing their valves, and similar reactions from the commensal guests.

In all probability, ghost anemones, polychaete worms, barnacles, and a host of other animals mentioned in "Life on the Oyster Bar" will have been brought in with the oysters. If you are lucky, there might even be some young oyster spat growing on the shells

The Oyster

of the larger specimens. These other diverse members of the animal kingdom are frequently even more entertaining and educational to watch than the oysters themselves. The commensals' food requirements are met by the frugal use of commercial preparations of suspended particles of proteins, carbohydrates, and fats designed for use in marine aquaria. These concoctions are available in tropical fish stores or pet stores. In addition to supplying the nutritional requirements of the commensals, these food materials will also be used by the oysters.

Decorative plants and salt-water fish should be avoided. The fish will disturb the oyster's commensals, and the plants will inhibit the growth of the algae required by the oysters.

Prospecting for Gold and Other Things

In 1972 a University of Maryland scientist was performing routine analyses of oysters taken from the Chesapeake Bay when an unidentified heavy metal appeared in one of his test tubes. After completing additional tests, the scientist determined the mysterious element to be gold, in a concentration of 1.68 parts of gold per million parts of oyster—certainly not enough to cause a new gold rush to the waters of the Chesapeake. The same batch of oysters tested also yielded a significant amount of the heavy metal mercury, which was not too surprising, as residues of mercury are frequently introduced into the Bay with pollution from manufacturing processes. The concentration of this dangerous element was found to be 1.3 parts of mercury per million parts of oyster.

Word of the discovery of these alien substances in Bay oysters was leaked to the press, and rumor has it some individuals did seriously consider going oystering to recover the gold. Other people were concerned about eating oysters that may have these heavy metals present in their tissues. The Maryland State Health Department quickly quieted these fears by announcing that a 150-pound human would have to eat thirty oysters a day for an indefinite period before he would amass an amount of these metals in his body that was generally regarded as being unsafe. The university researcher freely admitted that he had no idea where the gold in the oysters came from, but added that, like mercury, the gold could have originated as a by-product of some manufacturing process, the dregs of which had been illegally dumped into the waters of the Bay. This explanation seems more likely than the story that circulated declaring that the "pay dirt" in the oysters had entered the waters of the Bay from an undetected vein of gold, a real mother lode, located somewhere along the Susquehanna River in Pennsylvania.

As noted earlier in this chapter, the ability to accumulate various elements present in seawater at very low concentrations is common to many marine invertebrate animals, especially the filter-type feeders. Of particular interest is the proven ability of many bivalves to amass several of the heavy metals such as zinc, iron, manganese, copper, lead, and arsenic. Finding measurable amounts of gold and mercury adds a new dimension to this subject, because in polluted coastal waters shellfish may store these substances in concentrations dangerous to human health. Public health officials in the heavily industrialized states of New York and New Jersey have been aware since 1928 that oysters taken from the waters bordering their states had, on occasion, contained lethal amounts of arsenic trioxide and several compounds of lead. Though oyster beds in the Chesapeake system have frequently been closed because of bacterial or viral contamination, I know of no instance where beds had to be placed off-limits because of contamination with dangerous metals. The possibility of this occurring, however, is ever present, and routine tests made by public health officials in Maryland and Virginia should include procedures and methods to detect the presence of heavy metals.

Pesticides

Oysters, which are continually pumping water through their bodies, are excellent bioassayers and can be used to measure the amount of pollutants entering a given aquatic ecosystem. For example, it has long been known that oysters had a special affinity for DDT. Studies performed on oysters living in Long Island Sound in an area adjacent to a salt marsh that had been sprayed heavily for mosquito control with this persistent compound clearly showed that the oysters concentrated the toxicant in their tissues. The DDT content of the water in which the oysters resided was in the neighborhood of one-tenth part DDT to one billion parts of water, an infinitesimal amount. Detailed studies showed, however, that oysters with no DDT in their bodies when placed in the environment would accumulate seventy thousand times the amount of chemical in the water in a period of only thirty days. After a month's exposure to one-tenth part per billion of DDT, the oysters were found to contain seven parts per billion of DDT, a dangerous amount.

Studies such as the ones performed in Long Island Sound were repeated in other parts of the country with similar results, and the data thus accumulated played a significant part in the banning of DDT and other persistent pesticides in the early 1970s for routine use in the United States.

Radiation

At least once in the not too distant past oysters have been used to detect another type of environmental pollutant—radiation. Apparently the filtering mechanisms of their bodies serve to concentrate various types of radioactivity in the tissues, which may be monitored quite easily. In 1962 a merchant nuclear-powered ship, the *Savannah*, docked at Norfolk, Virginia, and the local authorities were concerned that some sort of dangerous radiation was being emitted to the waters of the harbor.

Knowing of the sensitivity of the oyster for gamma and other types of ionizing radiation, the Virginia State Health Department suspended bags of oysters over the sides of the pier at which the vessel was moored. After a time the hard-shelled detectives were retrieved and shipped off to a laboratory of the Atomic Energy Commission for testing. As far as can be determined, no report of the lab findings was made known to the general public.

Fossil Oysters

Ancestors of *Crassostrea virginica* are to be found in two locations in Maryland. The oldest specimens are easily collected along a little stream known as Back Branch, which sparkles and winds its way through southern Prince Georges County, three miles west of Upper Marlboro. Though this location is about a dozen miles from the Bay, geologists tell us that sixty million years ago during the Eocene era the site was actually the original floor of the sea.

The ancient fossilized oysters are numerous and lie partially buried in the sand and pebbles that make up the bottom of the stream. They are rather large specimens, measuring 4 to 6 inches in height. The usual color of these ancient rocks is gray on one side and dirty white on the other; some are as hard as flint or chert, but others may be crumbled easily into a paste by squeezing them between the fingers. Paleontologists give these extinct bivalves the generic name of *Ostrea,* and in the publication *Maryland Geological Survey—Eocene,* these oysters from Upper Marlboro are described as "an early ancestor of the modern Chesapeake Bay oyster." Be that as it may be, the fossil species exhibit one marked difference from today's oysters. The thickness of the shells is several times greater than the shells of modern oysters.

Another prime fossil-hunting area in Maryland is the Calvert Cliffs, which have attracted both amateur and professional fossil hunters for over 150 years. These palisades stretch for a distance of thirty-five miles and edge the western shore of the Chesapeake Bay from Drum Point north to Fishing Creek. The cliffs form the rim of a section of what was once the bottom of the Bay, uplifted during the eons of time and thrust as high as two hundred feet above the water's edge. Layers of the Pleistocene, Miocene, and Eocene periods make up the formations comprising the cliffs, with outcroppings of the Miocene being by far the most common. The Miocene period dates back about twenty-five million years, and the fossil record of life during that era is clearly written in the rocks of the cliffs. Among the fossilized shark teeth, fish bones, starfish, seals, whales, snails, and porpoises are numerous genera and species of bivalves, including *Ostrea.* These fossil oysters are about thirty-five million years younger than the ones from the Eocene of Upper Marlboro, but they are quite similar in structure and can be placed in the genus *Ostrea.* The thickness of the shells, however, is more or less intermediate between the condition found in the modern *Crassostrea* and their older cousins.

In any event, the original inhabitants of these fossil shells certainly never perked up the menu at a primeval oyster roast. In

The Oyster

Eocene and Miocene times even the earliest ancestors of man had not yet appeared on the face of the earth. It's probably just as well. The edible portion was much smaller than a modern oyster, and, if the massive thickness of the shell is any indication, shucking one of these oysters would have been a prodigious undertaking.

Freezing Oysters to Bring Out the Taste

Yes, it is possible to make oysters ("heaven on the half-shell," as they are sometimes called) more perfect. To do this the oyster is carefully chilled until about one-third of the free juices inside freeze. The part of the oyster "liquor" (which is made up almost entirely of the blood of the mollusk) to freeze first is almost pure water, and the remaining juices are saltier, with a higher concentration of the essences that give the oyster its distinctive taste. The freezing process must be done slowly, using equilibrium conditions, as the physical chemists say, or a thick magma of ice crystals will form, and this adds nothing to the taste. This method can be used to "Chincotize" an oyster out of water, if we may be permitted to coin a new word, but complete freezing should be avoided. Oysters that have been frozen for any length of time lose much of the taste for which we eat them in the first place.

What Substances Give the Oyster Its Characteristic Taste and Aroma?

Over twenty years ago two research biochemists at the University of Wisconsin analyzed the substances in oysters that are responsible for their taste and smell before and after cooking. This study was performed as part of a much broader program designed to track down the flavoring substances found in a variety of foods. The alchemists brewed up a batch of fresh oysters in boiling water and passed a stream of nitrogen gas through the mixture. The gas was exposed to certain indicator solutions, and the following chemical compounds were identified: dimethyl sulfide, methyl mercaptan, hydrogen sulfide, ammonia, diacetyl, and simple carbonyl compounds. The most abundant and readily identifiable compound was dimethyl sulfide, which was also found in fresh, uncooked oysters, but in smaller amounts. We can assume the characteristic aroma and the resulting taste of an oyster are caused by a combination of these chemical compounds acting in concert with each other, but in extremely low concentrations.

Most people are familiar with the smell of hydrogen sulfide (rotten eggs), but the aromas of its organic derivatives are not so well known. Dimethyl sulfide and methyl mercaptan are readily formed from hydrogen sulfide, and their odors are incomparably worse than that of the parent compound. Being of a higher molecular weight, they are heavier and more clinging and are considered by organic chemists to be the standard reference substances for illustrating the extreme limits of the human nose in odor detection. A chemistry professor at Salisbury State College commented on the smell of these compounds: "It takes a brave investigator to jeopardize his social standing by undertaking the study of the organic derivatives of hydrogen sulfide." Somehow, the oyster uses these extremely aromatic compounds to come up smelling like an oyster.

Goodbye to the Buy-Boat

The buy-boat is a facet of life on the Chesapeake that has become as extinct as the log canoe, and I wonder if the skipjack will soon not be placed in the same category.

The buy-boat served a definite need of both oyster catchers and processors until the middle 1960s. These large-capacity vessels would put to sea from the major oyster-processing ports of Crisfield, Baltimore, and similar sites, located primarily along the Rappahannock River in Virginia, to buy oysters directly from the oystermen working on the water. They came into existence to save time, but the truck that made steamboat traffic along Maryland's rivers and the Bay obsolete did the same thing for the buy-boats. The tongers and dredgers now unload their catch directly into trucks that back up to the dockside.

In the old days, a buy-boat would arrive on the oyster beds in the early afternoon, and the oystermen would be distressed if only one boat made an appearance. This meant they would be compelled to sell their oysters for the price the captain of the buy-boat was willing to pay that day. If two or more buy-boats arrived on the scene, competition would result. If one buyer appeared to be taking on most of the oysters from the tongers, the captain of another boat would hoist a bushel basket to the top of his mast (remember, this was in the days before citizen-band radios). This meant he was willing to pay five cents more per bushel than his competitor. If the oyster boats seemed to drift over to that buyer to take advantage of the new price, the first skipper might hoist two baskets to signal he was upping his price by another five cents. This bidding for the oysters did not get out of hand, however, as the buyers never raised more than three or four baskets during an afternoon.

The watermen would tie up to the buy-boat, and the skipper would give them a number that indicated the order in which they would be unloaded. A boom would swing a metal tub over to the tonger's craft to be shoveled full of oysters. The tub was a so-called "twenty-one-incher," named for the distance measured from the bottom of one side of the receptacle to the top of the other side. It became generally agreed among oystermen and buyers alike that a tub of this dimension would be used, and it was known as a Maryland bushel.

As the oysters were dumped into the hold of the buy-boat (some could carry up to eight hundred bushels or more) the captain would record each bushel by making a vertical mark on his tally board under the tonger's number. The tally board was usually a piece of sawed-off scrap lumber, and when five bushels had been transferred a diagonal mark was made through the four upright ones to present a figure as indicated: ₦₦. When the oysters were unloaded to the buy-boat, the watermen would be paid on the spot with cash, and the tally board would be used by the captain as a bill of lading to receive his payment when he unloaded at the processing plant. The word of the captain that the tally board was correct was accepted by the plant and the oysters were not measured again.

Sometimes a few oystermen would engage in a practice known as "cribbing," which involved various manipulations designed to place less than a Maryland bushel in the tub. If they were detected and if repeated warnings by the captain of the buy-boat

A buy-boat, or runner, formerly used on the Chesapeake Bay.

The Oyster

were ignored, the oystermen were apt to find themselves
"hawsed" the next time they attempted to sell to that particular
boat: The captain of the buy-boat would throw back the mooring
line the oysterman would cast to him as he came alongside and
attempted to tie up prior to unloading. Throwing the mooring line
back unmistakably indicated that the oysterman was ostracized by
that buy-boat, and usually by others working the same area after
the word had spread.

The same sort of thing happens today with crabbers and their
buyers. If a deceiving crabber tries to cheat the buyer by placing
number 3-grade crabs (females, or males called "white-bellies") in
the bottom of a bushel basket supposed to hold number 1-grade
crabs (prime, large, hard male crabs, or "Jimmies"), he will soon
find himself without a market. Frequently, these renegade crabbers will be encountered near the buying station, where they
attempt to induce other crabbers to sell their catch for them. Even
though a commission fee of several dollars per bushel may be
offered by the outcast, few legitimate watermen will run the risk of
being blacklisted themselves for selling someone else's crabs.

In the fall of 1980 I was sitting on the bulkhead in Bivalve
Harbor when a strange-looking boat steamed into the inlet. An
old-timer with whom I was passing the time of day said to me,
"Take a good look at that one, it may be the last buy-boat you will
ever see." It was, indeed, a buy-boat named the *Henrietta
Hearne,* with no home port indicated on the stern. My friend said
the *Hearne* used to ply the waters of Pocomoke and Tangier
sounds buying oysters primarily for plants located in Crisfield, but
he had not seen the boat in twenty years. The vessel carried a crew
of two, who proceeded to dock the boat along a portion of the
public mooring area, get into a pickup truck, and drive away. The
Hearne was leaking badly as the pumps worked continuously,
ejecting several large streams of water from the hold, and one
could readily see she was listing to the port side. The next morning
I returned to the harbor and found the *Hearne* reposing on the
bottom in eight feet of water, and she remained in this semisub-
merged state for about a month. Then one day a crew with several
large pumps arrived on the scene and refloated her. Late in the
afternoon of the same day a tugboat churned into the harbor, and

after making fast to the *Hearne*, unceremoniously towed her out of the harbor and into the setting sun. To this day, I still wonder what was the eventual fate of the once proud *Henrietta Hearne*.

CHAPTER TEN

Epilogue

A GENTLE west wind was blowing one warm, cloudless autumn morning as Officer First Class Bill Price of the Maryland Natural Resources Police maneuvered the sixteen-foot Whaler out of Nanticoke Harbor. As we cleared the breakwaters, he called to me to hold on as he shoved the throttle of the powerful outboard engine to full ahead. The patrol boat literally leaped out of the water as we headed up river to begin a routine patrol of Officer Price's area of responsibility. Having had Bill as a student in a biology class at Salisbury State College some years before, I was delighted to discover that he had become a marine policeman and was assigned to the area of the Eastern Shore where I lived. When he suggested I might find it interesting to accompany him on his rounds, I eagerly accepted the invitation.

As we approached a vast public oyster bar, known to the oystermen as Wilson Shoals, we noticed eight to ten boats working the area. Most of the boats contained two men, a tonger and a culler, but in two of the vessels women were performing the demanding task of culling. A lot of responsibility lies on the shoulders of the culler, so this individual must be an experienced oyster person. He or she decides which oysters are to be tossed into the "keeper" pile to be retained and which are to be returned to the bar.

A culler frequently taps an oyster with the culling hammer, checking to determine if the oyster is, in reality, a box—a dead oyster with the shells still closed. The hollow sound produced by the hammer against the shell is distinctive and identifies most boxes to the culler's ear. But if the shells have been infiltrated with mud, it is next to impossible to determine if you are dealing with a live or dead oyster. The culler also must be careful to separate any undersized specimens from legal oysters. Any miniature specimens adhering to a keeper will be counted in the 5 percent margin of error if, in the opinion of an inspecting officer, they could have been separated without inflicting permanent damage. A good, careful culler is a valuable member of an oyster crew, and the workboat captain who finds one of these individuals does everything he can to keep him happy and retain his services. In the final analysis, if a violation is found, it's the boat captain and not the culler who must pay the fine and have the black mark made on his record (unless, of course, the captain does the culling).

The workboat crews saw the patrol boat approaching when we were still at least a mile away, and as I observed them through the powerful binoculars, I could see the message that "The Man" was coming being transmitted from boat to boat. As we made fast to the gunwale of the first boat to be checked, the oysterman and Officer Price exchanged pleasantries. Questions about the health of the family, how the boat engine was performing after the recent overhaul, and the quality and quantity of the oysters being caught were bantered back and forth in a spirit of friendship and cordiality. Not once did Bill say anything like, "I am here to check your catch to determine if you are in violation of the law," but everyone, of course, knew why he was there.

While these exchanges were taking place, Price's trained eyes were inspecting the boat and its catch. By making a visual examination of the pile of culled oysters in one end of the boat, he could determine that the 5 percent law had not been violated. By observing other telltale signs he could also determine with a reasonable degree of certainty that there was no false bottom in the boat or other secret storage area where illegal oysters could be stashed. He used the same procedures as he checked the other boats working the beds—it's either check all boats in an area or none at all to indicate that no favoritism is shown.

As we went from boat to boat the disconcerting news crackled over the citizen-band radios that the dockside price that day would be eight dollars per bushel, down a dollar from the deflated price of nine dollars that had been holding for the past week or so.

Epilogue

One oysterman lamented that this time last year the dockside price had been thirteen dollars per bushel, with buyers anxious to acquire all the oysters they could get. Also, the rumor was spreading via the aquatic grapevine that there would be no market at all the next day or so for the remainder of the week. Where would the money come from to buy a new set of tongs to replace the set which had been broken? How could one get together enough money to meet the boat payment and the house mortgage? Would "they" repossess the pickup truck now that two payments had been missed? These questions and more must have been going through the minds of the tongers; they managed to present an outwardly calm image, but when I looked into their faces their eyes betrayed them.

Fortunately, no one was found in violation that morning. In fact, Bill Price did not even have to use his little measuring cup to determine if a violation had occurred. His visual inspection of the oysters the tongers intended to keep was sufficient. As we pulled away from the last boat that was checked, I commented on the apparent amiability that existed between the "Law" and the waterman. Bill gave a little laugh and said, "Sure, everything's fine now, but that's because I didn't have to give anyone a ticket this morning."

Bill sees his job as one in which he is sworn to enforce the laws of the state, but not to go out of his way to make life more difficult for the waterman. He knows how hard and uncertain their lives are, and, within reason, he gives them every break he can. For example, he knows that there is more than one way to stack a cord of wood, and he also is aware that the way the shells and under-sized oysters are placed in the cup used to determine if a violation has occurred can vary. Before issuing a citation, he makes absolutely sure the 5 percent rule has been violated. It is his policy to "throw in an extra point or two" to ameliorate any error he might have committed while filling the measuring cup.

The watermen know how he thinks and respect him. They know that he is not out to get them and is just doing his job when he monitors their catch—whether oysters, crabs, or fish. But they also know that if they purposely violate the law he will find them out and take whatever action is necessary to enforce the law. One young oysterman, who also has his own repair garage in Bivalve, told me the oystermen know that if Billy Price gives them a ticket they deserved it.

As we departed Wilson Shoals and continued north up the river to the Wetipquin Creek area to check on some signs that had been posted by the State Health Department placing certain oyster beds off-limits because of contamination with pathogenic bacteria, I settled back in the patrol boat and let my thoughts drift to more abstract and philosophical aspects of the relationship of Maryland oysters and men.

Here we are, in the mid-1980s, witnessing the taking of oysters from the Chesapeake system in much the same way as it has been done for over two hundred years, and I could not help but ask myself how much progress had been made to preserve and enhance this valuable natural resource. My thoughts wandered backward in time, and I pondered the thoughts, ideas, and predictions of Francis Winslow, W. K. Brooks, C. C. Yates, and Reginald V. Truitt. All of these pioneering oyster biologists had enunciated four principles that they considered absolutely essential to the survival of the oyster industry in Maryland. I took these four basic tenets, mulled them over one by one, and appraised the progress, if any, which had been made.

1. *The Oyster Fishery in Maryland Has Drastically Declined Primarily as a Result of Overfishing and Ineffectual Conservation Efforts.* In 1885, fifteen million bushels of oysters were taken from the Chesapeake; in 1984, less than one million bushels were harvested. This dramatic decline, which has progressed at a steady rate through the years, has resulted from the attitude on the part of many that the oyster populations are infinite—"Get em today and t'hell with tammar," and "Don't worry, God'll always provide enough arsters and crabs for us to catch." The oystermen themselves are not entirely to blame for these fatalistic attitudes; the state must bear some of the responsibility for not establishing and maintaining an effective conservation and education program. An educational program, in particular, has not been effectively implemented. If, as early as fifty years ago, the state had listened to its oyster biologists and allocated sufficient funds to

spread the message of conservation to all elements of the society, the situation would probably be quite different today. Now we find ourselves in the position of trying to treat the terminal illness of the industry by applying Band-Aids to the gaping wounds. It would have been far better to have practiced preventive biology at the outset of the illness. The critical condition would have been avoided, or at least would not have developed to the point where treatment is difficult, expensive, and has no assurance of success.

2. *Political Considerations Rather Than Biological Knowledge Have Frequently Hampered Efforts to Rehabilitate the Oyster Industry.* Over the past hundred years the Maryland legislature has exerted the primary influence on regulations governing the management of natural resources. Sadly, it must be recognized that many of the decisions made in regard to the taking of fin- and shellfish from the Bay and its tributaries were in direct opposition to the recommendations made by biologists and conservation managers. Political pressure brought to bear on elected and appointed officials by shortsighted self-interest groups has probably been the fundamental reason for the decline of the oyster industry in Maryland, and, as a matter of fact, for the dismal overall condition of the Bay we find today. With each general election, candidates for the legislature or State House almost always include in their platform a plank that calls for an effort to "Save the Bay," but nothing is really accomplished. The French have an expression that seems to be applicable to Maryland's efforts to effectively manage the Chesapeake: *Plus ça change, plus c'est la même chose* ("The more things change, the more they are the same").

3. *Private Propagation Has Been Eminently Successful in Parts of This Country and in Other Parts of the World. It Should Play a Major Role in the Operation of the Oyster Industry in Maryland.* Instead of doing everything possible to encourage the private propagation of oysters in Maryland as the early oyster experts had recommended, the state seems to do everything possible to hinder this vital operation and make it difficult if not impossible for new ostraculturists to go into operation. Few les-

sors of private grounds can remember when seed oysters from Maryland were last available for them to purchase, but they can remember the difficulties they encountered when they attempted to obtain a piece of barren bottom on which to invest their time and money and try to raise oysters. Of course politics is intimately involved here. Most of the watermen fear a takeover of the industry by large, powerful commercial companies who they think would end up being their employers—destroying, in effect, their preferred way of life. These concerns are registered with the lawmakers, who usually reflect the will of the people they think placed them in office.

The state seems to do nothing to abate these unfounded fears, and, in fact, sometimes appears to enhance them. In 1985, a high-ranking official of the Department of Natural Resources issued a statement that said in effect that the Chesapeake would soon no longer be able to support the number of watermen who were presently making their living from it, and in the not too distant future only a limited number of individuals would be permitted to harvest its oysters, crabs, and fish. This statement, which received wide coverage in the media, only served to upset the watermen and to confirm their fears that their way of life was rapidly coming to an end.

As noted earlier, only about 9,000 acres of bottom ground is currently under lease in Maryland, and, of this figure, a mere 2,500 acres are being cultivated actively. A few individuals may control considerably more than the 30-acre maximum set by law. Rumors to the effect that single individuals operate several hundred acres of bottom ground are prevalent and accepted as fact by many of the oystermen. This perceived skirting of the law by a privileged few with political clout does nothing to change their attitude that private propagation is not in their best interest.

4. If the Oyster Industry Is to Survive, Key Management Steps Must Be Taken. These Include: Conserving Available Shell for Replanting as Cultch; Protecting Spat through Cull Laws; Expanding and Protecting Natural Seed Areas. Looking back over the years, we can say that these recommendations of the early biologists were recognized as being of prime importance and have been implemented to a certain degree. Presently, 1,200 acres on natural oyster rock are designated as seed-production areas. Oystermen dredge the seed oysters from these areas for replanting on public fishing grounds. The efforts to produce seed oysters are far from adequate, however, and this is attested to by the fact that no one can remember when enough seed were available that some could be sold to private growers. Oystermen and laymen alike wonder why any seed oysters planted on private grounds must come from Virginia or from a "wildcat" oyster breeder like Max Chambers.

The oyster seed for planting on public rocks comes in the form of shell peppered with spat, and when replanted these young oysters will reach market size in two to three years. Fresh shell for the seed-production program comes mainly from the shucking houses, which by law must make available 25 percent (down from the 50 percent figure established in 1951) of their shucked shell. Shell is also obtained by dredging it up from beneath the sediments of long-abandoned oyster bars. Shell is also dumped on established bars to increase their productivity, but allegations have been made that much of this new shell cultch has been wasted by placing it on nonproductive areas.

The 3-inch cull law that Truitt was instrumental in getting through the legislature is rigidly enforced by the marine police, and this single bit of legislation has been of inestimable benefit to the entire industry.

All in all, I think the state deserves a passing mark for its efforts in heeding this last fundamental principle, but failing grades for what has been done about the first three.

In spite of the vast amount of knowledge concerning the biology of the oyster that has been gained through scientific research by numerous agencies, both public and private, there are still areas of great ignorance. For example, oyster genetics is in its infancy and could prove to be the ultimate solution to the problem. If techniques for oyster rearing in the laboratory could be perfected and standardized so that controlled reproductive experiments could be conducted with ease, new strains of healthier, larger, and faster-growing oysters could be produced. I have already mentioned the concept of cloning (the creation of a new organism from a single nonreproductive cell of a donor), and the far-ranging possibilities of this technique. With cloning, the basic laws of evolution could be circumvented in the search for a better race of oysters. Natural selection, which requires many generations to establish an advantageous characteristic in a population, would not be required. Only one oyster with the desired trait or traits would be needed, as this single specimen could supply enough cells to be cloned into countless new oysters genetically identical to the "parent specimen," and in one generation a new race or strain of oysters could be produced. Unfortunately, our knowledge of oyster genetics, cytology, and reproductive details is extremely limited. For example, we don't even know the characteristic number of chromosomes (bodies which carry the genes or units of inheritance) for oysters.

Another area in the life of the oyster in which much more knowledge needs to be acquired concerns the bionomics and behavior of oyster larvae while they float and feed in the water between the times of spawning and spatting. Though we have been able to study what happens during these two important times in the life of the oyster in the laboratory, practically nothing is known of what occurs in a natural environment. Observations made on an organism maintained under laboratory conditions may or may not be applicable to the creature in its natural settings.

The nutritional requirements of these larvae, and the juveniles and adults as well, need to be studied in detail. Little if anything is known about the sources of food available around the estuary.

Our understanding of the effects of pollutants—especially heavy metals, petrochemicals, and chlorine—ranges from very poor to nonexistent. Lastly, our knowledge of diseases among oysters, including both natural and hatchery-grown populations, is rudimentary at best.

Suddenly, all of these thoughts were jolted from my mind as Bill abruptly cut back on the throttle, and the Whaler responded appropriately. We had arrived at the entrance to Tyaskin Harbor at the mouth of Wetipquin Creek. Just north of this location some of the oyster bars, including both public and private tracts, had been quarantined over a year ago because of contamination with dangerous microorganisms. Signs prohibiting the taking of oysters or other shellfish from the area had a way of disappearing mysteriously in the past, and Bill was pleased when he found these to be intact.

Swinging the patrol boat around, and again shoving the throttle to full ahead, we headed back to Nanticoke Harbor, five miles downstream. On the way, Bill stopped two fishing boats to determine if the occupants possessed the new license required to fish in the Maryland portion of the Chesapeake Bay. Most users of the Bay and its tributaries strongly objected to the passage of this new tax, but, according to Bill, the majority of the anglers have complied with the regulation. In fact, he says that he finds that most people in his area of responsibility (from the mouth of the Nanticoke to the Delaware state line) obey the laws of the water, and his job of enforcement is relatively easy. In the three years he has been a marine policeman he has not yet had to draw his service revolver, and he hopes he never has to.

One of Bill's primary concerns, however, is the rampant use of alcoholic beverages by pleasure boaters and fishermen. Alcohol has been involved in almost all of the accidents on the water he has been called upon to investigate, and it is his belief that the stringent laws that have been enacted to deter drunken driving should be extended to drunken boating.

Disembarking from the patrol boat in Nanticoke Harbor, I thanked Bill Price for the opportunity to observe him at work and to learn more about his job. My work day was over and I prepared to leave. His was not. He explained that he thought he would remain in the vicinity of the harbor for the remainder of the afternoon and be present when the boats returned to harbor to sell their oysters to the buyers at dockside, some of which were already arriving. He explained that sometimes tongers become a little careless in their culling procedures, once "The Man" has checked them out that day on the water. Knowing that he might be waiting at dockside to have a look at the day's catch, they were reminded to continue to be careful in culling the catch.

As I drove away from dockside on an old road made of oyster shell, a flush of euphoric optimism came over me to replace the

The Oyster

mood of depression I had been experiencing as a result of my mental inventory of the oyster situation. I suddenly realized that the oysters of the Chesapeake will, in all probability, endure as they have for eons. In spite of mismanagement, overfishing, greed, pollution, political interference, and the adverse forces of nature itself, the oysters will survive.

They will endure because of the inherent resilience of the organism itself, which has been molded by the awesome forces of evolution for millions of years. And dedicated professional public servants, such as the man I had shared the day with, will help them along.

SELECTED BIBLIOGRAPHY

Bardach, John E., ed. *Aquaculture, The Farming and Husbandry of Freshwater and Marine Organisms*. New York: John Wiley and Sons, 1972.

Beaven, G. F. *Maryland's Oyster Problem*. Maryland Department of Research and Education, Education Series 8, 1945.

Blair, Carvel H. and Ansel, W. D. *Chesapeake Bay Notes and Sketches*. Centreville, Md.: Tidewater Publishers, 1970.

Bolitho, Hector, ed. *The Glorious Oyster*. New York: Horizon Press, 1961.

Brooks, W. K. "Development of the American Oyster (*Ostrea virginica* L.)." Studies from the Biological Laboratory, The Johns Hopkins University, v. 4, no. 1: 1-81, 1880.

———. *Report of the Oyster Commission of the State of Maryland*. Baltimore: The J. B. Ehler Company, 1884.

———. *The Oyster: A Popular Summary of a Scientific Study*. Baltimore: The Johns Hopkins University Press, 1891.

Capper, John; Power, Garrett; and Shivers, Frank R., Jr. *Chesapeake Waters*. Centreville, Md.: Tidewater Publishers, 1983.

Clark, Eleanor. *The Oysters of Locmariaquer*. New York: Pantheon Books, 1964.

deGast, Robert. *The Oystermen of the Chesapeake*. Camden, Me.: International Marine Publishing Company, 1970.

Galtsoff, Paul S. *The American Oyster, Crassostrea virginica Gmelin*. Washington, D. C.: Bulletin of the U. S. Fish and Wildlife Service, v. 64, 1964.

Hegner, Robert. *Parade of the Animal Kingdom*. New York: The MacMillan Company, 1947.

Hickman, Cleveland P. *Biology of the Invertebrates*. 2nd ed. St. Louis: The C. V. Mosby Company, 1973.

227

The Oyster

Kennedy, V. S. and Breisch, L. L. "Sixteen Decades of Political Management of the Oyster Fishery in Maryland's Chesapeake Bay." *Journal of Environmental Management*, v. 16: 153-71, 1983.

———. *Maryland's Oysters: Research and Management*. University of Maryland Sea Grant Program, Publication No. UM-SG-Ts-81-04, no date.

Lang, Varley. *Follow the Water*. Winston Salem, N. C.: John F. Blair, Publisher, 1961.

Lippson, Alice Jane and Lippson, Robert L. *Life in the Chesapeake Bay*. Baltimore: The Johns Hopkins University Press, 1984.

Maryland Department of Education. *Maryland's Sunken Treasure*. Conservation Series, Book 2, 1953.

Nichol, A. J. *The Oyster-Packing Industry of Baltimore: Its History and Current Problems*. Bulletin of the Chesapeake Biological Station, 1937.

Peffer, Randall S. *Watermen*. Baltimore: The Johns Hopkins University Press, 1979.

Sprague, Victor. "Diseases of Oysters." *Annual Review of Microbiology:* 211-30, 1977.

Truitt, R. V. "The Oyster and the Oyster Industry in Maryland." Maryland Conservation Department Bulletin, v. 4: 1-48, 1931.

Wennersten, John R. *The Oyster Wars of Chesapeake Bay*. Centreville, Md.: Tidewater Publishers, 1981.

Winslow, Francis. *Report on the Oyster Beds of the James River, Virginia and of Tangier and Pocomoke Sounds, Maryland and Virginia*. Washington, D. C.: U. S. Coast and Geodetic Survey for 1881, published 1882.

———. "Present Condition and Future Prospects of the Oyster Industry." *Transactions of the American Fisheries Society*, v. 13: 148-63, 1884.

Yates, C. C. *Summary of Survey of Oyster Bars of Maryland, 1906–1912*. Washington, D. C.: U. S. Coast and Geodetic Survey Report, 1913.

INDEX

Index

Index

Index

Index

Washington Post, 9
Water vascular system, 150
Waterview, Maryland, 52, 56
Waterview Hotel, 56
Wells, Dr. H. W., 100
Wesleyan University, 93
Wetipquin Creek, 88, 220, 222
Wetsuit, 186
Whaler (boat), 217, 222
Whelk, 146, 147
Whip mud worm, 115
Whitehaven, Maryland, 52
Whitney, Boyd, 94
Wicomico River, 52, 95, 96
"Widow makers." (see Shafts)
Wilson, Dr. H. V., 106

Wilson Shoals, 217, 220
Winslow, Francis, 53, 79, 181, 220
Winslow Report, 79
Wisconsin, University of, 210
Woods Hole Biological Laboratory, 17
Workboats, 164
Wye River, 127, 186, 188

Y

Yates, C. C., x, 86, 220
Yawl, 178

Z

Zinc, 192, 195, 207
Zoological status (of oysters), 26